Edwin B. Frost

AN ASTRONOMER'S LIFE

BY

EDWIN BRANT FROST

WITH ILLUSTRATIONS

BOSTON AND NEW YORK

HOUGHTON MIFFLIN COMPANY

The Riverside Press Cambridge

1933

The Riverside Press
CAMBRIDGE · MASSACHUSETTS
PRINTED IN THE U.S.A.

TO

MY WIFE

MARY HAZARD FROST

PREFACE

THE material collected in this volume was primarily written as a record for my children and grandchildren without being intended for publication. After a considerable portion had been dictated, I was persuaded by friends to consider its publication as a record of life in an academic community during the last thirty years of the nineteenth century and as an account of scientific work in astronomy in a Midwestern setting during a similar period in the present century. Of course the book does not profess to be a treatise on astronomy, but it would have been quite incomplete without a rather full and somewhat technical reference to that branch of science in which my life work has been done. I have been asked to include in the book the William Vaughn Moody lecture which I gave at the University of Chicago in December, 1930, as this had not been published elsewhere.

The reader will note that for evident reasons no attempt has been made to keep the record entirely chronological, but in dealing with different topics it seemed necessary to pass back and forth in the sequence of time.

It would have been totally impossible that these memories and notes could have been presented in their present form without the devoted interest and the untiring efforts of my wife.

Some of the humorous portions relating to the life at Hanover have been quoted by permission of the author, Professor Edwin J. Bartlett, from *A Dartmouth Book of Remembrance*, published by the Webster Press, and grateful acknowledgment is hereby made. The stories, as a matter of fact, were entirely familiar to me before they were so well written by him.

EDWIN B. FROST

WILLIAMS BAY, WISCONSIN
July, 1933

CONTENTS

I. GRANDFATHERS AND GRANDMOTHERS 1

II. HOTEL LIFE AND EARLY RECOLLECTIONS OF HANOVER 9

III. A GROWING BOY IN THE NEW HOME 20

IV. EARLY EDUCATION 38

V. COLLEGE YEARS 41

VI. ACTIVITIES DURING COLLEGE 47

VII. VILLAGE CHARACTERS 53

VIII. AFTER COLLEGE — WHAT? 57

IX. STUDY ABROAD 65

X. BACK TO HANOVER 89

XI. ROMANCE 101

XII. A NEW ENGLAND WINTER AND A EUROPEAN SUMMER 105

XIII. WINTER OF 1898–1899 109

XIV. LAKE GENEVA AND YERKES OBSERVATORY 114

XV. INFLUENCES AND PROGRESS 123

XVI. POLITICS 132

XVII. INCREASING RESPONSIBILITIES 138

XVIII. A YEAR IN EUROPE 150

XIX. AMERICA AGAIN 178

XX. WAR 182

XXI. BLINDNESS 189

XXII. IN THE DAY'S WORK 205

XXIII. Astronomy   228

XXIV. Years of 1931–1932   250

XXV. In Retrospect   269

XXVI. Fragments of Cosmic Philosophy   275

Index   287

ILLUSTRATIONS

EDWIN BRANT FROST   *Frontispiece*

EDWIN BRANT FROST AS A BOY IN HANOVER   12

IN THE CONSTELLATION AQUILA (SCUTUM): A SMALL AREA
     OF THE MILKY WAY   62
     Photograph by E. E. Barnard

BRIDE AND GROOM, 1896   104

THE YERKES OBSERVATORY OF THE UNIVERSITY OF CHICAGO   120

THE GREAT SPIRAL IN ANDROMEDA   230
     Photograph by G. W. Ritchey

BRANTWOOD   262

FATHERS AND SONS: SIX GENERATIONS OF FROSTS   276

AN ASTRONOMER'S LIFE

. .

CHAPTER I

GRANDFATHERS AND GRANDMOTHERS

IN ATTEMPTING to make a record of some of the events of a human life, whether of oneself or of someone else, we naturally look back to the line of ancestry to which we owe our being. It is remarkable by how slender a thread this existence has been maintained, especially for those of us whose forbears took part in the reclaiming of a continent for civilization. We often attribute an importance to that line which carries the family name, although in fact the dilution of blood has been so great with eight or ten generations that the actual impress of many other names of the good mothers, who bore more than their share in the struggle for existence, is quite as great as that of the line carrying the name.

My first Frost ancestor to come to America was Edmund, who was born about 1600 in Suffolk County, England. He set sail with his wife Thomasine and their son John on the ship *Great Hope* from the port of Ipswich, England, on October 16, 1634, in order 'to escape the more savage oppression of England.' The ship was wrecked off Yarmouth, but fortunately all the passengers were saved. The determination to seek liberty in the new colonies across the Atlantic was not thwarted by this misadventure, for we have the record that in the next year, August 10, 1635, they again embarked, this time in the ship *Defense*, and from the port of Gravesend, Kent County, for the Massachusetts Bay colony at Boston. After fifty-three days of sailing they reached their destination on October 2, 1635. The family settled in Cambridge, and Edmund Frost was allotted land on the westerly side of what is still known as Dunster Street between Harvard Square and Mount Auburn Street. He is said to have been a godly man, an Elder in the church, and greatly respected. That he had an interest in education is indicated by the fact that he made a contribution to the resources of Harvard College by the gift of ten shillings! This minute amount was doubtless considerable to him, as money was not easily obtained in the colony.

The line of descent of my branch of the Frosts is through Edmund's son Samuel, then Joseph, Jonathan, Elijah, and Benjamin to Carlton Pennington Frost, my father. This would place me in the eighth generation after Edmund. Our connection with the immortal company of the famous ship *Mayflower* was on my mother's side through the Allerton, Howland, and Tilley lines. There are, of course, many strong lines of family influence bearing other names well known in New England. For example, it was something of a surprise for us to learn a few years ago that my wife, Mary Elizabeth Hazard, and I were descendants in the eighth generation from Edmund Rice and his wife, Tamasine, who settled in Sudbury, now Wayland, Massachusetts, in 1639. At the same time we discovered that my brother, Gilman DuBois Frost, and his wife, Margaret Thurston, traced the same connection. Edmund Rice was my ancestor on the Frost side.

The Frost line was not inclined to push to the westward, but spread throughout southwestern New Hampshire and southeastern Vermont and into Maine. The name is a common one in those parts of New England, and I found as many as twenty-one bearing the name of Frost who graduated from Dartmouth College between 1845 and 1925.

There are some incidents, trifling enough, which occurred before I was five years of age, but which I recall as perfectly definite and genuine. Could I ever forget the palpitating excitement when the fire-engine tore past our house in the early evening on its way to the south part of our town, Brattleboro, Vermont, followed by an excited group of men and boys. Nor have I forgotten our disappointment when Father took my brother and me in the buggy behind Jenny, the sorrel mare, to see the ascension of the balloon which did not ascend. I remember, too, sitting in the carriage and being ferried across the Connecticut River. But this experience was followed by something much more exciting. On this trip we were on our way to a church picnic at Lake Chesterfield, New Hampshire, and I shall never forget how here Father took his two slender little boys with their pipestem arms and legs away from the group, and, after taking off his boots and stockings and rolling up his trousers, undressed us and took us into the water. The water was probably at least a foot deep, which was much deeper than the tin bathtub at home, and it seemed cold and terrifying. My grandchildren are much less timid, for at two years of age, little Jocelyn plunges into the shallow water of Lake Geneva with great joy, swallowing the water as if she liked it.

And with what numb surprise we saw Father, by profession a doctor, occupying the pulpit one Sunday morning, and reading the sermon for the minister who was probably his patient at the moment. There was also the sad occasion when for some necessary reason I was taken to church one evening. I had eaten blueberries for supper and the excitement was too great for my digestion, with distressing results to those near our pew. Arrangements seem to be better nowadays, for one little boy under similar circumstances made his exit successfully, and returning, explained to his mother that he had found a receptacle at the door marked 'For the Sick.'

Of course we were too small to go to school, but Mother had been a school-teacher, and education at her side was not neglected. She taught us to read and write and tried to instill in us her love of poetry. She was a great admirer of Tennyson and of the American poets. My brother Gilman, being two years older than I, began to commit poems to memory before I did. I can recall to this day hearing him reciting dolefully Wordsworth's sad tale of Goody Blake and Harry Gill. We both felt that its sentiments were overdrawn and unreal.

Remembrances of the town of Brattleboro are not very vivid, but farther up the street was a home with large grounds and beautiful evergreens where the children had a pair of ponies. Possibly this was the home of the Balestiers whose daughter became the wife of Rudyard Kipling. Brattleboro was quite a summer resort even in those days, with one or more hydropathic institutions, and it was conveniently located — only about two hundred miles north of New York.

There was a fine view, from some of the windows of our small house, of a high hill across the river in New Hampshire, Wantastiket Mountain, and it was my good fortune for the first twenty-four years of my life to have before me a mountain landscape and in the fore-ground the green hills hemming in the valley of the Connecticut.

Two of my mother's brothers, Gilman Bradford DuBois (named for Governor Bradford) and William Henry DuBois, were in the wholesale leather business in New York, and Brattleboro made a convenient stopping-place on their trips to the family home at Randolph in central Vermont. They often brought with them an assortment of shoes from which some appropriate to our feet could be found. I also recall how on one occasion they presented us with a large bunch of bananas, then quite a rarity, and these hung and ripened in the shed.

There were early recollections of vacation trips up the river to Thetford, Vermont, where my grandfather, Benjamin Frost, and his wife, Mary Catherine Brant, had settled in 1837 in order to have their three boys educated in the excellent Thetford Academy, which was a tributary to Dartmouth. This grandfather, with his father Elijah Frost, music teacher and farmer, had owned a large farm in the town of Sullivan in southwestern New Hampshire, but I find no greater preoccupation in the minds of Benjamin and Mary than that their sons should receive a college education. My father often told me of the family trek early in December over the snowy hills of New Hampshire on their way to a new home to be established in Thetford. They made the trip on a large sled, taking a part of their belongings with them, grandfather driving and seated on a Windsor chair. At this time my father was seven years old. With what high hopes and satisfaction in their souls must this ambitious couple have heard the ringing of the bell for morning chapel as they drove through Hanover, ten miles from their goal. It must have signified much to the young father and mother of the three small boys all of whom eventually graduated from Dartmouth College. My father cherished that Windsor chair which he later inherited. For years it was installed in our dining-room for his occupancy at the head of the table, and is still in the possession of the family. Mary Brant died when my father was in college, and her husband later married his brother's widow, Lydia Heald Frost whom I always knew as my Grandmother Frost. She often spent many weeks with us.

Elijah Frost eventually followed his son Benjamin to Thetford Hill.

There he married a widow who not only survived him but a third husband. She was thus always known to us as our step-great-grand-mother Blaisdell. She was a very bright woman and was accustomed to exchange witty repartee with my father who took care of her. She used snuff, a process which fascinated us boys, and she had a little hole in her cheek, probably from an ulcerated tooth of long standing. This always excited our curiosity. She was nearly eighty years old when I first knew her, and she lived to be somewhat over ninety. She died in 1881, and we inherited some of her fine mahogany furniture. The brick house in which she lived was built by my grandfather Benjamin, but later owned by his father Elijah. It commands a fine view of Mount Ascutney on the south thirty miles down the valley and extends to Mount Moosilauke on the north, one of the finest peaks of the Franconias. The house is kept by its present owners in perfect repair, and before it stands a row of maple trees which my father set out when he was a freshman at Dartmouth in 1848. And there still lives in the front yard a lilac bush gnarled and twisted and with a stem six inches in diameter. It was in this house that my mother roomed when she went from Randolph to Thetford Academy as a student, and it was here that she met my father.

The bedrooms in these New England houses were never heated. They were icy-cold and the windows tightly closed. The high feather bed in its four-poster frame had beautiful quilted or knitted covers, but the homespun linen sheets and blankets partook of the temperature of the room. A bed-warmer filled with live coals was passed around from one room to the other. Then it was a quick jump into that feather bed with the hope that slumber would be undisturbed until the morning's frigid plunge into cold clothes. If windows had been opened, there would have been less tuberculosis in the country.

My mother's family lived in or near Randolph, Vermont, in the valley of a branch of the White River. My mother's father, Earl Cushman DuBois, son of Joseph DuBois and Polly Spear, was born in Braintree, Vermont, October 6, 1799, one of a family of eleven children. On May 1, 1822, he married Anna Lamson, of Randolph, one of the younger members of a family of fourteen. They had six children of whom my mother, Eliza Ann DuBois, was the third, and the first daughter. It is not surprising that my mother had seventy-two first cousins. There was no talk in those days of race suicide.

I have always thought of my grandfather, who died about ten years before I was born, as a pioneer in transportation before the advent of railroads in that region. His business seemed to have been in carrying produce from the farms of Randolph to the market in Boston, and in returning with those products of the loom and industry that would find sale in Vermont. My grandmother told me that she used to send a barrel of cider applesauce to the Boston market with the profits of which she could indulge in some necessities and luxuries from the city. The season for transportation was the fall and winter, and the roads were difficult when the snows were deep. The trip of nearly two hundred miles often had to be made partly on runners and partly on wheels. There must have been considerable exposure in making such a trip in the severity of a New England winter. I recall a conversation I had with an old gentleman in Hanover who once kept a tavern on the route and who remembered very well my grandfather and his brothers as their slow caravan rested over night at his hostelry.

Grandfather died of tuberculosis when he was not much over fifty years of age. My grandmother DuBois, a saintly little lady, was a widow for nearly forty years as she lived to be nearly ninety. She was deeply religious and a member of the Christian Church. Her oldest child Gilman lived in Boston after his retirement from active business, and Grandmother found great joy in her occasional trips thither for a series of revival meetings by Dwight Moody in a building called the 'Tabernacle.' Even after she was eighty years old, she enjoyed going to 'camp meeting' in Vermont during the summer. Her family was somewhat reluctant to have her go, but she seemed to benefit by the simple life in cabins or tents. She often told me as a lad about the War of 1812 and the battle of Plattsburg. She could recall some of the songs that were sung in derision of 'General Prevost and all his host.' Some of her brothers, armed with pitchforks and other useful implements, probably including some squirrel guns, started to assist in repelling the British invasion, but could not reach Lake Champlain in time to participate. Grandmother quite vividly related to me an incident illustrating the necessity of self-reliance in the pioneer families of those days. The call had come for one of the boys to attend the annual Muster, and it shocked them to find that the young man had no suit of clothes fit to wear. With all speed a sheep was caught and sheared, the wool was cleaned and dyed and made into cloth. In an incredibly short time, with everybody helping, the homespun and homemade suit was ready.

I do not doubt that our thrifty pioneers are responsible for the disappearance of the passenger pigeon. My grandmother told me how they used to darken the sky in their great numbers, how easy they were to get both by trapping and shooting and how barrels of them were packed in salt. Perhaps in those days it was fortunate that in the rambling New England houses there was ample room for cold-storage. It was absolutely necessary that pork and beef should be 'put down' in various forms and that bushels of potatoes and barrels of apples should be stored for the winter.

My grandmother attended school as a young lady at Potsdam, New York, and she well remembered the somewhat fearsome trip over the ice on Lake Champlain. She told me about the wonderful meteors in November of 1833. It seemed to have been clear throughout New England and many thought that the world was coming to an end. She described the sky as looking like an umbrella, which meant, of course, that the radiant point in Leo was well pronounced. The meteors were in such tremendous abundance as to be wholly past counting, almost like the flakes of a snowstorm.

Perhaps this record of my forebears is not complete without a definite mention of my father and his two brothers, especially in regard to their services in the Civil War. Their mother, Mary Brant, did not live to know that only one of her three boys, my father, survived the ravages of that time.

My father was for seven months Surgeon with the rank of Major in the Fifteenth Vermont, whose colonel was Redfield Proctor, later Senator from Vermont and Secretary of War under McKinley during the latter part of the Spanish War. However, Father's war service extended over about three years as he was Surgeon of the Board of Enrollment for Vermont and stationed at Woodstock and at Windsor.

Uncle Edwin was captain of Company A of the Tenth Vermont and was in service for two years. Wearing a tawny beard, he was

called by his fellow soldiers 'Father Time.' He inherited from his
grandfather, Elijah Frost, a taste for music and had a fine bass
voice. In fact, after his graduation from Dartmouth, in 1858, he
traveled over the country for a time with a musical company known
as 'Father Kemp's Old Folks Concert Company.' He was known
both in his regiment and in his college days as a great wag. Possibly
he inherited his whimsicality from my great-grandmother, by name
Farrar, who was of the tribe of Artemus Ward, the New England
humorist. Uncle Edwin was killed at Cold Harbor, Virginia, on
June 3, 1864.

Uncle Henry Martin Frost, Dartmouth '57, was for a short time
chaplain of the Eleventh Vermont. His health was so seriously
impaired that he did not long survive after the war although he was
rector of an Episcopal church in Louisville, Kentucky, for some
time before he died of tuberculosis at his home in Thetford, Vermont, February 20, 1866.

Reminiscences of the days of early childhood of threescore years
ago may be somewhat dangerous and deceptive. If some decisive
change happens in the status or location of a family, it may definitely punctuate such recollections. In our case there was a change
of base, because in December of 1871, when I was five and a half
years old, my father was called from my birthplace in Brattleboro
to a professorship in medicine at Dartmouth College, sixty miles
farther up the Connecticut River and on the New Hampshire side.
He had lectured there during the autumn terms for the three preceding years. I do not vividly recall the trip to Hanover. Trains
were still something of a novelty, and Mother was car-sick and a
bit nervous with her two restless charges. I do remember that we
were solemnly cautioned not to lose our hats as we looked out of
the window in passing a high bridge near Claremont, New Hampshire. We were much impressed by the sad tale of a boy who had
lost his hat on such an occasion. I have always made it a point to
look out at that bridge high over the stream below whenever I have
passed that way.

CHAPTER II

HOTEL LIFE AND EARLY RECOLLECTIONS OF HANOVER

FOR two shy little boys, it was quite a change to pass from a quiet home to the life of a hotel where we were to live for four years. It was something of an ordeal at first to sit at the table with the elderly group of permanent guests, and when a family with children came we rejoiced in their youthful companionship.

The hotel was in two parts, one of brick and one of wood, and was connected in the middle by a long hall forming a large H. If anyone dared to race around, it gave an ample field for exercise. Mr. and Mrs. Horace Frary who presided very strictly over the hotel were lenient with us. They were both odd characters. Mrs. Frary was an excellent cook, but woe to the guest who complained of the food. 'What ails the biscuits this morning? I made them myself,' she would say in a voice which was far-reaching. Or, 'Wants his coffee hot, does he? Well, then, he better come to breakfast on time.' She shuffled as she walked with flapping heels and showed lively satisfaction when she had successfully squelched a boarder. She was really a woman of dignity, and with some grace greeted the Governor or any important guests of the college. Mrs. Frary liked cats. 'How many cats have you?' someone asked. 'Oh,' she replied, 'half a barrel.' They were never any nuisance so far as I know.

It was the funniest thing in the world to see Mr. Frary stand at the serving table and carve the side of beef. He would wipe his knife on his white trousers, and then, cutting off a slice of meat, would pick it up delicately with two fingers and lay it on the plate. He scorned a fork. But he loved Shakespeare and could quote long passages. Dr. Oliver Wendell Holmes, when he was a member of the Medical Faculty, knew Mr. Frary well and greatly enjoyed him. 'Hod,' as he was always called, was devoted to my father, but his sense of humor prevailed once in an illness when he remonstrated with his wife: 'Damn it, this is no time to be sending for a doctor. I'M SICK!'

At this time, oatmeal was being introduced from Scotland. Dr. Samuel Johnson defined 'oats' as 'A grain which is generally given to horses, but in Scotland supports the people.' Porridge was supposed to be good for children, but as there were always some hard grains and husks, we heartily disliked it. Each of us therefore received a reward of five cents a week if we ate our oatmeal and brushed our teeth. This was our spending money. My brother was less successful in saving his, two cents being his standard reserve. I was the better banker of the family.

The dining-room was a large bare place and offered little that was pleasing to the eye, nor was sustenance the only consideration. There was brilliant conversation and quick repartee among the distinguished people who gathered there. Of the permanent guests the most notable was William H. Duncan, 'Squire Duncan,' a celebrated lawyer and a fine Latin scholar. He married one of two sisters, heiresses of the village, and Rufus Choate married the other. Their father, Mills Olcott, was for many years treasurer of the college. Squire Duncan's wife died early, leaving him desolate. He decided to remain in Hanover, his academic home, to live alone with his books. He never allowed a woman to enter his sanctum over Cobb's hardware store to mollify the dust. Squire Duncan boarded at the hotel for years due to an impetuous arrangement in a moment of gratitude after he had successfully defended Mr. Frary in a lawsuit. In his last illness Mr. Frary made it clear that he had tired of his promise, for when his wife bent over the bed and said, 'Horace, this is Mr. Duncan come to see you; you know your friend, don't you?' Hod's choleric reply was, 'Know him? Damn him, I should say that I do know him. He hasn't paid a cent of board for twenty years.' But Mr. Frary was really devoted to his friend and was proud to have him grace the head of the table to which came all the notables, the Governor, the Trustees of the College, and the eminent lecturers. When Squire Duncan died, we inherited from him a good many books and quite a bit of furniture, including a Chippendale couch and chairs and a beautiful secretary at which must have often sat Rufus Choate, his famous brother-in-law.

For a late summer and autumn term in the Medical College, there were many members of the faculty at the hotel who were recruited from other centers, mostly from New York and Boston. The medical students, a hundred or more, were most fortunate in obtaining instruction from these distinguished doctors and surgeons. My father and one or two others constituted the resident nucleus of the Medical College, my father acting in the capacity of Dean. During the winter, the instruction was given chiefly by him with the assistance of the demonstrators of anatomy, by Dr. Edwin J. Bartlett for chemistry, and later by Dr. William T. Smith for physiology and related branches.

Another Vice-Regent in the dining-room was Auntie Haddock. Her husband had been sent by President Polk as Minister to Lisbon. She was much impressed by the glory of the Court. In England she had danced in a quadrille with Queen Victoria and Prince Albert, and her reminiscences were enjoyable. She was very deaf, however, so that her conversation often took the form of a monologue. She took the *New York Herald*, which was supposed to be rather a *risqué* thing in that sober town. She had many relics of departed glories in her room. Every table, mantel, and whatnot was covered with curious little things placed at certain angles, each article always remaining in its definite place. In those days it was regarded as a proper thing to have a parlor filled with knick-knacks. I am surprised to find that this was true all over Europe. It was evidently the influence of the Second Empire. We boys thoroughly enjoyed our Sunday call upon Mrs. Haddock, although we detested those little velvet suits given to us by the Fairbanks family after several children had outgrown them. We were supposed to look so elegant, however, that we had to be photographed in them.

One of the hotel guests, M. Prudhomme, often called upon Mother that they might speak French together and discuss French literature. Mother was an excellent French scholar, and always enjoyed reading her French Bible. She had not only taught French and art, but was much interested in botany and astronomy. Both of my parents kept from their student days their copies of the large celestial atlas known as *Burritt's Geography of the Heavens*.

Among the distinguished lecturers was Dr. John Lord whose histories were widely read even up to recent years. He smoked a pipe right in the sacred precincts of Dartmouth College. We little boys were very much awed to see him smoking a pipe at his work.

In those days a college professor did not smoke, or at least if he did, he sneaked away somewhere. Many college professors were ministers who were called back as teachers on account of their scholarly attainments. They didn't always make the best instructors for the rough-and-ready boys who came to Dartmouth in those years. But the senior professors were indeed stately and preserved the traditions of Daniel Webster. They all wore tall hats and frock coats and were very dignified.

We stood in awe of one hotel guest, a magnificent big speciman of a man who was supposed to be a Chief of the Cherokees. He had the blackest of hair and a mahogany face. Dressed in a Prince Albert coat, he was particularly impressive. His son was a student in the Medical College. It is an interesting item, by the way, that in the charter of 'Moor's Charity School,' from which Dartmouth College grew, free education was to be provided for Indians as well as for English youth. Before 1915, when this school was officially dissolved, it was the custom to give free tuition in the college to any Indian who came properly prepared. There were very few who applied for this, but occasionally an Indian student entered the college and was graduated.

A picture of an enormous pair of boots standing outside of a door on our floor persists in my mind because I used to hide in them, at least up to my armpits. The boots belonged to a tremendous man, G. B. N. Tower, a teacher of engineering, christened by us, 'Great Big Normous Tower.' The boots were daily cleaned by Vail, the half-wit to whom we presented a knife at Christmas; it was probably a dangerous gift!

There was a circulating library kept in the home of a kindly lady on Main Street not far from the hotel. Here I was accustomed to go for books during the years before I went to school. I still recall the vividness of J. S. C. Abbott's stories of the Punic Wars. Excitement ran highest when Hannibal came down over the mountains toward Rome with his armored elephants. The *Pickwick Papers* also amused me greatly, but somehow, as I grew older, I could not seem to keep my interest in the works of Dickens which seemed to me so detailed as to leave nothing to the imagination.

Across the street from the hotel in Cobb's Block with its mighty pillars was Deacon Downing's drug-store. I used to make frequent

EDWIN BRANT FROST
As a boy in Hanover

trips thither, carrying with me those big old-fashioned copper pennies. I insisted on the logic that the larger amount of metal called for a larger stick of candy. This reminds me of a time somewhat later when Sam Bartlett and I were assigned the duty of filling a coin box for the missionaries. To hasten our task, we gathered together all the big copper pennies that could be found in the community.

There used to appear occasionally on Main Street a poor man who was known as a 'jumper,' one who has the peculiar physiological reaction to a sudden noise. When this afflicted man came to the village on Saturday to do his weekly shopping, he was pestered by the boys in a spirit of youthful meanness as they would suddenly pop around the corner and shout, 'Bolt, Jimmy Wright!' just to see him jump. He was naturally annoyed and sometimes gave chase. This man lived in a little cottage on the road to Lebanon near a tract of land once given to the college. This property included a ridge ironically called 'Mount Support,' because no financial returns from it could be foreseen. For some generations the name has degenerated to 'Mount Sport.'

At the south end of Main Street, the long hill leading down to Mink Brook was called 'Nigger Hill.' I am not sure how it received its name, but I remember as a very small boy 'Aunt Sophie,' a former slave, who lived in a cottage near the crest of this hill. She was quite a mystery to me, and I was somewhat afraid of her.

Guests coming to Hanover arrived in stage-coaches, which were important items of life there. They were strongly built in the Concord style and provided seats for about a dozen people inside and an indefinite number on top. They were commonly drawn by two horses, but a pair of leaders were put on when traffic was heavy. The coaches made their circuit around the village picking up passengers and stopping last at the hotel and the post-office. One of the best of these coaches has fortunately been preserved in the college museum. In winter there were stages on runners which were built much nearer to the ground. They were really comfortable vehicles and were often used for parties going to neighboring towns for some fraternity dinner or other social function.

Besides these covered stages, the stables also possessed for winter use what were known as 'barges.' These were large affairs with a big curved front and room on each seat for at least six persons. They were well supplied with straw and real buffalo robes, and added to the gaiety of winter.

While we lived at the hotel, Father kept his horses at Allen's livery stable, and it was fun for us lads to get into the stable where we knew all the horses by name, each horse having his name over the back of the stall. Our little brown mare, Kit, whom Father drove up from Brattleboro, was an excellent saddle horse, but used to cut up quite a bit, somehow finding a way of getting her halter untied. I remember that once she tipped over the whole tub of water from which the horses drank, rolling it up and down the floor. And once she started up the stairs to the hayloft, breaking down several steps. Mr. Allen, the proprietor of the stable, was already on in years when we knew him, and had retired from the active adventures of youth when he used to drive the mail over the Andes. He was rated as a worthy person and had a fine farm on the way to West Lebanon. I remember him more particularly as he sat in front of the grocery store on a keg, generally with a whip in his hand, tall hat, a Prince Albert coat, and high boots. He was a typical character of his time.

On a sharp winter's morning in Hanover it was quite a picture to see the ox teams, each hauling cord wood, gathered in the small square at the corner of the Common. Every load carried its snack of hay for the oxen, making quite a bucolic scene. The students dickered with the farmers, and toward the end of the afternoon there was a tendency for the price to fall. In those days, each student provided his own stove, usually purchased from some previous occupant of the room. The task of getting the wood sawed and split and carried up to a small closet was a difficult one, but the problem of keeping it was another matter, as there was quite a little borrowing back and forth. It was always a wonder that some of the dormitories were not destroyed by fire half a century earlier than actually happened and long before beautiful old Dartmouth Hall perished in the flames in 1904. I know the room which my father had in Old Dartmouth. It was in a corridor vulgarly known as 'Bedbug Alley.' My father was in the class of '52.

In the village our most distinguished guests during the summer were Mr. and Mrs. Hiram Hitchcock, of New York, who had developed a beautiful summer home just west of Faculty Avenue on Main Street, and leading with well-kept paths through Webster Vale down to the river. Mr. Hitchcock was proprietor of the Fifth Avenue Hotel and a gentleman interested in many important under-takings, such as the Metropolitan Museum in New York and Madison Square Garden. He was at one time president of the Nicaragua Canal Company. His wife was a charming woman and was for some years our Sunday-School teacher. She must have spent a long season at Hanover, because I seem to recall a picnic in Webster Vale under her auspices at about the time of my brother's birthday, May 7. Mr. Hitchcock was a trustee of the college and a close friend of my father, and it was a great satisfaction to the latter that when Mrs. Hitchcock died, Mr. Hitchcock erected as a memorial to his wife the Mary Maynard Hitchcock Hospital. For many years this had been my father's ambition for the Medical College and for the benefit of the student body and of the community. The hospital was built on a beautiful site in the northwest part of the village on the way to 'Stump Lane' and 'Rope Ferry.' It was built slowly and thoroughly, and my brother became its first medical director. He had then received his medical degree at Dartmouth and Harvard and completed his service as interne in the Boston City Hospital. Miss Margaret Thurston was sent from the Boston City Hospital as the first head nurse, possibly with some designs, as she and my brother had been pretty well acquainted in their joint work in Boston. They were married in the early autumn in 1895, about eight months before my father's death in May, 1896.

Professor Charles Augustus Young, son of a professor of natural philosophy, and grandson of an earlier member of the faculty, was one who played a decisive part in my own choice of a field for work. He occupied the Appleton professorship of natural philosophy which carried with it the instruction in astronomy. He was a remarkable teacher and inspired with a zeal for research, especially in solar spectroscopy. Professor and Mrs. Young and their daughter, Clara, were our very dear friends, and the younger son, Fred, was our chief playmate. It was quite a familiar experience for two lads somewhat tired of the monotony of hotel fare to run across the Common to the hospitable Young house and there find that Mrs. Ashley, the cook, had saved a little of that rice pudding for our dessert.

Professor Henry E. Parker was another courtly figure in the faculty. He had come from a pastorate in Concord with his well-to-do wife and had built a handsome home. His daughter, Alice, was a contemporary and often joined us in our play. Professor Parker was an accomplished Latin scholar, and with Professor John K. Lord was our instructor in that language during our college days.

We attended Sunday School regularly and I can remember the terrible sheets distributed on the occasion of the quarterly temperance Sunday. These portrayed as graphically as possible the road to perdition as induced by alcohol. One accomplishment which I learned during those hours was how to touch my nose with the tip of my tongue! That bit of wisdom was imparted by him who has now for many years been the popular undertaker. But there were also a great many other things brought to our attention in addition to the usual routine of the lesson sheet. It was here that I made my first acquaintance with the Nebular Hypothesis, and it certainly made a great impression upon me.

I, myself, later taught a class in this same Sunday School. I cannot guarantee the success of my ministrations, for one of the boys was later incarcerated in the State Prison at Rutland for some offense — what, I know not. Perhaps he would otherwise have arrived there sooner. I remember a pair of fine twin boys who were added to my class one Sunday. In trying to distinguish between them, another boy came to my help with the terse statement, 'This is Beef and this is Pork.' They were named from the 'Corn Beef' and 'Salt Pork' boxes hanging from the rear of their father's butcher cart which in those days daily visited the kitchen doors of the householders.

Sunday School used to be quite a perfunctory affair, following the forms of the printed Lesson Helps and in general with little preparation on the part of the pupils. Children were taught the precepts of the Bible in what would now be called the 'Fundamental' way, and these tenets were accepted without much question. Today it is quite difficult to make a fourteen-year-old boy believe that 'the meek shall inherit the earth.' His idea is that he must go out and get such part of the earth as he may desire for his possession, and he cites illustrious cases of wealthy men who are far from meek. He is even apt to question the applicability of the Biblical doctrines to modern life and frankly argue about the facts of creation. It is sur-

prising to me, by the way, that in the light of modern science there
are so many who still believe in the literal interpretation of the first
chapters of Genesis. Only recently, in a certain part of the United
States, a lecturer on astronomy was warned just before the address,
'We believe that the earth was created in six days of twenty-four
hours each.' My father used to tell me that when the velocity of
light was accurately measured and it was shown that thousands of
years would be required for light to reach the earth from distant
stars, there arose some lively discussion as to the bearing of this
upon the idea of instant creation on the 'fourth day.' Old President
Nathan Lord, who was head of the college when my father was
a student, summarily dismissed all doubts by saying, 'The Lord
created the light streaming all the way.' From his point of view, it
was a sufficiently good argument.

Going to church on Sunday morning was not without some excitement for two lively boys in the early days. First, breakfast at the
hotel had to be accomplished with fishballs, baked beans and brown
bread, the conventional morning repast of a Sunday, the beans
having first been served on Saturday evening. Then we would be
dressed up in those velvet suits which we so cordially detested and
arrive at our pew rather far front. The first question that occupied
our minds keenly was whether poor old Elder Richardson, paralytic,
would get up to the 'amen' corner in the very front where he was
supposed to sit, or whether he would fall into some lady's lap as he
staggered along from pew to pew the whole dreary length of that
church. It probably took him ten or fifteen minutes to make it. We
were under the strictest orders not to laugh at anything, however
funny. His maiden sister, Jane, could not, of course, struggle along
with him or help him, so she came whirling up the aisle at about
the time he should have reached his goal. Then we looked for a woman and her daughter who came rather late with great speed and
whom we always called 'the engine and the tender.' Behind us sat
a woman with an excellent, rather overpowering voice. We were
apt to get some entertainment, rather suppressed, from her singing.
The excitement quite subsided after the second hymn, and after the
long prayer I dozed off with my head on my father's lap and under
his beard, and there was no occasion for my taking further notice
until they rose to sing the last hymn. But meanwhile I had followed

a mesmeric device of my own and had for years indulged in various adventures on the horns of a splendid reindeer who could carry me anywhere over ford or hill to visit my relatives or see new parts of the unknown world. This practice of napping in my father's lap continued until I was probably twelve years old. It was broken on one Sunday when Father was away and the 'sextant,' as we called him, perhaps with some deviltry in his mind, ushered a couple of young ladies to our seat. They were the daughters of one of our visiting medical professors. On week days we were on the best of terms, often riding bareback together on the same horse, but on Sunday, when we were dressed up and the eyes of the congregation were upon us, it was rather a serious matter. I was grievously afraid that I should fall asleep and put my head in the lap of one of the girls, which I knew would entertain the audience.

This church served also as the public hall for lectures by distinguished guests of the college and for concerts occasionally presented during the year. We lads were not allowed to sit up late in the evening and went out only under exceptional conditions. I remember the concert by Camilla Urso, the violinist, and a fine chorus of Swedish voices. And Mr. Stoddard used to come with his lantern lectures, descriptive of his travels in Europe. They were well presented, but the change of the pictures with their varying illuminations always bothered my eyes and put me to sleep in short order. I was already a junior in college when Matthew Arnold came to lecture. I found him thoroughly dull, but there was an incident worth relating about his visit. He was entertained at Professor Parker's, and the thing that seemed to interest him most in the college was that an Indian was a student. This was Charlie Eastman, of the class of '87, and Charlie was invited to meet him at Dr. Parker's. The English author was probably expecting something quite different from the neatly dressed young man who came to call, and the tables were turned because Matthew had very little to say, and the Indian was certainly not inclined to be voluble.

It was a great treat to us boys, and a pleasant change from hotel fare when we were sometimes invited to accompany our parents to the homes of other members of the faculty. I remember going to a supper at the Sanborns' and how subdued we had to be. We sometimes got a peek into Professor Sanborn's office with that extraordinary wallpaper from England where the whole side of the room represented one picture. Professor Sanborn distinctly represented the scholar of the forties. He was professor of belles-lettres and was greatly in demand as an orator for the Fourth-of-July addresses and at the County Fair. His wife was a niece of Daniel Webster. Their son, Edwin Webster Sanborn, was a Hanover boy of an earlier academic generation than mine. He had much wit and was a favorite after-dinner speaker in New York. His sister, Kate Sanborn, was a brilliant woman who lectured at various women's colleges and wrote a number of books which were widely read. She held naturally rather a dominant position among the young women of Hanover and doubtless would be properly said to have passed her college widowhood there. After her father's death, she lived in New York, engaged in literary work, and there had a somewhat belated romance with a man of means and of distinction. He died before the wedding bells had been rung and left her a large fortune. This passed to her brother Edwin at her death, and was left by him to Dartmouth College for the erection of the beautiful Sanborn Hall recently built near the library for the department of English and serving as a memorial to his father. In that building is Professor Sanborn's office, furnished as it was originally, even to the famous wallpaper. Our nephew, J. Frederick Larson, was the architect who had the pleasure of making plans, not only for this building, but for all the recent fine construction at Dartmouth.

CHAPTER III

A GROWING BOY IN THE NEW HOME

How we did enjoy leaving the hotel and going to our new home! The carpenters were not out, but we couldn't wait. I still remember the delicious roast ham sent to us by that gracious lady, Madam Dixi Crosby. My brother and I sat on nail-kegs and ate our dinner in a little annex to the kitchen, rejoicing in the freedom from the restraint of the dining-room of the Dartmouth Hotel. This was in the summer of 1875.

The house to which we moved had been built about 1810 on the most conspicuous lot in the village at the southwest corner of the Common. It had been the president's house during the administration of Francis Brown in the forties, and was a beautiful specimen of old colonial architecture. It had been moved away to a new site to the eastern edge of the village and was purchased by my father from Mr. Gibbs, the tailor. I will digress here to say that the position of tailor to the faculty and students of Dartmouth College was no lowly function. Mr. Gibbs, I believe, was the immediate successor in that office of Levi P. Morton, who absorbed the academic culture necessary to serve admirably as Minister of the United States to France and afterwards as Vice-President of the United States.

The college dormitories were in such poor condition that they were unpopular with the students. Although the college recouped itself for its loss in revenue in rentals by assessing a small charge against the student body for unoccupied rooms in dormitories, the students preferred private homes. Accordingly my father added a third floor with a mansard roof, providing four suites for students, each suite with a study and bedroom easily capable of accommodating two students. For the next twenty years these rooms, which had their own stairs and access at the side of the house, were occupied by a fine set of young men, for the most part sons of men and women who had been friends of my father and mother during their residence in St. Johnsbury (1857–62), or at Woodstock and Windsor, where they lived during the years of the Civil War. The young men were quiet and orderly.   Each had his own stove with a coal bin in the barn, and the boys made no appreciable trouble for the family.   Of course there was sometimes a keg which sprung a leak and let the cider trickle through to the ceilings of our rooms below.   Occasionally Jim Morrill, son of the venerable Senator of Vermont, would stumble upstairs a little late, but in general our association with these fine young men was very pleasant.   We lads were accustomed to run up-stairs and talk with these men of the classes of the late seventies and early eighties, or listen to their practice in oratory.   In later years some of our own classmates occupied those rooms, and during our collegiate period my brother and I had the southwest suite for our own study.   One of the last of the group was Dean Craven Laycock who occupied the southeast suite for three years, and in those days we formed a firm friendship which has continued.

Occasionally sons of classmates of my father came to our house only for their first days in Hanover until they could be located in some dormitory or boarding-house.   Richard Hovey, the poet, was one of these men.   He was already deeply interested in literature, but he had another basis of common interest with us in his accurate know-ledge of birds, which he had studied carefully in the region of Wash-ington, D.C.   Nature lore appears less in his poetry than I for one could wish.   He felt the effect of Oscar Wilde, who was then some-thing of an æsthetic fad among aspiring young poets of the day and Hovey was a picturesque figure on the campus, with his long hair, his striking style of dress, and a sunflower in his buttonhole.   His poetry bears the flavor of his days at Dartmouth and will doubtless endure.

When our own barn was built, the old style was followed of having all the parts measured and fitted with tenons and mortices.   The kindly old carpenter who performed this rather laborious job was a wizened little man called by us 'Captain Jinks' (of Mother Goose, I suppose) 'of the Horse Marines, who fed his horse on corn and beans.'   When everything was ready, there was a grand 'raising.'   All the parts were gradually brought together and the framework of the structure fastened by strong hardwood rods or bolts which had been prepared for every joint.   There was some danger of an accident or collapse in this process of 'raising,' so that we were not allowed to participate as we would have liked.   This barn gave us a fine place to play on rainy days, and the boys of the neighborhood gathered there with us in various enterprises. The cupola was an excellent place to discuss our diverse interests and to spy out the land. We found a way of removing a slat so that it gave no offense to the architecture of the building.

College students always needed jobs to help pay their way, and during these years Father was fortunate in having a medical student care for the horses. Mr. Hyde was a man of wide experience in the Southwest country and he had an accurate knowledge of birds. It was he who gave us our first start in identifying and learning the characteristics of the birds, which were very abundant in the college park abutting our property just beyond the barn. My brother and I were greatly indebted to Mr. Hyde for this early start in natural history. It has been a perpetual source of satisfaction to us both.

Beyond the site of our house was the home of Charles Henry Hitchcock, Professor of Geology. He was thoroughly absorbed in his profession, which he inherited from his father, President Hitchcock, of Amherst College, but he was not quite alert enough for the human element of his audience to make a good teacher. He generally lectured with his eyes shut and often walked around the street apparently in the same way. He had made a special study of glaciation in his capacity as State Geologist of both New Hampshire and Vermont, and we sometimes later went on short expeditions with him. He was building a large relief map of the two States and when we were a little older he entrusted us to secure for him with an aneroid barometer the altitudes of some of the lofty hills in the vicinity. His oldest daughter was a contemporary of ours and joined us in an enormous industry of making mud pies during the construction of our house. There was plenty of material for the purpose, and day after day we produced vast numbers of loaves of bread, biscuits, and other articles which could be fashioned and baked, but never disposed of.

It seems to me that I had considerable patience for a boy of twelve when I often played by myself in a way that was a little too juvenile for my older brother. I recall the episode of my pet turtle. I made a harness for him, attaching a little wheeled cart built of cigar-box wood. I often spent an hour or so driving him the hundred feet from the stable to the street. I do not recall that he showed any marked signs of intelligence, but I at least learned some of the peculiarities

of turtles. Just last year, I was much interested in a wholesale migration of turtles from an artificial lake which had completely dried up.
At one point the highway was quite covered for a time while the
turtles with some deliberation crossed the road on their way to the
waters of Lake Geneva, Wisconsin.

When we were young we were always little spindle shanks, and how
we could run! We always ran — never walked. Little wonder that
we were restless at night and that when we slept with any of our relatives they complained of being black and blue the next morning
from contact with our sharp angles. It is not surprising, too, that I
was something of a somnambulist. It was not an infrequent experience to find myself on the stairway wondering where I might be.
One night the family was somewhat electrified to hear an unusual
racket in the hall and rushed out just in time to see me coasting
down the stairs on a great metallic serving tray.

There was perhaps something typical of the era in the contents of
the bookcase which hung on the wall of our bedroom. I remember
well the works of Racine, Corneille, and Molière which belonged to
my mother. Then there was a copy of *Napoleon and his Marshals* and
beside it *Godey's Lady's Book*. There were only a few books for boys,
some of Oliver Optic and a set of the Rollo Books passed on to us by a
cousin who had outgrown them. And I well remember the extreme
unction with which my brother would sometimes read to me, a little
before it was time to get up, what must have been a celebrated sermon by the Reverend John Todd. It was entitled *The Oiled Feather*.
I do not know where was kept the *Thomas Nast Almanac* for 1872
which had made a definite impression upon me when I was six years
old. This was before Nast, by his powerful cartoons published in
Harper's Weekly, had assisted effectively in the exposé of Boss Tweed
in his corrupt politics in New York City.

I shall never forget Nast's picture of the firemen pulling Mary's
little lamb out of the fire by the tail. I cannot guarantee that after
sixty years my recollection of the version of the variation on 'Mary
had a little lamb' which accompanied this picture is absolutely
verbatim, but it must be nearly correct. The last part of the ditty runs
this wise:

> But round and round the room it ran
> And did not seem to tire,

Until at last the stove upset
And set the house on fire.
The bells then rang,
The firemen came,
And made a dreadful noise.
They quenched the fire
And saved the girls
And nearly all the boys.
When Mary missed her little pet
She raised a dreadful wail,
Just then a fireman pulled it out
And saved it by the tail.

For more than one season, we played a game of 'farm' that was invented by my cousin George DuBois. The hand scroll-saws had been in use for some time, and we collected all the cigar boxes available. Then we searched the agricultural reports sent to Father by friends in Congress, finding patterns for all the varieties of cattle and sheep, which were sawed out and sometimes painted. Each boy had a certain area for his farm and there kept his stock which was allowed to increase under fixed rules. Dump carts and other implements were made, and we were well entertained, building barns for our animals and implements as rapidly as time permitted. We really learned quite a bit about different varieties of domestic animals, but found more practical opportunities when the great barn of the State farm of the Agricultural College was erected less than a quarter of a mile beyond our house. Here they kept some eighty head of cattle, experimenting with their feeding and frequently weighing them. There were also sheep and pigs, and we learned something about the raising of them. We were accustomed to spend considerable time in this big barn, where we knew practically every animal and had a name for each. We did some dangerous acts of walking on the beams high above the haylofts, but fortunately without accident.

The feline habits of our cat were largely responsible for his absurd set of names, 'Captain Jonah, Mighty Purrer, Gentle Howler, Felis Domestica, John, Everywhere and Anywhere, Monocular, Winkie, Antigyp-et-snow, Tom, Nimrod-Grasshopperorum, Thomas Smith Frost, F.R.E.S. (Fellow of the Rat Exterminating Society).' I used to put him on the back of a chair and make him say his prayers when he was naughty. He and our hundred-pound dog 'Dom' were good friends. Dom was, strictly speaking, 'Lord Edward,' from Frank Stockton's story. We shorted it to 'Dominus Edwardus,' and then to 'Dom.' People used to call us 'the three Frost boys.' I used to punish Dom by putting a great bag over him and setting him up on a wheelbarrow in full view of those who passed by. He was afraid to stir for fear he would fall. On the bag was painted, 'This is a bad dog repenting of his sins.' Dom went everywhere with us, nothing, even a stepladder, daunting him. He often followed us along the shore of the river when we were in the boat or sat excitedly in the bow until, grasping him by collar and tail, we threw him out for a swim. One adventure I shall never forget. I picked up somewhere the chassis of an old baby carriage, converting it into the semblance of a wagon which Dom could draw with a harness I made for him. One day I went down to the station riding on this thing. The dog was afraid of trains and very restive and unexpectedly dashed off while I was precariously balanced without a good hold on the reins. We went flying over the dusty road into the old covered bridge, but he finally lost his wind as we started up the hill. In winter, we sometimes skated up the river twenty miles, the dog with us, and came back on the evening passenger or freight train. Once when I saw Dom on the ice on the college campus where it was flooded and consequently made pretty good skating, I counted a chain of thirty-two children who were being carried around by his caudal appendage. He was often a trial to my mother with his long hair and his ravenous appetite. Every day there was a loaf of molasses brown bread baked for him. He was not permitted in the dining-room, but sat in the doorway, full of hope. A resounding snap of his big jaws indicated that a morsel of food had been surreptitiously thrown to him by one of the three men at the table. Mother really needed a daughter to defend her from masculine domination.

There were two points of special attractiveness to small children within the limits of the college park. One was the garnet rock, near the old pine, the crystals being of considerable size and a constant resource for the entertainment of children. The other attraction was the so-called 'polliwog pond.' This occupied a cleft in the rock near the Medical College and had about the contents of two bathtubs. The supply was rainwater, but it was sometimes polluted by careless medical students with waste from the dissecting room. I suppose that several generations of faculty children sailed boats on this diminutive pool. I used it as the place for experimenting with spring-driven side-wheel steamers which I made myself.

It was unfortunate that poison ivy had spread widely through the college park, with frequent painful experiences for us children until we carefully learned to avoid the three-leaved variety of ivy. I fear that even now this has not been exterminated.

New England thrift was displayed in all of our toys and outfittings for sport. In walking in the woods one always kept his eyes open for a crooked stick to serve in playing hockey on the ice. Sleds were often homemade, and the local blacksmith would be called on to supply the runners and the angle irons. The spirit of New England has been summarized in the words, 'Eat it up. Wear it out. Make it do.' All of this is in strong contrast to the modern tendency to extravagant buying of machine-made toys which are quite lacking in durability.

The local barbers, of Portuguese origin, had wonderful full-rigged ships of diminutive size with which they let us play at times and in moments of leisure could tell stories of the Azores and of the sea. Both men had aspirations to complete a medical education, but the exigencies of family life prevented them from carrying out their intention. Their own children received the education which they had sought. It has been interesting to see the absorption into American life of the infusion of foreign blood and the rapidity with which the new generation finds its place of influence.

The local bookbinder's establishment was a place of special interest to us, and Mr. Colby was very patient in showing us how he did his work. Although he has passed on, we have not forgotten his kindness to a couple of small boys.

We were not allowed to go to evening parties in our early youth and thus escaped the penalties of the silly games of that day, 'Post-Office,' 'Clap in and Clap out,' etc. We were far from being girl-minded and rather scorned social games. But when it came to coasting on the crust on a moonlight winter's night, there were no parental restrictions.

I had a cousin, Charles DuBois, who afterwards became Comptroller of the American Telephone and Telegraph and President of the Western Electric Company. He had a little printing press, and with another lad edited and published in Randolph, Vermont, a little paper (three by four inches in size) entitled *The Golden Reaper*. Charles constantly asked me for copy. I wrote everything I knew about birds and sometimes a verse or two. My mother was very fond of poetry and probably had ambitions for me, as she treasured for years an absurd little piece of doggerel which I wrote on January 1, 1875, when I was nine years of age. I hesitate to repeat it, but on New Year's Eve, just fifty years later, when I was dining in Washington with my former playmate, Fred Young, he referred to it and proceeded to repeat it *verbatim*. Moral: Beware of publishing too early!

> The old year goes down
> The New Year comes up,
> And all the ladies in town
> Invite the men to sup.
>
> The old year of '74
> Is gone and is no more.
> The New Year of '75
> Is born and is alive.
>
> Eddie Brant Frost (With apologies, '32.)

At this time we made frequent trips to Randolph where we had a host of relatives. My grandmother made her permanent home there, although she always spent a month of two of each year with us.

The partnership between my uncle Royal Turner DuBois and his brother-in-law Willard Gay, husband of my mother's only surviving sister, was a remarkable one and deserves mention in these days when people often lack faith in their fellow men and may even distrust their relatives. These two men were partners in various enterprises in Randolph and for many years had a private bank known as DuBois and Gay. They also owned a business block and, what was of immense importance to us boys, the fair grounds where the circus was held. This ordinarily meant to the nephews and nieces free tickets to the shows and an opportunity to see some of the intimate life of the people of the circus while the tent was being erected and the food was being prepared for the horses and the wild animals. My uncles were said to be thrifty Yankees and usually knew how and when to strike a bargain, often, however, helping a farmer when he needed some ready money and had a wood lot to dispose of. The two partners took out their rent for the meat market in the form of supplies for their respective home tables, and both families bought their dry-goods at a store whose proprietor was a tenant of the building owned by them. The two families lived on a similar scale of comfort, but not extravagantly, and for forty years the two men had no accounting between them. This duty, so far as it could be undertaken, fell to their heirs.

It was in the autumn of 1876 that my brother and I made our first trip out into the big world. It was highly exciting to us, but Mother kept us well in hand. Uncle Gilman DuBois and Aunt Ellen lived in Boston and had rented one of the 'brownstone front' mansions on Beacon Street for the season. They invited us to be their guests. The stately furniture was protected by linen covers and the ceilings seemed to us intolerably high, not our idea of a homelike atmosphere, but we had a grand time and our hosts treated us most graciously. I remember that we were there at Thanksgiving and it was a pleasant occasion. My uncle was retired from business, but usually walked down past the Common to the bank of which he was director and where he had a desk. He took part of the day to amuse us, and I remember very well going on board a steamer just in from Halifax and studying the mysteries of shipping. We saw the chattering flocks of English sparrows which had just been imported from Britain and which were objects of much interest to the citizens. They were maintained in excellent quarters at the city's expense, and little did anyone realize that in a few decades the 'bloody little birds' would be scattered all over the United States and a general nuisance, particularly to bird lovers.

Besides his pair, which Patrick kept in good order in the stable on Charles Street, Uncle Gilman had a favorite horse, a fine traveler, and in the afternoon he took us for long rides into the suburbs, sometimes going to the home of our ancestors in Randolph, Massachusetts, and then around through Brookline.

It was customary for our Uncle Gilman and his wife to drive up from Boston to the White Mountains and stop with us for some days or weeks on their way. Uncle brought along an extra saddle horse and thus took his exercise regularly while with us or at the White Mountains. It was a great sorrow to us and an irreparable loss to him when Aunt Ellen died suddenly of what must have been appendici-

tis, just before surgeons had learned how to perform an appendec-
tomy. Thereafter Uncle made his home at the then popular Bruns-
wick Hotel and was a devoted attendant at Trinity Church, presided
over by Phillips Brooks.

Our first bird book, E. A. Samuel's *Birds of New England*, was presented to me by Father and Mother on my tenth birthday and is still
one of my treasures fifty-five years later. We made a small collection
of eggs with only one specimen for each species, and we never traded
in eggs as did some other boys with unfortunate results for the nesting
birds. My brother and I remember to this day the exact circumstances of the discovery of this and that nest that was either actually
rare or new to us. Thus, I recall how one day in May I flushed a
whip-poor-will from the ground out by the 'Bottomless Pit' on the
road to Etna. These birds do not build a nest, but merely choose a
little hollow on the leafy ground. For some reason, I definitely con-
cluded that this bird had selected a site for a future nest, and a few
days later, on returning and finding the spot, I was happy to see the
two eggs in that little inconspicuous depression. We were also satisfied that the white-throated sparrow was breeding in that swampy
area and searched most diligently for her nest. We finally found it,
but the eggs had not been laid, and our search had been so thorough
that the bird never did occupy the nest. Out there, too, we became
acquainted with the olive-sided flycatcher, rather a rare bird, and
my brother and I adopted its call for our own. I doubt if there were
any two boys in New England who chose that particular call for their
special use. So far as I know, it was never imitated by other boys,
and if one of us missed the other in as large a crowd as at the Barnum
and Bailey Circus, which occasionally came to White River Junction, connection could immediately be re-established by giving
that whistle.

A really rare find that we made was the discovery, very early in
the season in the college park, of a couple of nests of the American
siskin, or pine finch. We spent hours and hours in an effort to find the
nest of the red crossbill which habitually spent the winter in the park
and stayed so late into the spring and early summer that we felt sure
it must be breeding there. Our strenuous efforts were not rewarded.
We were also interested in trying to find the breeding place of the
lesser yellow-legs (*totanus flavipes*). We made several early trips be-

fore sunrise toward Dotham, Vermont, in order to locate it, joining forces with our friend Allen Hazen, of Christian Street, in Hartford, Vermont. These birds have that interesting peculiarity of holding their wings aloft when they settle on a fence-post as if uncertain whether it would support them. We learned many of their habits, but never found a nest, although we felt quite sure that they might occur in the region which we were searching. For a single summer a pair of red-headed woodpeckers lived somewhere in the college park. They are very common in most parts of the United States but not near Hanover, and such visitors were a real novelty to us. In winter we had quantities of the pine grosbeak feeding on the cones of the Norway spruce which were abundant in the park, but in summer it was a special delight when we could locate the rose-breasted grosbeak, charming singer and beautiful bird. There were many scarlet tanagers around the college campus, and when the sermon seemed somewhat dull on a summer Sunday morning, one could always make quite a little study of natural history through the open windows. This has been a resource to me ever since.

It was my duty in natural history surveys to climb the trees, because I was entirely fearless in respect to height, while my brother became dizzy. Thus I had the satisfaction of learning the sustaining qualities of the different kinds of trees and barks. A beech with its smooth bark and its elastic branches could be trusted out to the very tip, while the elm was somewhat treacherous. Maples could be depended upon to hold you wherever you could go, and these were some of our finest trees. I learned to shinny up quite like a monkey, even when the trunk was far too large for me to reach around. Sometimes it was necessary to bring an egg down from a nest in a tree, which required a careful descent. I remember very well one such occasion when we drove ten miles south to a heronry in order to add a specimen of their eggs to our collection. The stunted evergreen trees had very brittle branches and the eggs were rather large to be carried in the mouth. I recall that a branch broke unexpectedly and I found that the heron's egg was distinctly fresh. I had to go up again to get another one.

One of our boyhood associates of the vigorous Vermont type was Dean C. Worcester, of Thetford Hill, whose father was the local physician and with whom my father had begun his study of medicine.

Dean was keenly interested in nature and particularly in birds, so that we compared notes as often as we could together, occasionally joining him in an expedition in search of rare species. These early interests were continued throughout his life. After graduating at Ann Arbor, he became an assistant professor there in the Department of Zoölogy. It was not surprising that he was invited to go as a scientific adviser to the Philippines during our early occupancy of the Islands. He wrote several delightful books about the natural history of the Philippines and ultimately became for some years Secretary of the Interior of the Insular Government.

When we were considered qualified to own a boat we bought the *Psyche*, which was a good-sized dory, and tied it up near the Ledyard Bridge. It was a common joke for people who read the name and knew that it was owned by the doctor's boys to ask if it might not be a new way of spelling 'physic.' We never ventured on the river in a canoe. In the freshets of the spring and early summer, the current was too strong and treacherous and has been the cause of occasional fatalities among students who were inexperienced in handling a canoe under these conditions. After such a tragedy, a resident expressed herself thus: 'I should have thought if he couldn't have swum he wouldn't have went.'

After we acquired a boat our later trips in studying the habits of birds took us on the river, where we had especial pleasure in getting up speed with our oars and then drifting quietly along shore, studying the birds, who did not seem to notice the noiseless approach of our boat. Our ownership of a boat meant a great concession on the part of Mother, who had a great horror of water. For the same reason, we had rather a hard time learning to swim, but there was a possible place, called by us 'Deep Hole,' in Mink Brook about half a mile upstream from the West Lebanon road. There we occasionally had an opportunity to practice swimming, but my brother and I were not experts and never liked to dive. Later, however, on the New Hampshire bank of the Connecticut near the mouth of Mink Brook, we disported ourselves in the free and easy manner of youth unencumbered by bathing-suits or towels. The process of 'drying off' was a simple one — to run fast in the breeze.

I have always loved the banks of that part of the Connecticut River above which Hanover is situated. The slope is steep, and the graceful white birches among the stately pines mirrored in the waters of the river below make a picture of great beauty and serenity.

I have a very definite impression of the trees in Hanover, some of which were well over a hundred years old. Even as a little boy I loved them and had among them my special friends. In the spring I was much interested in guarding the secret of the growing nuts of a couple of chestnut trees in the college park, and later in the fall I enjoyed scuffling through the leaves of a special row of scarlet maples. White pines, which a century earlier covered this whole region, were splendid trees — great sentinels. Four of these pines when felled would enclose an acre, which means that they were two hundred feet high. Later the streets in town were dignified by magnificent elms whose branches meeting overhead made a graceful arch. One of the largest of these elms was still standing in the seventies on the southwest corner of the Common, and I well recall its mighty fall after men had chopped on it for days. Professor Young told me about a particular elm tree which was hollow when he was a lad (1840) and that he could hide in it. This tree was patched up by building a box around it, the bark finally encircling it. This tree still stands. on the northeast corner of the Common opposite the entrance to Rollins Chapel. It is a magnificent elm, and few residents seem to know that it used to be hollow.

Stump Lane was a relic of the days of the mighty pines which everywhere covered the plains around Hanover. This lane led northward from the village toward the rope ferry which was operated in the early days over the Connecticut River near the first island. The gigantic stumps and roots were placed on their sides as a substitute for a fence and some of them rose from ten to fifteen feet above the ground, offering a confusing obstacle to cattle who might wish to pass. There were many of these great stumps left while I was a boy and I have seen a good photograph of them at a still earlier period, but they have now probably vanished from the landscape. The early morning rides on my horse through Stump Lane and down to the river with its low-hanging mist gave me great joy.

Near-by was the Vale of Tempe, well known as such to generations of students. Shut in by steep wooded slopes and shaded by tall pines, its tiny brook followed a winding course to the river. Water from the springs along the slopes gave the brook its meager

water supply. We often had picnics here, and it was in this rather secluded spot that we found our first redstart's nest. In some of its
shady places patches of snow often lingered until the second week in
May. I always hoped to find the trailing arbutus here, but it grew
higher up on the hillsides where it was abundant in the acid soil of
disintegrated granite rock.

In my later boyhood days, Sam Bartlett and I were interested in
the production of gunpowder. The Fourth of July was approaching
and we needed explosives. So for some days we secretly conducted
operations in the protection of a bare ledge in the college park. We
somehow acquired the necessary saltpeter and other constituents,
following the formula of the encyclopedia. But the product lacked
the one quality of inflammability. However, we had expected to
make the big effort on the morning of the Fourth, and a candle had
been set alight timed to burn down to the level of the powder by four
o'clock. Sam lived in the Dartmouth Hotel at that time and it was
not convenient for him to be called by his parents who were not informed on the subject. So Sam fastened a strong string to his toe,
hanging the string out of the second-story window at a height calculated to be reached by me from my saddle horse. A dismal rain set
in about midnight and added the final touch to the safe quality of our
gunpowder. Naturally, I did not get up early. The string worked,
however, because the hotel porter in sweeping off the steps that
morning discovered it and angled to see what he would get. It was
only a moment before a foot came out of the window following his
vigorous pull. Thereafter we bought our firecrackers with what
little money we could gather together for the occasion.

In the late seventies, active boys with a fervor for making collections were greatly interested in learning the names and numbers of
the locomotives on all railroads within their purview. My brother
and I felt the importance of this matter very keenly and it always
added interest to our visit to Randolph, Vermont, that the main
line of the Central Vermont went right through the village only a
few feet from the bank, then owned by my uncles. There were
eighty-four engines as far as we could ascertain, and we felt it a part
of our duty to commit the names and numbers to memory. I can repeat quite a few of them to this day, although I cannot guarantee
that I could keep the numbers with the names. The J. O. D. Hatch

was number one and the Arctic was number eighty-three. It was quite a satisfaction to us when they named one of the engines for our uncle, W. H. DuBois, who was a director of the road, and that by a signal to the conductor when we boarded the train he could ensure free transportation for us from Randolph to White River Junction. The names and numbers of these engines were carefully kept in special notebooks with a chapter for each railroad, and in case it was impossible to see personally every engine on every railroad, it was legitimate to swap names and numbers with other lads who lived on the Erie, for instance. I do not suppose I can ever forget the Emmons Raymond (number fifteen on the Passumpsic Railroad), passing through the stations of Norwich and Hanover on the morning mail; or the handsome Magog with a red smokestack which pulled the fast White Mountain Express in summer. Our visit to Boston yielded a harvest of names because the Boston and Lowell still used that system. We found one old engine with a very low number, number four, and its name was the Comet. It was during this period that a transition was made from wood-burners to coal-burners. The great flaring funnel was replaced by a long straight one, and it was no longer necessary to stop beside a vast pile of chopped cordwood while the train crew threw it up into the tender. Passengers who were in a hurry and were willing to take the exercise gladly assisted. There was often a tame bear on a chain at these 'wooding-up' stations, presumably to amuse the French-Canadian workmen who were at the endless task of getting more wood to throw into the next tender. I should add that, besides getting the names and numbers of the engines, we also trained our ears so that we could recognize the individual whistles and this practice has stood me in good stead for all the years since. My children have shared my interest in knowing the engines by number whenever we have traveled, and we have our favorites on the Chicago and North Western Railroad and the Chicago, Milwaukee, St. Paul and Pacific.

My brother and I got well acquainted with the details of the dissecting room in our tender youth, as we often took telegrams for Father to the Medical School Building, where he supervised the instruction in anatomy. Anatomical material was not in those days so readily obtained, but the State Prison furnished an occasional cadaver from some notorious character who had been executed. Thus there was a murderer named Evans whose skeleton was frequently 'borrowed' from the Medical College on the occasion of some special celebration and was found on the campus in the morning hanging between the poles where the campaign flags usually swung in the breeze. I can recall a portly cadaver sitting in a chair in the large lecture room not used in winter, waiting for his turn to be taken down to the tables below. Formalin had not at that time been discovered, and the odors in the dissecting room were not suppressed as they are today. We boys, however, could stand anything that the medical men could, and we learned something of human anatomy by the kindness of students who showed us how they were tracing out a system of nerves, and so forth. This winter class came to Father's office about five evenings in the week for recitations, first at the hotel and afterwards at our house. As bathtubs were not current equipment of students' rooms, or even of the gymnasium, the first process after the students left was a most thorough ventilation. I do not recall that students wore laboratory coats or uniforms and therefore they carried about with them a distinct impression of the dissecting room.

In this connection I recall having assisted a medical student to assure the complete cleanliness of a new thoroughly wired skeleton by hiding it for him in a spring in a sequestered spot. After a few weeks the constant circulation of the water over the bones produced the desired result. It should be added that this particular spring was not the source of any water supply. One may imagine, however, the possible surprise of some exploring botanist looking for rare plants to find this rattling good specimen of the *genus homo*.

The hygiene of the New England towns was not all that could be desired. There was, of course, no water supply in the main dormitories, Old Dartmouth, Wentworth, and Reed. And the students who had ablutions to perform must perforce go to the college pump on the campus. It must have been cold on some mornings when a man had forgotten to supply his needs the afternoon before. The pump was of iron, and the student put his hand over the outlet and drank from a little hole in the pipe. Thus, if a man happened to have typhoid, he could readily distribute it to the rest of the college. My father had typhoid when he was in college, probably communicated in some such way. There was occasionally an unfortunate amount of typhoid fever even in the well-protected homes of the faculty. I recall also when there were one or more cases of smallpox in town, which of course my father cared for. Then there was a period that I was not allowed to sit in his lap at family prayers. After breakfast I always expected to sit in his lap and then to find a place under his arms when he knelt after reading the Scripture. I greatly loved and respected my father. He used to call me affectionately, 'Little man.' I did not call him 'Dad' until I was quite a young man, and always answered him, 'Yes, sir.' We looked upon my father as an example, not a dictator. Until we entered college, family prayers did not have to be hurried, and no such untoward incident arose as in an authentic case in another family. The head of the house often came in hurriedly and began reciting the Scripture before he sat down or even opened his Bible. That family was somewhat electrified to hear him say one day, 'The Lord is my shepherd, I shall not want. Damn that cat!' as he unexpectedly sat on Tabby.

Sunday in a Calvinistic college town of New England was not a day of rejoicing and resting one's soul. As a matter of course a boy went to church and then to Sunday School, but it was not considered good form, and was indeed not a practice, for healthy youngsters to do more than take a sober walk in the afternoon. My brother and I were especially fortunate. The Doctor must, of course, take what were long drives to see his patients. We were thus able to visit new fields for the study of birds or to tramp to some hilltop near the home of the patient. My father's parents had stern memories of 'The Great Awakening' of the days of Jonathan Edwards, Whitefield, and Eleazar Wheelock. It was therefore the wish of my grandmother, Mary Brant, that her first-born, my father, should be a missionary and help the so-called heathen before it was too late to rescue them as brands from the burning. My father's interest in medicine led to a compromise with the thought in his mother's mind that he might become a medical missionary. This did not come to pass, but there lingered the tradition that medical services rendered on the Sabbath Day might well be gratuitous. Thus there were long rides to visit chronic patients, doctors or members of their families, and forty miles in a buggy with a single horse gave an outing to us youngsters. We abstained, however, from riding our saddle horse, and without any precept on the matter so far as I recall. Nor did it ever occur to us to use our boat for a row upon the river. In the nineties there was a relaxation in the severity of the observance of the day, and it became proper to invite some young lady to take a ride on Sunday afternoon before the chapel hour.

In the early days, five o'clock was the hour for chapel, quite similar to the routine morning service. But it was followed by a required exercise consisting of reading from the New Testament in Greek or Latin for those who had studied these subjects, or in appropriate variations, as in French for those who had not studied the classics. The task of instruction was divided among the professors. On the part of the students there was little complaint that their afternoon walk had been shortened by the religious requirements of the hour.

CHAPTER IV

EARLY EDUCATION

AFTER our early and rather irregular hours of study at home with Mother, she seriously carried us through *Colburn's Mental Arithmetic*. It was a severe discipline but a useful one, and gave us the habit of thinking quickly and clearly without depending upon the use of pencil and paper and those awful unsanitary slates. We thus early acquired a habit of forming a mental picture of the whole problem straight through to its solution.

Thank Heaven that we learned to spell by syllables, and not by whole words as is the practice today. It is difficult to believe that the new method leads to the accuracy of the old way. A young fellow in reading aloud today often struggles over comparatively simple words because he doesn't know how to break them up into syllables.

Before entering high school I attended for a few weeks a parish school established by the Episcopal Church. This was my first experience in any schoolroom. We had an excellent teacher and a thorough training in the use of the Prayer Book. I always accounted to Mother for the wearing out of my pants and stockings at the knees by the fact that I had to get up and down so often at prayers.

Lewis Parkhurst, of the class of '78, was the principal of the high school during the first season after the building was erected, and was thus my first teacher in the public school. He was a powerful man and could keep order even among some of the larger boys, practically men, who came to receive a belated education. I was a timid, slender lad, and took refuge by sitting under the wing of Dave McNally, a big fellow who had already served in the United States Navy. In geography, Dave couldn't very accurately visualize on the map the ports which he had visited as a sailor. We had new and interesting books, or so it seemed to me whose home studies had been chiefly with books of the previous generation. I have never forgotten those excellent maps showing three red dots in the vast spaces of Siberia where were the towns of Omsk, Tomsk, and Tobolsk. I was thoroughly scared at first when called upon to recite, and so made rather poor work of it in arithmetic. But when I got over to the part called 'mensuration,' which concerns itself with areas, slant heights, rhomboids, and so forth, I was greatly interested, and with a pretty good memory could run off the rules for the different cases quite glibly. Accordingly, at the grand finale of the winter term I was awarded the prize for the best general improvement in arithmetic, a small volume of Tennyson's poems which of course I still possess. That was in 1878. At this time my brother was appropriately ahead of me in mathematics, but we began our Latin and Greek together, the former when I was eleven, and the latter at thirteen.

We continued our study in the high school at Hanover for two or three years, and with fine teachers. But as the school could not start us in Greek, we presently took all of our college preparatory studies in our own house under college students of high standing. I recall with special pleasure Herbert J. Harriman ('79), who was then a medical student. We had the satisfaction of infecting two of our tutors with mumps, which gave us a few days of holiday, but by the same token, we communicated the disease to our good old Grandmother Frost, who was visiting us at the time — something of a joke to us, but more serious for her at eighty years of age. My brother had had an excellent preparation in mathematics and in fact used to tutor freshmen in their algebra in classes as early as 1883. Meanwhile, I was catching up in these subjects, and we went on together in the classics. We had a blackboard in one of the rooms on the ground floor of our house and there had our lessons over a period of two or three hours a day, taking up the Iliad, Ovid, and other Latin and Greek authors. With only two of us in class and a certain spirit of humor in the whole undertaking, we rollicked along through much more than was required in preparation for college. I generally drew cartoons on the blackboard representing the principal actions of the day, such as Hector and Achilles chasing each other around the plains of Troy, with old Priam, Helen, and the rest of them occupying poses which seemed appropriate to me, but which were not wholly classical. We used to adopt the Greek and Latin names for common articles around the house and barn, and in this way succeeded in fixing them rather definitely in our minds, although without that intention. We had a lot of books inherited from my father and my uncles as well as from the library of Squire Duncan, including excellent classical geographies which told us of the haunts of the 'blessed Ethiopians' and of the unicorns (symbolic rhinoceroses). I feel sure that at one time we knew the provinces of Greece and Macedonia far better than we ever did the counties of New Hampshire.

About this time (when I was fifteen) I was given the task of reading and recording the weather observations at the observatory during the winter vacation. I also kept the fires going so that the batteries wouldn't freeze. To be at the observatory at 7 A.M., 2 P.M., and 9 P.M. — and in all kinds of weather — was something of a responsibility for a young chap, but I felt that I was taking part in a scientific undertaking and did not much consider the fact that I was making these twenty-one trips a week for one dollar.

I was also appointed clerk of the Dartmouth Scientific Association and for my services received the munificent sum of forty cents a week. Two definite tasks were assigned to me. The first was to keep the records of the scientific publications, and the second was to deliver the copies of these periodicals to the members of the Association. The latter task did not take long, as I always rode my horse bareback on these errands. The task of binding *Nature* gave me the opportunity of becoming acquainted with this periodical when I was quite young. On the occasion of the appearance of its two thousandth number, I had the pleasure of dining with the editor, Sir Norman Lockyer, in London.

And so it befell that in June, 1882, we, with a few others, took the entrance examinations for Dartmouth College. Most of the men entered from academies or high schools by certificate and without examination. These boys had the advantage of being drilled so that they would do creditable work in their freshman year. We worked on these examinations for three days, morning and afternoon. This was about a month before my sixteenth birthday. We were certainly lacking in the study of English grammar and English literature, although we were well drilled in Latin and Greek grammar. We were admitted, and I remember that Father told us to forget our books until the college term opened in September. So we went over the hills in search of rare birds, and visited relatives at Randolph. I remember driving home with Kit in the single buggy, making a long détour *via* the so-called 'rabbit track' over amazingly steep hills through Chelsea, Vermont. We found college men along the way and made quite an adventure of this trip of exploration.

CHAPTER V

COLLEGE YEARS

I THINK that family prayers were suspended in our house when two or three of us had to make a hurried scramble to get to chapel at three minutes to eight. The bell rang for four minutes, then tolled for three minutes and ended with a double stroke, after which no entrance was permitted, and those who arrived too late could only gnash their teeth. Students often came to chapel without full completion of their toilet, but a large overcoat covered a multitude of omissions. It was always arranged that classes immediately followed chapel, and there was a hasty exodus from the building to the various classrooms. Most of these were heated by an iron stove and there was a small room adjacent, called the 'guard-room,' wherein lived the student charged with keeping up the temperature in the classroom. This system of heating seems rather crude today, but it was on the whole very efficient and we seldom had cold rooms. The student who acted as stoker also served as a monitor, checking off attendance at certain classes.

The morning exercises in the old chapel in the central part of Old Dartmouth Hall were always likely to have some unexpected finale. The president and faculty sat on a raised platform at the front with only one entrance on either side. There was never quite complete certainty whether the organ would work or might have been tampered with in the night so as to emit sounds not appropriate in a religious exercise. Back of the stage a window-curtain might fall during the service, bearing incriminating remarks about certain students or the faculty. Or a sheet might be found in the hymn-books having some 'grinds' on an unsuspecting college officer or upon a member of the student body who might be in temporary disfavor.

Then there was always the question of emergence. The juniors sat on the south side and behind them the freshmen, with the seniors in front on the north and the sophomores behind them. President Bartlett usually gave a pretty fair hint as to when the final prayer was approaching the end. It took the form of the phrase, 'Hasten the time when all the earth shall,' and so forth. This was parodied once in the college annual, 'Hasten the day when prexy will pray some other way than "Hasten the day." ' The form of ending became a matter of speculation to those inclined to wager. Someone therefore set the president wise and he frequently used an alternative phrase, 'May the time soon come,' so that sporting chances were still taken. But when these final phrases came from the lips of the august president, the juniors who sat in front of me had their hats ready and no time was lost. Not a second after the Amen began, they started for the door. And it was with some delight that the freshmen followed them so closely that the front array was generally pushed from the stone steps and carried off, as it were, on a wave of descending piety to the walk below. Once in a while there was a sprained back or leg as a result of this prompt dismissal, but on the whole there was a business-like air in hastening to the classrooms and an apparent ardor for learning which would hardly have been expected. This procedure had been followed for over a century. I always remember Josiah Quincy, of the class of '84, who sat not far in front of me and could be seen for the last few minutes of the prayer getting his little derby in position so that he would have a grand start.

When college opened in the autumn, it had less novelty for us than for most of our classmates. We had hung around the outskirts of the crowd at all college sports enough to be familiar with them, and we had seen so many freshmen come in and adapt themselves to the new life that we were inclined to regard ourselves as somewhat sophisticated. This was not the case in the classroom, because we had not been used to reciting before other students and we were both rather shy. The schedule was: Algebra, Latin (Livy), and Greek (Herodotus, Æschylus, and the lyric poets). While I realize very fully the limited acquaintance with the classics which the average boy picks up during the six years of Latin and four years of Greek under the old academic system, I nevertheless have no moment to regret for the time that I thus spent. I feel that my knowledge of these languages, although limited, has stood me in good stead every day for more than fifty years. I never was a good scholar in Latin and I could never see reason in the sequence of Latin composition. I know, too, that most of the students abhorred it. I remember the weekly exercises under Professor John King

Lord and how I offered some reflections on the 'Ceruleus Connecticutus.' The professor didn't smile, but dealt with it seriously as perhaps it deserved.

I always liked Greek better than Latin. One of our instructors was Professor John Henry Wright, an excellent scholar who had lately come back to teach at Hanover after completing his studies in Germany. He thought that there was virtue in the German lecture method and tried it on us in Greek composition. Thus we had to take notes, and were obliged to write down *verbatim* his introductory paragraph, which I committed to memory. When called upon to make some remarks at our reunion forty years later, I thought it would be amusing to repeat that paragraph: 'The object of this course is, by a series of exercises, interspersed with notes on various matters, first, to secure familiarity with the Greek mode of expression, and, second, to make more vivid, exact, and comprehensive, the knowledge to be gained by reading.' Several of my classmates called out, 'Letter perfect.' Naturally, that was the only thing about the course that I did remember. It is sometimes easier to commit a thing to memory than to forget it.

As I had a slight gift of caricature, my personally illustrated notebook on the history of philosophy, as presented to us in lectures by Professor Gabriel Campbell, had some notoriety among my classmates. To me, the sketch of Anaxagoras toiling up the hill to the Parthenon and pushing a wheelbarrow filled with γοῦς (the philosophy of intelligence and reason) made unforgettable to me the fact that he was the first man to bring philosophy to Athens. I also recall my sketch of Socrates and his δαίμων (demon), who was really his good angel and controlled his life, persuading him to keep away from a wineshop. There was another picture of Alcibiades celebrating in a hilarious mood under a lamp-post on the hill of Athens.

In the spring term all freshmen were required to take a practical course in surveying. This was one of the most interesting of all courses, both to those naturally industrious and to those naturally lazy. We went out in groups of about four each in charge of one of the more trustworthy students. We used the plane-table for a survey of the campus and laid a base-line measuring the distance to Mount Ascutney, which is a fraction under twenty miles from the observatory. We wound up with making a survey of some irregular piece of land with a rail fence and plenty of bushes, requiring offsets. It may seem strange to a modern youth that all students were required to take such a course, but it was certainly a valuable one to most of those who took it. For well over a hundred years in the history of the college this was a required exercise.

After sophomore year was finished, we were allowed some electives, and my natural tendency toward the study of the physical sciences led me to choose all the laboratory work possible in the ground floor of Reed Hall. The college really had some remarkable equipment, especially in the line of optics. This had been purchased chiefly by Professor Charles Young and his father before him. I took great pains with my notebook on the physical experiments, which I illustrated much more elaborately than was necessary, little realizing that in a couple of years I should be installed as an assistant in the same laboratory.

One of my special pleasures in college was the opportunity of being in the classroom of Professor Arthur S. Hardy who taught us analytic geometry, calculus, and analytic mechanics. He was a remarkable teacher and a many-sided gentleman — poet, novelist, and author of a volume of quaternions. He gave up teaching about 1895 and became editor of the *Cosmopolitan Magazine* in New York. Shortly thereafter he was appointed Minister to Persia and so journeyed to Teheran. Later he was transferred to the position of Minister at Athens, and thence after some years to Berne, and finally retired from the diplomatic service after having been Ambassador to the court of Madrid for some time.

Senior year at Dartmouth in 1886 provided rather a large range of electives. I had been greatly interested in a course in descriptive astronomy given by Professor Charles F. Emerson (familiarly known as 'Chuck'), and had up to then used the telescope, with which I had been more or less familiar for many years. This term was probably the only one in which I had a higher rating than my brother, and to pass ahead of him required being about at the head of the class. I was considerably in doubt as to whether my work would be in the line of physics or astronomy. The tradition of Professor Young's brilliant work in the observatory was still strong. My personal acquaintance with him and the family added to the interest. It happened that at this time (in August, 1885) a new star, or Nova, was suddenly discovered by an English astronomer. It was in the heart of the Great Nebula of Andromeda and was a star of about the seventh magnitude. It thus became the only individual star distinguishable in this nebula, which at that time we supposed to be a purely gaseous body. From what we now know, this star almost certainly became twenty million times brighter than our sun. The distance of the nebula was then not regarded as greater than that of the stars in our portion of the Milky Way, but it is now known to be vastly more remote — of the order of 900,000 light-years, and is composed of stars instead of nebulous matter. Among astronomers, as well as the public generally, it was thought that we might be observing the sudden transformation of the nebula into a star along the lines of the theory of Laplace. I was familiar with the appearance of the nebula and was immensely excited over the new phenomenon. Perhaps it was this that led me somewhat definitely to enter the field of astronomy rather than that of physics. I had just passed my nineteenth birthday at this time and had a right to youthful enthusiasm.

It had been the requirement at Dartmouth that every senior should deliver before the college an original oration during the course of the year. This exercise occurred at one-thirty on Wednesday afternoons under the conduct of the professor of English literature, who censored in advance the speeches to be presented. After the two or three so-called orations were over on a given Wednesday, the rest of the afternoon was free. This made the audience somewhat restive, as all the boys had some program of activity to set in motion as soon as the last speaker had finished, and it was a highly critical audience, not hesitating at all to applaud at the wrong place as circumstances might seem to require.

When my turn came, I had the temerity to choose as my topic this remarkable new star in the Andromeda Nebula. Perhaps it was out of consideration of my youth, for I was the youngest in the class, that the audience was tolerant and let me by without any undue disturbance. But it rather committed me to the astronomical field. I used the telescope a good deal during the year, learning how to observe the prominences or solar eruptions and to study the bright lines in the spectrum. I remember well how I pored over the big blue book of Norman Lockyer, entitled *Solar Physics*. I did not then realize that before many years I should have the pleasure of becoming acquainted with this distinguished scientist. He belonged to a little different school from that which I was entering. Both at Princeton and later in my studies at Potsdam, Germany, under H. C. Vogel and J. Scheiner, we looked somewhat askance at Lockyer's tendency to build up a theory like his Meteoritic Hypothesis on inadequate observational data, and the same thing applied to his Hypothesis of Dissociation, but he was a man of great genius and could often reach important inferences from a modicum of observed data.

In June, 1886, we graduated in the regular course, after a year of hard, interesting work. I specialized in physics and received 'final honors' therein, while my brother received his in mathematics. We had to write theses as a part of the extra requirements. My brother gave the salutatory address and I ranked somewhere around sixth in the class. I made rather a juvenile speech on the influence of astronomy on literature. Graduating day was quite an ordeal for the audience, for not less than fifteen of us spoke, and we followed the ancient practice of appearing in dress suits, though the time was forenoon.

The class of '86 was not a brilliant one, but most of them were hard-working men who have made honorable records. Some of them have attained distinction. They went into the usual professions open to college graduates, lawyers, business men, physicians, and engineers predominating. Three of the class went into the ministry. They have all been faithful to Dartmouth, and the reunions, at all of which I have been present, have been well attended. I have kept rather intimately in touch with a good many of the men of '86 and it hurts to see the thinning ranks. Every five years a class report has been issued, and as a frontispiece in the one prepared for our fortieth reunion, the secretary selected a photograph of my cousin, Mary Brant Little, standing between my brother and me. The picture was taken soon after my graduation and in the report it was given the caption, 'The Roaring Eighties,' the picture having been snapped as I was telling what must have been a good story.

CHAPTER VI

ACTIVITIES DURING COLLEGE

IN THE early days, before organized sport had become of absorbing interest in college life and before winter sports except skating had entered into student life, there were few outlets for the students' natural effervescence. Of course, many of them went out to teach school immediately after Christmas, as was the tradition. My father and his two brothers, Edwin B. and Henry M., all taught in the winter, probably in each year of their college course, and generally in the vicinity of Cape Cod. There was a long vacation of four weeks, which in earlier years was even longer, so that the student lost no college exercises.

The town was rather a snowy waste during January, but this made little difference to a pair of young fellows who had a horse and sleigh at their disposal, plenty of sleds, and two pairs of good skates. Coasting was a sort of passion with me and I must have made walking pretty risky for some of the older citizens living in our neighborhood. As a boy I used to ice the sidewalks where the track of my sled would be well marked and bank the corners so as to make in safety what would otherwise have been hazardous turns. I can remember one bitterly cold night when I was out icing my track that I looked at the observatory thermometer and found it stiff at 39° below zero. This is the lowest reading that I have ever seen. The latter part of the winter, extending even into April, when the sunshine would be strong by day and the air very cool by night with frequent zeros, the situation was ideal for forming a crust. I have seen the crust so strong that oxen could walk on it, and again, I have skated on it. It was then one of our great delights to go wandering about over the hills and dales.

A grand old elm tree stood on the crest of the hill a couple of hundred yards south of the observatory, and it was a test of skill to make the turn around this splendid old tree, and go crashing down over the bump into the valley below. Later, probably after I was an instructor, some of the young ladies used to like to trust themselves to my steering. But with five on the sled, there was a pretty strong chance that the slippery turn could not be made and that there would be a general spill, some of the passengers perhaps going over the edge. It happened that this particular spot was in full sight of the chemical laboratory in Culver Hall, and I came to learn that these episodes were quite distracting to the class who should have been in their places at the long tables of analytic chemistry instead of hanging out of the windows, hoping to see a grand upset.

My single sled 'Shoo-Fly' was given to me in the early part of the winter of 1872. I have it still. When Professor Young's family went to Princeton in 1877, they gave us their whole retinue of sleds: 'Bummy,' a little yellow sled that Professor Young had built when he was in Hudson, Ohio, for his daughter, Clara, about 1862 (and this I still have), and a double-runner which belonged to Fred Young and which bore the appropriate names of 'Comet' and 'Meteor.' I doubt if the second generation has any such enthusiasm for coasting as mine did. There were times when River Hill, leading into the old covered Ledyard Bridge, and Nigger Hill toward West Lebanon, and 'Potash Hill' on the Lyme road would be very icy, and there was real sport for a heavy double-runner on those hills. Balch Hill to the east, nearly three quarters of a mile long and very steep, was chiefly used by the farm sleds bringing wood down to the village. Chains had to be put on the rear runners, and this tore up the road. Therefore it was a real achievement if one could successfully make a descent without an upset. It lured me very often and I think I sometimes accomplished it, but it took so long to climb the hill and so short a time to descend that it was an ill-balanced sport. On the crust, however, one was as free as air and could go from one hill to the next and sometimes meet the most surprising drops which could hardly be foreseen in advance. Skiis did not begin to come into use until the end of the eighties. I inherited a pair from Arthur Fairbanks, my classmate, who shared them with C. S. Cook, whom I succeeded as instructor in physics in the Chandler School and assistant in the laboratory of the academic department. These skiis were so long that a pair of old shoes had been attached to the rear for a second passenger. The situation got very painful for the man riding behind when the leader began to toe in and the skiis spread at the rear.

We used snowshoes now and then, but generally speaking, unless the snow was particularly favorable, a man who trusted to his own legs for a hundred-yard dash could usually beat the man on snow-shoes.

This reminds me that one of the great phases of student activity of special delight to small boys was a track meet which was held once a year on the campus. Few of the citizens, students, or faculty will forget the mighty walkers that were developed, a leader among them being my early teacher, Lewis Parkhurst. He could walk a mile in seven minutes. Mr. Parkhurst later became an important member of the firm of Ginn and Company and an influential Trustee of Dartmouth College.

There were various annual episodes in that country in the time of high water in the spring as the ice blocks came rushing down the Connecticut, bumping the pier of the old covered bridge. Some-times the débris from other structures higher up the river came floating down and for some rods near the bank the water over-flowed. A little later, in June, came the annual log jam — big spruce logs, filling the whole stream and extending for a length of some three miles. Indians and half-breeds were the log drivers, setting up their camp along the shore and letting us have a bit of their salt pork and brown bread. They kept the logs from getting too firmly jammed. It was an interesting trick to cross the river, stepping from log to log. There was enough of a hazard about it, at least of getting one's feet wet, to make it good sport. And I remember once of trusting too much to a log and going in up to my neck. It was, unfortunately, at a moment when I had on a suit of new clothes, and it took the good offices of my aunt, who was visiting us at the time, to get them dried and pressed before Mother should worry about the subject.

In the spring and summer we liked to row up to the second island about two miles above the bridge. This had quite a beach and was a fine place for picnics. The big curve in the river and the railroad just before reaching the island made a pretty picture. There never seemed to be much life on the island, which was perhaps a quarter of a mile long, but there was plenty of driftwood so that a fire could easily be built, and we often went there on summer evenings with our friends, boys and girls. We were rather girl shy, but could still be persuaded to help entertain young women who might be visiting friends in the community.

There is an attractive bayou about a mile below the bridge at what was always called 'Nigger Island.' It was really a peninsula most of the time except at high water, but there was something particularly attractive in the overhanging trees along the edge of the island, where the wood-duck made its nest. It was also a favorite picnic ground and offered considerable variety of trees and undergrowth. Beyond here was Chase's Island, a small one on which Charles P. Chase, then college treasurer, had built a little cottage where the rest of us boat owners were frequently entertained. It is astonishing that we had any voices left after the strain that we gave them in singing on summer evenings. But there was generally some bright talk around the fire and we rowed home against a sluggish current at a late hour.

A large dam was built across the river about 1880, replacing the old one at Olcott Falls, a mile or so below Chase's Island. Twelve thousand horse-power was developed for the manufacture of paper. They made pulp in large sheets from the logs which they had floated down the river, and soon quite a little village was built up on the Vermont side. It was given the name of Wilder.

It is, of course, quite impossible to get a heavy boat past the Olcott Falls, as this involves carrying it more than half a mile beyond the lower falls. But we could go as far as the mill and tie up for a picnic in the woods on the New Hampshire side, a favorite place. We always hoped that we could sometime float down the river to the Sound, the mouth of the river being at Saybrook (near Lyme), Connecticut. But the boat was too heavy to be undertaken by a party of two or even four, as there were also some falls in Massachusetts. We did sometimes go as far northward as Orford, twenty miles, and tie up for a trip over to the Franconias. I recall one such expedition when we spent the night at Orford at the home of our friend Joe Willard, '87. The next morning we climbed over Cube Mountain and started down past the Tarleton Ponds. Thereupon fell a mighty rain. We had to walk to Wentworth and four or five miles up the railroad track to Warren, where we arrived toward evening drenched to the skin, our shoes oozing water at every step. We put up at the hotel and had a room on the third floor. There were three or four of us in the party. There was nothing to do but to send our clothes and shoes to the kitchen, and, as there was not a dry rag on us, everything had to go. I do not know what arrangement was made about supper, but I suppose it was left on a tray at the door.

Next morning our garments and shoes were dry, but stiff, especially the shoes, as if they had been made of iron, and we were pretty footsore by the time we reached the top of Moosilauke, forty-eight hundred feet above the sea. This is one of the most attractive mountains in the East, and I have spent not a few nights at the comfortable house on top or at the Breezy Point Hotel on its slope. In the summer after my graduation and the following year I made observations here in assisting my friend C. S. Cook to experiment with the use of the 'rain band' as an aid for the prediction of coming storms. The 'rain band' is a group of very fine lines in the yellow part of the spectrum, and its intensity varies greatly with the amount of moisture in the line of sight. Spectroscopes were made by the United States Weather Bureau for the experiment and could be accurately leveled and pointed to the desired altitude. We made simultaneous observations from the two stations, Mr. Cook at the top of the mountain, and I generally at Breezy Point, three thousand feet lower. The hotel at Breezy Point as well as the house at the top of the mountain belonged to the Woodworth family of Concord, and I was greatly pleased when many years later, Ned Woodworth of '97 and his brother Charles of '07 presented the whole top of the mountain to the college for the use of the Outing Club. It had magnificent views, especially at sunset, when the Adirondacks, a hundred and twenty miles away, came definitely into view, and sometimes in the morning we thought we could see the ocean far to the east. The view from here of the other members of the Franconias and many of the Mount Washington Range was splendid. Old Tripyramid, with its characteristic 'blaze' due to an avalanche which had taken down all the trees, was especially fine. One summer my brother and I and one other boy joined our classmate Arthur Fairbanks at a point near Mount Washington as he drove over from St. Johnsbury with a buggy in which to carry our impedimenta. We left the horse and our effects with one boy at some lodgment while the rest went across one of the mountain passes. On this occasion we went up from Crawford to Mount Washington and as far south as Mount Kearsarge and Chocorua.

In subsequent summers we sometimes had a larger party and traveled light. We usually spent the night at a fairly good hotel, and it was the duty of an advance scout to size up the hotel clerk, who was generally a college boy, and find out what fraternity he belonged to. Then the member of our party who was of the same group, whether Delta Kappa Epsilon, Alpha Delta Phi, or Psi U, would approach him and, by making friends, secure accommodations within our means. A few college fellows were not unacceptable to the younger guests at the hotel, but we were rather a tough-looking lot. I remember that on the occasion of our climb to Mount Washington we reached the hotel rather late in the day. I was the advance agent and could make no progress with the hard-boiled clerk, who thought that we would certainly not venture down the mountain at that hour. However, after consulting with my friends, we decided to move on and proceeded down the trail to the Glen House, where we found a hospitable hotel with a D. K. E. student acting as clerk, and soon had comfortable quarters.

CHAPTER VII

VILLAGE CHARACTERS

MY FRIEND Mildred Crosby Lindsey, daughter and granddaughter of the famous Crosby doctors, has often told me of the humorous sayings of the real character of the village, Jason Dudley, the driver of the hearse.

'Mildred,' said Jason, 'I never seen your grandmother consarned mad but twice; once when they was rowin' about the bridge and arrested the old doctor and put him in jail over at Woodstock. He sent a man clear over from Woodstock to break it gently to his grass-widder. The man said, "Don't be askin' for your husband, Mum, for they have jailed the old fool in Woodstock, and as far as I am concerned I hope the old New Hampshire idiot will stay there." And the other time was when she got all ready for a big family funeral — cakes, mince pies, ham, calves'-head soups, and so forth, and I myself had fetched the coffin-stands up, and she met me at the door, mad clear through. "Mr. Dudley," says she, "there will be no funeral; the corpse has rallied."'

And meeting Mildred herself one day, he said cheerily: 'I done some measuring down to your lot today and if we bury you in the north corner of the lot in the curve where we calculated to, your legs will be part in the highway. We was lottin' on your bein' short like your mother, but you got one of these figgers that nothin' stops your waist but your heels.'

Mrs. Edwards, in the cemetery arranging for the interment of her aged aunt, Mrs. Johns, said, 'I think, Mr. Dudley, that by placing auntie's head this way by uncle's feet you could make room for her and a small headstone.' 'Well, Miss Edwards, this ain't no sardine packin' factory, and while I am the head of this cem'tery, heads will match heads or the old woman won't be planted,' replied Jason; and the matter was settled.

And Mrs. Edwards in eulogy of her uncle, the elegant Professor Johns, declared, 'It was a great loss to the college, and the village, when he paid the debt to nature.' 'Well, I swan,' roared Jason, 'if he paid the debt to nature, it was the fust debt he ever paid; old Duncan never could see how he kept out of jail.'

These are only a few of Mildred's good stories. We had a pleasant revival of these and many others when not long ago we accepted her invitation to détour from our automobile route and visit her and her husband, Judge Edward Lindsey, at Warren, Pennsylvania. It was an evening of jollity and good-fellowship among old friends. Mildred recalled at this time how my father gave her a vaccination certificate in preparation for a trip abroad. In a spirit of fun he clipped off a piece of parchment from a spoiled diploma with its ribbon still attached, and wrote the necessary data. At one point in her travels, Mildred had to show her passport, which to her consternation she had either lost or mislaid. With some bravado she produced her certificate of vaccination. To her surprise it not only served the purpose, but the official, bowing low and clicking his heels together, insisted upon escorting her to a first-class carriage while Mildred smiled in derision at her mates who were receiving no such favored treatment.

I recall that when we retired that night in Mildred's home, my son Ben accompanied me to my room and there saw hanging upon the wall a picture of the three Fates, Clotho, the Spinner who spins the thread of life; Lachesis, who determines its length; and Atropos, who cuts it off. They were pictured in their customary vocational work, and my son, to whom these mythological characters were not familiar, asked me their names. I dodged the issue somewhat, and in the spirit of the evening, suggested that they should at the present time be called, 'Nemesis, Paresis, and Sclerosis.' This was believed to bring the matter up to date.

In the sixties Dr. S. P. Leeds came to minister to the needs of the great white college church, one of the most beautiful of that type in New England. Every pew was privately owned and, as was the custom in the old New England meeting-houses, had a door which could be locked with a catch if one cared to do so. The whole college was required to go to church, but of course the Catholic boys and the Episcopalians were given the privilege of attending services in their own churches. There was a monitor, however, who kept a check on their presence at each Sunday morning service. The students called the new pastor 'Pa Leeds,' and while their attitude was decorous, it is not so certain that they heard the sermon, as it was quite possible to read from a worldly book and appear to be wrapped in religious thought. The seniors sat across the front of the church, the juniors up in the east gallery, the sophomores in the west gallery, and the freshmen on the two sides of the church under the galleries, so that the congregation was last and sat behind the seniors in the body of the church. The organ was in the back gallery, and it gave a little variety to have the audience rise and turn toward the organ for the second hymn. Dr. Leeds had a rare wit and was not above having a little joke secreted in his message. I well remember as a lad of six the amusement that spread over the church one Sunday morning when Professor John King Lord brought his bride to church on the first Sunday after he reached town. Dr. Leeds gave out the hymn, 'Joy to the world, the Lord is come. Let earth receive her King.' I mentioned this to Mrs. Lord a year ago at Northampton when I was giving a lecture at Smith College, and she confirmed it.

John Brown and Sam Phelps were two good Yankees who came down from the hills of Vermont to practice the trade of mechanics in a little shop containing a lathe and a few other tools. They were clever men and kind to young boys having interest in mechanical matters. John Brown very promptly learned how to make telephones after Bell's invention had been developed. Mr. Bell's father-in-law, Mr. Gardiner G. Hubbard, was a prominent alumnus of the college and he soon sent telephones to Hanover. The homemade receivers served very well for some years, but the transmitters were not made locally. A transmitter was installed on the pulpit of the college church as early as 1880 or 1881. Whenever the instruments at the observatory had to be cleaned or repaired, John Brown was an invaluable helper. After his death, Sam Phelps came into the employ of the college as mechanic and was installed at the college shop. He was a kindly soul, a bachelor, who lived with his maiden sister at the old Rood House on the site where now stands Webster Hall.

It was through the mischievous machinations of Mildred Crosby that Sam was encouraged to let his fancy be turned toward a good 'widow lady' who kept a boarding-house for students. His suit was successful and the nuptials were arranged for a certain evening, the ceremony to be performed at the parsonage by Dr. Leeds. But on that selected evening I had other plans, namely, for the production of a little local playlet called *Indian Days*, in which Mildred was to have a prominent part. The bride and groom consented to postpone the ceremony for a day. After the marriage the question was where they should live. Of course, the maiden sister could not be put out. This delicate matter was finally adjusted by running a calico curtain across the room with the sister on one side. The arrangement did not work out so well for some reason, and Sam, who was becoming dissatisfied with matrimony, accordingly took himself to an attic room which had been vacated by a student. He added a spring lock to the door and carried off the essential parts of the bed. This serious matter was brought to the attention of Dr. and Mrs. Leeds by the wife and her sister-in-law, and after due deliberation the ladies were advised to watch for an unguarded moment in which the spring lock was not set, when they could extract the bed and burn it. I believe this remedy proved successful. At least, all went well, and later Mr. and Mrs. Phelps were installed in the addition to Conant Hall. While there Sam fell sick with pneumonia and when my brother was called, he at once insisted upon the removal of Sam's celluloid collar. His wife objected, however, saying, 'I ain't never seen him without it.'

Luman Boutwell was our veteran cabinet-maker of Hanover as well as a veteran of the Civil War. Many a piece of fine mahogany furniture had been fashioned by his hand and he was most skillful as a restorer of those genuine antiques which could hardly resist the effect of furnaces which at this time began to be used and which brought heat even into the 'front parlor.' A daughter of a member of the faculty called upon Luman's wife when he was *in extremis* to inquire for the patient. 'How is his appetite?' she asked. 'Oh, fine,' said the anxious wife. 'He et a piece of apple pie yesterday and it set real neat.'

CHAPTER VIII

AFTER COLLEGE — WHAT?

COLLEGE over, the next question was the future, and we had to make our arrangements while enjoying the pleasures of summer vacation. It was at this time that Sam Bartlett and I took a trip out into the world, going down to a summer hotel on the Sound at Niantic, Connecticut, for a few days. I had had very little experience with the sea and found the sailing a bit rough, but we had a good time, and then went over to Newport to give that resort our youthful inspection for a day. It was evidently not for us, but we had a pleasant time.

My brother found a position as sub-master in the Holderness School near Plymouth, New Hampshire. This was a church school under the direct supervision of the Episcopal Bishop of New Hampshire. It was a strange sight to see my brother robed in churchly habiliments marching with the processional and singing his best. Mother and I drove over to Plymouth on an autumn day and spent the week-end looking over his situation and meeting his friends at the school.

As for me, the family felt that I could afford the time to take some more courses in chemistry which I had not yet done in view of my extra work in physics, so I was enrolled as a post-graduate and started on the study of chemistry under Professor Bartlett. He soon found that he needed a little more assistance in his elementary course for medical students and asked me if I would be willing to give a couple of hours in the afternoon as assistant. I hope that the medics did not realize how I hustled every morning to complete each experiment which I was expected to teach them in the afternoon. I was hardly one jump ahead of them and certainly quite inadequate for the job, but my knowledge, little as it was, was certainly fresh and we got on all right. Later Dr. Bartlett asked me to assist similarly with some of the senior work in the Chandler Scientific School. I am sure that many of the men knew more about the subject than I did, but nevertheless in those days we did what we had to do whether we could or not.

When the fall term was practically over, I had an urgent call from the small town of Hancock, New Hampshire, for a Dartmouth student or graduate to conduct their so-called 'high school' for the winter term. I knew of some others who had had this post; indeed, one of the professors in the Chandler School had held it in the early days. I agreed to take the job. The town board printed their advertisement of the session of the school, stating that Mr. Edwin B. Frost, a graduate of Dartmouth and well recommended, would conduct the school for twelve weeks. By a curious coincidence I found an identical advertisement in a scrapbook of nearly forty years earlier in which the only change was in the names of the board, and that of the teacher who was my father. His school was in the next town, Harrisville. I even found one good woman who remembered him quite well.

What was done in the name of education in those days seems rather incredible, and yet there were positive results gained from even those meager opportunities by energetic and ambitious young people. Hancock is a little town in the southwestern part of New Hampshire on the line between Nashua and Keene, only about six miles from the peak of Monadnock. During the winter all the district schools in the township were closed and the teachers and the more advanced pupils came into this high school for which the munificent sum of two hundred dollars was voted by the citizens at the town meeting. Notice what this amount must cover: the salary of a lady who served as assistant at four dollars per week and who must naturally be a resident of the village; rent of the school building (which did not belong to the town, but to one of the churches and was above the auditorium of the meeting-house), amounting to one dollar per week; the services of a janitor; fuel; and the cost of light and oil for the Lyceum course held in the evening. The principal took what was left. I remember that I got home with seventy-seven dollars after a twelve-weeks term, which I think was doing pretty well. I paid four dollars for my room and board. I chose between the two opportunities for these lodgings on my way from the railway station to the village, taking the counsel of the stage driver. The room in which I slept received a limited number of calories from a small iron, wood-burning stove not any higher than the seat of a chair; but I was warned that the chimney was not very safe and that the fire must not be allowed much headway. It was rather a cold winter and naturally my room reached a low temperature by morning. After I had difficulty in breaking the ice in my water pitcher for the first few mornings, the man of the house very kindly brought me warm water from the kitchen when he gave me the rising call. My hosts were very simple people and made me quite at home. There were twelve hens to be seen out in the back regions near the stable — one for every Sunday dinner during the term.

The schoolroom was certainly a museum piece. It was probably a hundred years old, and the floor was made of pine, the knots of which had not worn down like the rest of the surface so that it was difficult to find a square foot that was all on the same plane. There were no regular benches, but long pine boards were provided, supported by X-shaped ends, and centers. Five pupils sat at these eighteenth-century school desks. Owing to the irregularities of the floor, the slightest pressure of the elbow by a pupil at the end of the desk could cause considerable disturbance to the other occupants. It had not been the custom to replace window-panes as they became broken in the natural wear and tear of many decades. On the contrary, it was found easier to patch the glass on the inside. I remember counting the number of broken panes in the room, but I wouldn't dare to repeat the figures now at this long interval. I had forty-nine pupils, counting a half-wit who habitually went to high school and probably would continue to do so for the rest of his life. Some of the teachers then enrolled as 'pupils' were older than myself; I even had an interesting engaged couple. Sometimes mischievous young misses would intercept notes passing between this couple and lay them upon my desk during the recess. Discerning the intention of the notes without reading them, I tried to deliver them without being caught at it by the rest of the school. You may be sure that sharp eyes watched me, and when somehow I managed to get around during an exercise to the point of delivery, I could hear a sigh of relief from the pupils and sense a feeling of general satisfaction.

The Lyceum met weekly in the schoolhouse with a program planned by the older students. It was remarkable to see how accurately those boys and girls knew their American history. Their dates were at their tongue's end, and the teacher had to be alert in order to keep up with them.

It was a matter of regret to me that I could not make the climb up Monadnock, but it was a serious undertaking in winter and no native would think of such a thing. It could not be attempted alone, but almost every day after school I walked around the corner and up the hill to get a commanding view of the majesty of that peak.

There was a family in the village which seemed a little unusual. Two sisters lived together and made much of music and literature, and it was always a pleasure to be invited there. There was in the family one of my pupils, an attractive lad, a nephew of these ladies, by the name of Virginio Torlonia Patten. His father married an Italian lady of that distinguished family whose name was carried by the son. The ladies were taking this boy to Europe the next summer and asked if I could not continue to teach him privately after my return to Hanover. My mother had no objection to having a bright young lad in the family, and so I tutored him for several weeks, particularly in French! This was not because I made any pretense of being a French scholar, but I studied *Whitney's Grammar* intensely. As a matter of fact, I also tutored another student in that language in the person of my friend Allen Hazen who was about to enter the Institute of Technology at Boston and must improve his French before examinations. It was to his credit, not mine, that he passed the tests successfully.

At the end of the winter, in response to an invitation by Professor Young, I went to Princeton to take a practical course in astronomy, being a guest in his household. This was certainly a valuable experience in every way and I was able to go through the better part of a year's course in observational astronomy.

In that summer of '87 there was again the question of what I should do for the next year. The president of the college recommended me for the position of principal of the high school at Rutland, Vermont, which carried with it the responsibility of overseeing twenty-five teachers and some two thousand students in the different schools. It could not have been on the strength of my having taught for one winter in a country school that the president did thus rashly recommend me. I suppose that with the courage or audacity of youth I might have attempted this difficult task, which provided a

good salary, but some friends on the faculty advised me to lie low
and not undertake this, as there was something else brewing. A
little later I was informed that my friend and instructor C. S. Cook
was to become Professor of Physics at Northwestern University and
the college authorities had unwarranted confidence that I might
take his place as instructor in physics and astronomy in the Chandler
School of Science and as assistant in physics in the academic department, which carried with it presumptively the responsibility of the
observatory. No one today would dream of taking so young and
inexperienced a person and placing him in that position, for I had
just passed my twenty-first birthday. I knew the conditions, however, and realized that my parents would be glad to keep me at
home for a while longer. So I undertook the task, for which I was
to receive the munificent salary of seven hundred dollars!

Until 1900 the main scientific gathering of the year was the annual
meeting of the American Association for the Advancement of Science.
Like its British prototype it migrated from one city to another and
this greatly stimulated interest in science throughout the section
of the country in which it met. Scientific men were not then sur-
feited with meetings, conferences, and committee sessions to which
they must travel, often over very long distances. This was the
main event of the year, and members were frequently accompanied
by their wives and daughters, thereby adding to the attractiveness
of the sessions for the young fellows who were just beginning their
scientific life. An attendance of about a thousand was regarded as
very satisfactory, and this included sections for all the important
branches of science. I naturally wished to get acquainted with
scientific men and hear their contributions given in public lectures
and sectional papers.

The first meeting which I attended was that held in Toronto in
1889. The attendance was excellent, the weather was fine, and the
citizens of Toronto were most courteous in their hospitality. It was
especially interesting for a person as young as I to be cordially
received by the recognized workers in the field of astronomy and
physics as if I were already one of them. I saw or met for the first
time such distinguished men as Professor H. A. Newton of Yale,
Professor Simon Newcomb of Washington, and representatives of
many other fields of science. There was a garden party at the

spacious home of some representative of the Dominion Government and a delightful overnight excursion to the Muskoka Lakes. We spent Saturday and Sunday in that attractive resort, which seemed to combine the elements of natural wildness with comforts of civilization. I remember that it was the point farthest north ever reached by two or three of us who were traveling together, and yet upon reflection we recalled that we were nearer the Equator than the Pole, although not more than one, if any, line of railroad crossed the region north of us, and there were comparatively few settled communities. Steamers traversed the chain of lakes, stopping from point to point, giving us a delightful view of this unspoiled region. The programs of the meetings were not so crowded as they now are. There might have been fifty to a hundred chemists in attendance, but what was that as compared to the present membership of more than fifteen thousand in the American Chemical Society alone! This comparison gives an idea of the tremendous development of science, both pure and applied, in the forty-odd years since I joined the Association. Young men naturally stayed in the background, and I remember meeting another young fellow who was lingering in a back seat to let the older generation leave at the end of the session. We introduced ourselves and have been friends ever since. This was W. W. Campbell, then instructor at the University of Michigan. He has not continued to linger on a back seat, but has held all the important offices in this and many other scientific societies, including the Presidency of the National Academy of Sciences. After his retirement as Director of the Lick Observatory he became President of the University of California.

I missed one or two of these meetings when I was in Europe, but later attended several interesting assemblies of the Association at Rochester in 1892, at Brooklyn in 1894, at Buffalo in 1896, and at New York in 1900. I was secretary of Section A (Mathematics and Astronomy) in 1896, and in 1912 at Washington was chairman, and consequently one of the Vice-Presidents of the association.

In the summer of 1888, Professor Young was working intensively upon his series of textbooks, the first and largest of which was the *General Astronomy* bearing the imprint of 1888 and published by Ginn and Company. Professor Young asked me to read the proof, which arrived about twice a week and kept me pretty

IN THE CONSTELLATION AQUILA (SCUTUM)
A small area of the Milky Way

busy. It was my first experience at proof-reading, and I wished to solve all the problems used for exercises in order to check their accuracy. My small assistance to the publisher and author was of course of far less consequence to them than the value of the experience to me. The book was a great success, being widely used in colleges. The art of making half-tones had not then been sufficiently developed so that Ginn and Company cared to use them in their textbooks. Within a few years, however, the improvements in engraving were so great that half-tones on special paper were inserted, thus furnishing a much more accurate picture of the sky and of the nebulæ than could be reproduced by the hand of any engraver on wood, no matter how skillful he might be.

With the opening of the autumn term I was also to teach the senior class of '88 in electricity in the Chandler School. The men, with one or two exceptions, were older than myself and they were certainly very tolerant. I tried to have them feel that we were students together. We used Silvanus Thompson's excellent little textbook of electricity and magnetism which was published in many editions. I was glad to meet the author a score of years later in London and tell him how much we had liked his book. Dynamos and motors were rather new inventions in 1887 and some of the newer appliances were quite exciting as portrayed in *Dynamo-Electric Machinery*.

Being the youngest member of the faculty in the Chandler School, I had thrust upon me the additional responsibility of teaching Greek history for one term and English history for another. I did not pretend to have any adequate preparation for teaching Greek history, but I do remember my reply when a New Hampshire boy with great earnestness asked me to compare Daniel Webster and Demosthenes. I said, 'Please ask me that a thousand years from now.' During the senior year, the courses in physics were given in the autumn and winter and followed by astronomy in the spring, with the classes meeting at least five times a week. When I reflect that I was also on duty as assistant in the academic physical laboratory for four afternoons in the week, and tried to do some work at the observatory in the evenings, I can truly say that those were days of hard work. After two years in this position I decided that it was time for me to get away for graduate work. I first planned to study at the Lick Observatory in California. However, after considerable discussion with the college authorities, I was persuaded to stay one year more, with release from the teaching of history in the Chandler School, but with the taking over of the academic courses in descriptive astronomy with the class of '91. I was to receive a substantial increase of two hundred dollars a year in salary. I felt a little shaky about my first experience in teaching a large academic class, but '91 was very friendly. The work was not less during this year than before, but more to my liking.

At the end of the year, I felt that graduate study could not longer be delayed and made arrangements to sail in June, 1890, for England on the old Cunarder *Cephalonia*, which was the only steamer of that line plying between Boston and Liverpool.

When I went to Randolph to bid my little grandmother good-bye, she said, 'I will wait for you until you come back.' She gave me a warm welcome upon my return from Europe two years later, and lived into her ninetieth year, passing away on January 21, 1893. I am said to resemble her rather more than any of her other grandchildren.

CHAPTER IX

STUDY ABROAD

As OUR sailing was to take place early on Saturday morning, it seemed best to spend the previous night on board the ship. The Celtic temperament made the evening a very mournful one for those going back to Ireland for only a summer vacation. Later, after the weeping was over, there were at least two thousand sides of beef slid into the hold, *via* the roof of our cabin as it appeared to us, so that the circumstances were not conducive to sleep. I believe that we sailed at six when there was still much sadness of parting in the steerage.

It was a distinguished company on board this little ship of about five thousand tons, Bishop Phillips Brooks, Ex-Governor Russell, and many others in the group. My roommate was Allen Hazen who had at this time graduated from Massachusetts Institute of Technology and was intending to spend the summer visiting European experts in sanitary engineering, his own specialty.

In comparison with the steamers which now cross the seas, it may seem odd that the *Cephalonia* carried sails. Whenever the captain thought that the wind would help our progress, the boatswain's mate blew his whistle and up went the sail to the rhythmic call of the men straining at their task. We sat on the deck without any covering over our heads and kept warm by staying on the lee side of the smokestack. We were off Queenstown in about eight days and the fresh vegetables and fruits from Ireland tasted very good for the next twenty-four hours until we reached Liverpool. Here we stopped no longer than was necessary to collect mail before going on to Chester, where we spent our first night in England, proceeding the following day to London. I had letters of introduction to some famous English astronomers and had the great satisfaction of spending an afternoon with Sir William Huggins in the suburb of Brixton. Sir William and Lady Huggins were most courteous, showing me the observatory and the telescope and spectrograph with which Sir William had done such marvelous work in astrophysics. I also made a brief call at Greenwich Observatory, meeting for the first time their then chief assistant, H. H. Turner. After a fortnight or so in London, where I also met some American friends, I went over to Paris where I stayed another fortnight. At the Paris Observatory I was turned over to Miss Dorothea Klumpke who was the first woman to take a Doctor's degree in mathematics at Paris and who was already beginning to measure the photographs of the astrographic charts, an international undertaking which has not been entirely completed in the forty-two years that have elapsed since 1890.

Miss Klumpke was one of four brilliant San Francisco girls who were in Paris with their mother to complete their education. Miss Anna was a portrait painter. She secured permission to paint a portrait of Rosa Bonheur at her château at By-Thomery and from that time made her home there and inherited Rosa Bonheur's property. Her life of this famous painter is most interesting.

After seeing the sights and inspecting the best-known art galleries in Paris, I went to the German Embassy and procured my passport visa to Strassburg, without which the Germans would not allow anyone to enter from France.

Strassburg was said to have the best-equipped observatory in the German Empire at that time. I intended to call upon the Professor of Astronomy and decide whether or not I would matriculate there in the autumn. Professor Ernst Becker received me most kindly, but we had great difficulty in conversing, since he knew no English and my German consisted only of a short acquaintance with the grammar and very little reading some six years earlier. We used Latin and Greek words when necessary to piece out the conversation, but this experience did not deter me from deciding to enter the University at the opening of the winter semester.

From Strassburg I went through the Black Forest, reminiscent of Vermont, up to Schaffhausen and Zurich. Hazen and I were planning to meet and take a walking trip in the Berner Oberland. I arrived at Lucerne just as a heavy rain set in which lasted two or three days. My American friend was not able to join me and so I sallied forth with a young Englishman who proved a welcome traveling companion. We walked through the Brünig Pass to Meiringen and thence to the Rhone Glacier. From there we went down the valley to the proper point for the climb up the Eggishorn.

It was not over seven thousand feet high, but commanded a fine view of the Oberland and made a good beginning for an amateur climber. Arriving at the hotel near the top, late in the afternoon, we found it completely full. They were able to feed us, however, and we had quarters in the hay above the barn, where we promptly fell asleep, listening to the soft wind and the merry voices of the goodly company of English boys and girls who were given quarters in the hotel. The ladies, at least, had a semblance of a place to sleep on, as the dining-room tables were reserved for them. We were up early the next morning in time to reach the peak by sunrise, and were rewarded by a view of thirteen glaciers below and beyond us, a dazzling expanse of eternal snow. We next went up the valley from Visp toward Zermatt, a very pleasant walk, and we found this village had an excellent hotel.

The Matterhorn was in full view and I wished very much to try the ascent, but guides were required and the cost was about fifty dollars, which my purse would not allow. We therefore contented ourselves with the easy climb of the Gorner Grat, about ten thousand feet high, with one of the excellent Seidel Hotels near the top. It was a fine day, and the view, especially of the Matterhorn, was magnificent. We were reluctant to leave this attractive region, but had to move on, and our next stop was at the Baths of Leuk, partway up the Gemmi Pass. At this hotel rheumatic patients spent large parts of the day in the warm water with floating tables and floating checkerboards for entertainment. The climb up the steep pass of the Gemmi next morning was interesting and a local thunderstorm with lightning flashes between the peaks slightly above us added to the impressiveness of the scene. We moved on to Berne, where I had to wait for at least three days for my grip. I had passed it once and succeeded in persuading the postmaster to let me open it for a necessary change of clothing. I felt rather uncomfortable in my soiled walking outfit, especially before some nice American girls at the hotel. Thence to Basle and Heidelberg, alone. Here I made the acquaintance of Dr. Max Wolf, who was then a *privat-docent* at the university. This began a friendship which has lasted for forty years. He has done a most distinguished service to science as Director of the Heidelberg Observatory on the Königstuhl. I deeply regret his death in the autumn of 1932.

Thereupon I took the train for Göttingen, where I had engaged accommodations in the well-known *pension* of Fräulein Schlote. There were many American women and men here, among them Mrs. White of New York and her daughter Anna, who later married my friend Frank G. Moore when he was a member of the young faculty at Dartmouth; also several graduates of Wellesley and Smith, Gaylord White of the Union Theological Seminary, New York, and Benjamin Snow who later was Professor of physics at Madison. Among others were three fine young Greeks from Athens, one of whom I especially liked, Gounaris by name, a student of law. Many years later he became Prime Minister of Greece and was cruelly murdered in a revolution while he was a victim of fever. Charles Downer Hazen, whom I had known while he was in Dartmouth as a member of the class of '89, soon came to the *pension* with his sister. At the *pension* we were assessed a small fine for speaking English at table, and some of the company nicknamed me 'Später' because of my constant use of that word which enabled me to defer answering a question in German and gave me time to consult the small dictionary which was always in my pocket. Hazen joined me in intensive tutoring during the daily walks with our instructor. This was especially necessary for me if I was to be prepared for the lectures the coming semester. I was glad to be able to spend nearly three months in this ancient University town.

It was not the custom for the German universities to make an actual beginning until about two weeks after the scheduled time. Therefore, it was not until the early part of November that I left the pleasant associations of the 'Schloterei' and journeyed alone to Strassburg. On the street the next morning, somewhat low in my mind from a sense of loneliness, I was greatly cheered by seeing Buffalo Bill with some of his braves traveling down the street. I felt like embracing them on the spot. It appeared that they were going into winter quarters near Strassburg and I learned a good many interesting things regarding the show from one of the men whose brother was a student of physics at the university.

There were many distinguished professors at Strassburg, and the German Government had spent much of the reparation funds which they had collected from the French in 1870 before they left Paris in building up the ancient university into as modern and fine an institution as possible. This did not prevent the venerable registrar of the university from using a goosequill for a pen or from scattering sand over a written document in order to dry the ink.

The physics department of the university had as its chief professor Friedrich Kohlrausch. He was an excellent lecturer and conducted a valuable course in practical physics. I found special interest in working with the various clever instruments which Professor Kohlrausch had designed for the measurement of the electrical resistance of liquids and of the earth's magnetism. I also made a special study of the spectral absorption of liquids. Dr. Hallwachs made some important discoveries on the emission of electrons or photons from metallic surfaces. Dr. Wiener, an assistant, had just made some discoveries on 'Standing Light-Waves.' He later became Professor of Physics at Leipzig.

As is usual for beginners in a foreign university, I elected too many courses and could not give much attention to some of them, considering them more as review. Professor Becker regarded my progress in the German language during the three or four months since I had met him as highly satisfactory. He remembered the extreme difficulty of our first conversation. I was able to follow most of the lectures without much difficulty, but I am no believer in the lecture method for mathematical subjects. It was rather a surprise to me toward the end of my study of orbits to discover that the professor who copied his formulæ on the blackboard from his notebook, gave very nearly the presentation made by J. C. Watson, leading American astronomer, in his work entitled *Theoretical Astronomy*. It would really have been better if we had originally used the textbook in English instead of trying to make a satisfactory copy of notes from the blackboard. We were generally far enough behind so that we could not fully complete the elucidation of the formulæ ably given by the professor.

The other students in the astronomical courses were Friedrich Ristenpart, a bright young student from Frankfort with whom I formed a lasting friendship; J. Riem, for many years a member of the staff of the Rechen-Institut at Berlin-Dahlem; and Hans Paetsch of Berlin, who later was employed in the Prussian Academy's project of compiling the history of the positions of the stars (*Geschichte des Fixsternhimmels*). The youthful and extraordinarily brilliant Karl

Schwartzschild did not come to Strassburg until the next semester, after I had left the university. It would have been a pleasure to be associated with so gifted a fellow student. He died during the World War. We had the astronomical seminar about every fourteen days, and it was not long before it became my turn to speak to the group, something of an ordeal with my broken German. The professor assigned to me the duty of reviewing the work entitled *Harvard Photometry* which had recently appeared, and my fellow students were considerate in overlooking my blunders of speech.

At the boarding-place near the university we had some associates who were American and some Englishmen. I particularly enjoyed the society of Joseph Thompson, who was an alumnus of Amherst and who was completing his graduate work. There was also on the same floor a very attractive young man from Milwaukee, a graduate of the University of Wisconsin, William Brumder. He was studying law prior to taking a hand in the large interests which his father and other relatives had in his home city. In later life I had the pleasure of meeting him occasionally and greatly regretted his too early death. On the evening after Einstein had given the first of his three lectures in 1921 at the University of Chicago, I met Brumder just as he had entered the Ryerson Laboratory to pay his respects to this famous center of research. He had come down from Milwaukee to hear Einstein's lectures in Mandel Hall.

One of the American students with whom I was intimate was Walter Le Conte Stevens who had had a responsible position in teaching physics in Brooklyn and had made not a few contributions to physiological optics. He was a Southerner by birth and had always regretted his lack of opportunities for graduate instruction. Finally, when he was about forty years old, being unmarried, he resigned his position and went to Europe for study, a lifelong desire. He found it more difficult than the younger American students to adapt himself to the peculiarities of the language and their customs, but he was very conscientious, hard-working, and a man of the finest character. His middle name, taken from his distinguished uncle, a geologist, who was one of the first presidents of the University of California, sometimes caused him a little trouble because everyone thought that he was a count. In consequence he was overpersuaded to take a large room in a suite which had just been vacated by a

Russian prince, and no doubt when his name was known had to pay a little more for anything he bought than did the rest of us. There were about twenty American students in Strassburg and we had Thanksgiving dinner together.

There was another interesting man completing his graduate work at the time, Peter Lebedew, a sturdy big bear from Moscow. He was a brilliant student and later was distinguished as the discoverer of the pressure of light, which was simultaneously found by my friends Ernest F. Nichols and Gordon Hull at Dartmouth. This discovery had been predicted by J. C. Maxwell and by Bartolli on mathematical grounds, some years before. I kept up an occasional correspondence with Lebedew until his untimely death about 1910. At the observatory and in the classroom Professor Ernst Becker was most friendly and I was frequently invited to dine in his hospitable home. Of course, my three years of teaching and personal work at the Dartmouth Observatory had given me a little more experience than my German fellow students had enjoyed. The assistants were *Privat-docent* H. Kobold (meaning 'gnome'), a little bearded man who fitted his name, and who has been for the last thirty years editor of *Astronomische Nachrichten* at Kiel. The second assistant was J. Halm. The latter received an important position in the observatory at the Cape of Good Hope, where he did excellent work. I have had the pleasure of continuing the acquaintance of these two gentlemen by correspondence during all the years since 1900. Another man on the faculty was Walter Wislicenus, a tall, slender young man who did not seem to have very strong German characteristics. He had no equipment for astrophysical research nor an opportunity to work at the observatory and so devoted himself to theoretical considerations. I shall not forget the review which he presented at the colloquium in physics of a new work entitled *Spectral Analyse der Gestirne*. This had just appeared from the pen of Julius Scheiner, assistant in the Potsdam Observatory. This presentation of the newest discoveries in celestial spectroscopy by one who had had a hand in the important advances made at the Potsdam Observatory impressed me very much, and I decided to translate the book for English readers with the author's and publisher's permission.

The political situation in Alsace was still rather difficult, although it was twenty years since the Franco-Prussian War. The Vice-Consul

for the United States was an Alsatian who had studied in America and
had served in the Union Army during the Civil War. We soon became
acquainted with his family, but there was no mixing between their
friends and the families of the faculty who were Germans. Strassburg was very active in the construction of new buildings, bridges,
and other improvements, but I was always impressed by the fact that
they were trying to make it an important German center as it had
been prior to 1681. Many streets in the old part of town had the
French names effaced and new German names substituted. It had
been the battlefield of the Teutonic and Gallic races for many generations.

> 'Oh Strassburg, Oh Strassburg,
> Du Wunderschöne Stadt,
> Darinnen liegt begraben
> So Mannicher Soldat.'

There was a garrison of about twenty thousand troops in the city, the
population of which was fifty thousand, so it will be seen that the
military element was very strong.

On Sunday noons we liked to go down to the Broglie Platz (now
Place Broglie) for the changing of the guards and for the brief concert by one of the excellent military bands. The theater was managed
by the city, although there may have been supervision by the Government. I tried to make it a point to hear some opera or play every week.
This was valuable for the improvement of my German and gave me
an opportunity to hear some operas which I had never heard in New
York. I recall in particular the operas of Wagner, *Rienzi*, and a
presentation of *Parsifal* which was sung before the curtain without
any acting, because at that time no license had been given for the
production as an opera except at Bayreuth. I had heard several of
the Wagnerian operas in New York and was enthusiastic about them,
but even as late as in the nineties I found many Germans who were
doubtful whether one could really prefer the stately themes of Wagner's operas to the more melodious and sprightly arias of the Italian
style. Not much later the distinctly German operas, with their marvelously stirring strains and recurrent motives, were widely acclaimed.

It has always been evident that any new style of music, of art, or
of literature must pass through a period of probation before the ac-

ceptance of those new elements which are of permanent value and the discarding of those which are purely temporary or bizarre. This history is being repeated today in many of the modern musical productions, and who can judge of the lasting qualities of some of the present outbursts in art and literature?

Toward the end of the semester I sent my letters of introduction to Dr. H. C. Vogel, director at Potsdam, with a request that I be allowed to come there as a volunteer during the spring and summer. Although I did not use the formal language in making this request, which I learned later was expected on such occasions, I nevertheless received the desired permission. I planned to leave Strassburg as soon as the lectures were over and to begin at Potsdam about April 1, hoping to secure other material from which I could prepare a doctor's thesis and return later to Strassburg to take a degree.

I had a plan for a walking trip in the Vosges Mountains near Strassburg with my friend Friedrich Ristenpart, but the weather was not favorable and the plan had to be given up. I therefore hurried on with my small belongings toward Berlin, with a month or more of leisure before my opportunity for work at Potsdam should begin. After spending two days in Nuremberg I was joined by my friend Stevens and enjoyed acquainting him with some of the many interesting things I had found in that old city, one of the most attractive in Europe. When I arrived in town, I did not go to the table d'hôte, at my hotel, but went to a large *Lokal*, where music could be heard and meals could be secured along with good beer. The room was blue with smoke of bad tobacco, but I finally was able to discern a vacant table, where I engaged in conversation with my neighbor. Of course, he recognized from my speech that I was not a Bavarian and that there was something peculiar about my accent. He asked me from which province I came, to which I replied, 'Strassburg in Elsass.' He did not seem suspicious, but quietly replied 'Ich bin aus Cleve-e-land.' So I had to confess that Elsass was not my permanent home. His German was not much better than mine, and he had certainly not acquired much of the English language, although he had been in America fifteen years.

The treasures of the Germanic Museum gave striking evidence of the vigor of the Renaissance in that ancient town. It was a progressive one, too, with a fine educational system and a school for the textile industries, with a permanent exhibition. The first electrical railroad built in Germany ran between Nuremberg and the suburb of Fuerth. The great Schuchert electrical works, for the manufacture of dynamos and motors and electrical machinery generally, were located here and Stevens and I were permitted to make quite a thorough inspection of the work in progress after we had given assurance that we were students and not engaged in technical engineering. I have been in Nuremberg at least three times since this visit, but I shall never forget the tremendous impression I received of the virility of the revival of art and science by Hans Sachs and his contemporaries.

As admirers of the work of Wagner, Stevens and I made a visit to Bayreuth, where we saw the new Wagner Theater and paid a visit to a house in which had lived Wagner and Liszt. In March there was no apparent activity in the operatic field, but rehearsals may have been going on for the next summer. We then went to Dresden which was an active center for arts and science. To this day I cannot forget the beautiful rendering of Schubert's *Serenade* by a small orchestra in a restaurant on the river-bank where Stevens and I went with many worthy citizens for coffee on a snowy or dull afternoon. The collection of birds in the Zwinger Museum was fascinating enough, but rather overpowering because they had so many specimens of the different kinds of birds from all over the world; it was difficult to find even a genus which might be common in America, but was lost here among great numbers of others of slightly different genera. At the hotel by prearrangement I met my classmate Tom Harris. By some kind of chance which I do not need to fully understand, there were one or two attractive American girls at the same hotel at this time. We had a lively time for a few days. I rather expected results as far as Tom was concerned. Of course, I shouldn't say this, since I was an usher about five years later at his wedding to charming Lena Breed, an accomplished 'cellist. Her presence at our class reunions has added much to the satisfaction of such gatherings.

Our next stop was in Berlin, and here I found a room in the Dorotheenstrasse, not far from the Friedrichstrasse and the university. I paid thirty marks a month, including morning coffee. Benjamin Snow had a room adjoining mine and perhaps suggested these quarters. He had been in Berlin for some time and studied there for about four years, taking his degree in the department of physics. I soon made the trip to Potsdam, which is sixteen miles from Berlin and is situated on either side of the river Havel which expands into lakes at frequent intervals. I completed my arrangements to enter the observatory about April 1. Returning to Berlin, I acquainted myself with the buildings and principal features of the city and of the university. I had one opportunity to hear a lecture in physics by the celebrated Professor Kundt. The lecture hall was packed, as all medical students had to attend, and the presentation was as beautiful as was to be expected from the author's reputation.

Professor von Helmholtz was then just about to leave the University and take over the presidency of the Imperial Institute (*Reichsanstalt*), which was to take the responsibility of testing all kinds of units like liter measures, thermometers and electrical measuring instruments, for the German Empire. This institution soon grew to be a very large one, conducting research into the properties of all sorts of material and taking one of the most important places for investigation in physics and mechanics to be found in Europe. The United States Bureau of Standards at Washington was later developed along similar lines largely as a result of the efforts of our Professor S. W. Stratton, of Chicago, who directed it with great efficiency for many years. I saw Helmholtz at Berlin, but did not hear any of his lectures.

I called on Professor Förster, head of the Department of Astronomy at the university, which had its observatory on the Lindenstrasse at Enckeplatz. He encouraged me to take lectures in astronomy at the university coincident with my research work at the Potsdam Astrophysical Observatory. I later discovered that this arrangement would not have been agreeable to Director Vogel, who was particular about keeping free from any entanglements with the Berlin Observatory, an entirely independent organization. Later, however, Dr. Scheiner did hold a Professorship of Astrophysics at the university and gave lectures there, perhaps twice a week.

Berlin was developing very rapidly at that time, and the young Kaiser had succeeded his father about two years before. He desired to have a hand in everything that went on, and the government was decidedly paternal. The imperial family spent only a few months at the palace in Berlin, occupying 'Friedrichskron,' the rather rococo structure beyond the original park of Sans Souci. The palace was surmounted by statues of three distinctly human graces who were dressed even more scantily than modern women.

At the appointed time, I moved to Potsdam and found an attractive room in a large apartment building at the foot of the Telegraphenberg, less than one-half mile from the observatory. This house bore a great sign on its roof carrying the single word, 'Salve.' This was visible from the railroad station, so that my American friends having been told that I lived in the 'Salve house' could readily find my room. The service was far from immaculate. In the morning about eight, a dull-witted maid shuffled in with my morning coffee and a couple of rolls, which served well to sharpen one's teeth. I was an extravagant boarder and paid extra for butter to eat on those rock-like rolls. It helped decidedly to lubricate them. The coffee, of course, was very bad and only a small amount of it grew in Brazil; the greater part of it was home-grown chicory. Since it was customary for everyone to have his *Zweites Frühstück*, I adopted the plan of putting a couple of these hard biscuits in my coat pocket, masticating them about eleven o'clock. Dinner was my main meal which was procured at some hotel or restaurant across the long bridge in the main part of town. At first I ate alone in the cheap restaurant *Aux Caves de France*. Later I joined some of the other unmarried men from the Observatory and the Geodetic Institute, and had dinner at the hotel on the Havel. There were always several young soldiers and officers at this table d'hôte. When the weather was fine, we sometimes ate out-of-doors where we could throw the hard biscuits to the swans in their dignified rounds below us and could watch their comical efforts to swallow them.

To the first restaurant on one occasion I took some American friends, young men and women who were spending the day with me in Potsdam and who wished advice and guidance to see the important places. All of them had recently arrived in Germany and were not familiar with that awesome attitude of silence prevailing in such a restaurant, at least during the daytime. My friends were laughing and talking loudly in a very natural American way. I could see the horrified looks upon the faces of the regular guests (*Stammgäste*). James Breasted was the leader of the party and he was amused by my efforts to keep the company within the bounds of quiet. But it took several weeks for me to re-establish myself in that restaurant as a sedate person. In my first autumn, at the request of a mutual friend I looked up a Berlin *pension* for Breasted, for which he should be, and certainly is, profoundly grateful to me; for did he not meet there, residing at the *Pensionat*, Miss Frances Hart of San Francisco, and did she not in the fullness of time marry the aforesaid James Henry Breasted after all the complicated legal formalities incident to such a marriage in a Prussian city had been accomplished? 'Where is your birth certificate?' is one of the questions difficult to answer upon such an occasion. And Will Rogers would answer, 'Well, you can see I was born, or I wouldn't be here.'

In the spring it was delightful to hear the song of the nightingale as I came home from observing. But on Sunday mornings there was a pestiferous destroyer of sleep from the rifles of the sharpshooters in the Schützen Verein, not fifty feet from my window. They began in summer at sunrise and kept up their target shooting until all hope of sleep was gone.

On Sunday noon and sometimes on other days of the week, at the changing of the guard near the Stadtschloss, a fine concert was given. I liked to linger near this when on my way to dinner. Speaking of these bands, recalls an instance when in 1913, with the whole family, I spent a fortnight or more in a *pension* at Potsdam. I learned that the Kaiserin and her family were to attend a special service in the Garrison Church in the crypt of which lies the bones of Frederick the Great. The children were interested in seeing Her Majesty and delighted with the resplendent regiment. It happened that at this same time there was near-by a celebration of the hundredth birthday of a brisk little man who had once held the post of cabinet-maker to the famous First Regiment of the Foot Guards. For the occasion, one after another of the military bands came and played a salute in honor of the event. Some of the princes came to the door to pay their respects, and the Empress sent a cake. The uniforms were gorgeous and it was quite an unusual event. The Germans were most meticulous in their attention to all such celebrations, particularly if one of the crack regiments was involved.

But what excessive attention was often given to insignificant matters by the civil servants of the Government. I had sent to America for a couple of fountain pens to present to German friends. When they arrived in due course, I was summoned to the postal branch of the customs house to attend to any duty that might be levied. The pens had to be explained to the officials and I mentioned that they were of gold. I suppose that the men still used quills, for they said it was quite impossible that the pens could be of actual gold and that they were therefore not subject to any duty.

Even thirty years later we met with another example of wasteful red-tape. I went to the postal branch of the customs house in a Moabit district of Berlin for a package with a tag bearing my name and a franc postage-stamp. The package contained nothing more or less than my tall hat in its leather box. I remarked to the official in uniform who waited upon me that I should like to have the stamp on the tag. He told me courteously but firmly that this was quite impossible. The case had frequently arisen and the decision had been affirmed and reaffirmed that the stamps and tags must be left at the office. I naturally acquiesced and started on my way. On the street, my small son confided in me that in spite of the clerk he had succeeded in removing the cancelled stamp and had placed it in his collection. This seemed an amusing ending to the discussion and we forgot the matter. Not liking our *pension* on the Linden which was rather dingy, we moved to brighter quarters at one of the small hotels, *Christliches Hospiz*, near the Reichstag. About a week later I was called from the breakfast table by a postal messenger who held in his hand that identical tag upon which I recognized my own writing as I had made it at Geneva. He ominously pointed his finger to the place where the stamp had been and solemnly said, 'Where is now this stamp?' I called my lad, who reluctantly went up to his room, took it out of his collection, and showed it to the official. It fitted perfectly. One could even see where the cancellation overlapped. The official was slightly appeased, but not wholly satisfied, probably thinking that a microscopic examination would be necessary. He departed with the words, 'We shall see.' Some considerable part of a week had evidently been spent in tracing us in order to find this foolish cancelled stamp. I don't know what would have happened if we had meanwhile left for Paris; perhaps extradition papers would have been necessary!

A case was related to me by an American friend about a fire that happened in Berlin. The alarm was pulled and the fire-engine came.

Before starting active measures to quench the fire, the captain had to investigate the credentials of the person who sent in the alarm, his name, age, number in the family, etc. But just as the formalities were completed, so that some thought could be given to the extinction of the blaze, the official discovered that the house was outside of his district and that the alarm across the street should have been pulled in order to bring the proper company. Accordingly the engine was taken away and the alarm sent in through the proper channel. We can only hope that meanwhile the fire had not gotten beyond control.

A pleasant feature of social life in Berlin in the winter of 1891–92 came to me through the kindness of Mrs. Mary B. Willard, sister-in-law of Miss Frances Willard. Mrs. Willard had an excellent school for American girls in the Nettelbeckstrasse. James Breasted and I were known to be steady boys and so were often invited to parties at the school; in fact, I had a standing invitation for dinner on Sunday if I came in from Potsdam to the American church. Mr. Clemens (Mark Twain) and his family were spending the winter in Berlin and we often had the pleasure of meeting them. Mr. Clemens had a marked interest in astronomy and asked me many questions. He must have been writing his little book entitled *Captain Stormfield's Visit to Heaven*, which, by the way, should have a broadening influence for Fundamentalists and which involves some astronomy. Mark Twain was very popular in Germany, and his books had been read by almost everyone. He was regarded as one of our greatest American authors.

One day toward spring I was walking near the old Sans Souci Palace with a few scientific friends from the observatory, when I saw Mr. Clemens and his party. My friends were immensely pleased to see the great man. I was not sure that he would remember me, but before we had reached their group Mr. Clemens saw me and called out, 'Here's Mr. Frost!' and gave me a cordial greeting. I had the pleasure of introducing my German friends to him and to his party and I could see at once that I rose mightily in the esteem of my Teutonic comrades!

On another occasion I had ridden to Berlin in a compartment with the American Consul who was spending the summer in Potsdam. He invited me to ride with him in his carriage across the city. By some good fortune I happened to pass some of my German friends who were making their way to the station for Potsdam, and the spectacle of an humble would-be astronomer riding in a droschky was almost overpowering to them.

Speaking of cabs, I heard the story of one distinguished professor at Berlin who always attended the meetings of the Verein of those studying his specialty. It was late when he called a cab and started for home. He fell asleep and woke to find that the driver was making a circuit around a pond in the Thiergarten, evidently without enough consciousness to find the professor's address. The latter was by now quite wide-awake, and decided to exchange places with the sleepy driver in order to reach home safely. When he dismissed the cab at his doorstep, the driver asked plaintively, 'Now who will drive me home?'

The concerts at the Philharmonie were conducted by von Bülow and were exceedingly fine. When the weather was so definitely cloudy that I could not use the telescope, I went to Berlin to hear these performances. One could get his supper, or its equivalent, in the hall, and occupying one or two boxes were always some of Mrs. Willard's girls who were not averse to having another American boy join their party. We heard some splendid music, brilliantly presented. On one occasion I persuaded my director to go with me to the Philharmonie, something that he had not done for years, and I am sure that he enjoyed it. His life was rather lonely, as he had never married. It was in that winter that Mascagni's *Cavalleria Rusticana* had just reached Berlin, and one frequently heard the Intermezzo with the accompaniment of a great organ, especially at the Koncerthaus. Some of the music in the churches at the Christmas season and in Passion Week was also especially fine.

One of the annual outings of the Thursday Evening Club at Potsdam was the so-called 'walk' to Berlin on some fine spring day. Some of the members were rather portly, and the term 'walk' had to be interpreted rather broadly. We first walked about half a mile until we reached a restaurant where could be found some fluid nourishment, preferably *Kümmel* (extract of caraway-seed). Then we took a tram for a few miles until we could reach a passenger boat on the Wannsee. This brought us a few miles nearer Berlin. Then followed a short walk in the Grünewald, after which we reached the street-car system of Berlin or Charlottenburg. By this time we were ready for supper and then for some sort of show; living pictures were just then the novelty. Later we returned to Potsdam by a fast train and thus completed our walk to Berlin by covering the distance from the station to our respective homes or rooming quarters.

It was rather a late spring, that of '91, and the supply of fuel at the observatory had been exhausted, so that I had to learn to adapt myself to studying in a room at a low temperature. Having no subject assigned to me at first, I began reading through all the quarto volumes of the publications of the observatory. This was good practice and familiarized me with the work of the institution from the beginning. Whenever I thought that I had found a typographical error I could go to the author and check the matter with him.

I first studied the periodic errors of the fine spectrometer that had just been installed at the observatory. Soon Professor Vogel suggested that I investigate the amount of radiation over the different positions of the sun's disc, using a thermopile. I built the thermopile myself and attached it to the eight-inch equatorial. This telescope has been used for many years by Professor Spörer in his study of sunspots, and although quite an old man he still did much observing. I soon began to get some interesting results which confirmed some that I later found had been made by S. P. Langley at Allegheny and rather sketchily described in the *Comptes Rendus* of the French Academy. Sun-spots which radiated less than the adjacent photosphere, when they were near the center of the disc, began to radiate relatively more a few days later when they approached the edge of the sun. Indeed, in some cases I recorded the greater radiation of the sunspots near the edge than from the adjacent photosphere equally distant from the center. This was due to the relatively greater absorption by the solar atmosphere of the photospheric light than of the dark umber or center of the spot. I then had some idea of taking this observational material and working on the theory of it at Strassburg in the next winter's semester, but circumstances, as will appear later, changed my plans and I did not leave Potsdam.

There were two other volunteers at the observatory at his time, F. Blumbach of St. Petersburg and Shin Hirayama of Tokyo. A. Belopolsky of the Pulkova Observatory spent some weeks at Potsdam, as he was planning to undertake at the Imperial Russian Observatory spectrographic observations according to the Potsdam observational methods. He and I shared the same birthday, but he was twelve years older than I. He is a very able and industrious observer, of pure Russian stock, and I learn that he is even now, at nearly eighty years of age, still keeping a part in the observing program. He visited us in the summer of 1899 at Williams Bay, Wisconsin, and seemed to enjoy helping us move from the little house which we called the 'Cracker Box' to one which we occupied for six years. I have never seen Blumbach since, although we have occasionally corresponded. He has lived in London since the revolution and has acted as scientific agent for the Government. I suspect, although he has never said so, that he regarded the air of England more healthful than that of Soviet Russia. Belopolsky, Blumbach, and I took our exercise together in the parks around Potsdam, and I often heard small German boys say, *'Da sind die drei Russen.'* By the way, it is interesting to note how widely Cooper's tales were read by the small boys of Germany. I recall once seeing a group of them playing around in the woods in a mysterious manner, and I asked them what they were doing. 'Oh,' said they, 'we're Indians. Those over there are Sioux [they pronounced it sy-oox] and we're Apachen.'

There was in Potsdam an informal group known as the *Donnerstag Abend Gesellschaft.* The membership was composed of scientific men connected with the Observatory and Geodetic Institute, some gymnasium teachers and a doctor or two. We met at the *Lokal,* where there was good beer. The session was supposed to begin about nine o'clock, but one dropped in at his convenience until midnight. The party generally scattered by one o'clock. It was then a question of who would escort Dr. Scheiner up through the woods to the observatory. He was a reserve officer and of course not afraid, but he liked company and some one of us generally escorted him up the hill. There were some rather spicy stories told at the sessions with Scheiner as the leader. There was a quaint ceremonial which was quite new to me, namely, that of passing the snuff box. This was usually provided by one of the older members of the club, and a sufficient quantity of snuff was inserted in each nostril to give a mighty blast, saying, *Eine Ausgezeichnete Priese,* as he passed it on to his neighbor. It was decided that we should have a Christmas celebration at the club in 1891, and a committee secured a keg of the Munich product. I was told later that the fourteen members present consumed fifty-three liters on that evening, which would seem to be a pretty good average.

This was soon after the passage of the McKinley high tariff bill. The prospects of higher tariff were not particularly agreeable to the Germans. I was presented with a wooden jumping-jack named 'McKinley' and I myself was jokingly designated on the inscription as *der Zechende Temperenzler* ('old soak') — I could drink a liter in the course of an evening.

There was a club in Potsdam, the Stadtklub (City Club), which claimed to be organized in a democratic English fashion, and all titles, which play so prominent a part in German life, were supposed to be omitted. Each person was 'Herr' so and so. I was very courteously invited to attend this club which had rooms in the central part of the city. One was supposed to introduce himself by rising, clicking his heels together, and giving his name. On one occasion I was sitting at a table with some others when one of the burgomasters came and seated himself with us. I immediately arose, for by this time I had learned some of the formalities, clicked my heels together and said '*Fröst*'! He looked at me quizzically and apparently in some doubt. I repeated '*Fröst*,' but could not make the name clear to him. I learned later that as soon as I left the table he had inquired of the others as to my name, '*Wie hiess denn der Herr?*' He thought that I said '*Pros't*,' meaning 'your health,' which without the necessary accompaniment of a stein of beer would have been quite out of order.

An excellent physician, a member of the club, was greatly entertained when I called at his office with a sore throat and asked him to decorate it. I used the verb *malen*, which would mean to paint as an artist does, whereas I should have used *streichen*, meaning to swab my throat. This amused the others and I was beginning to learn the language well enough to be amused myself. This Potsdam Club gave a grand celebration in the course of the winter with a dinner and a play. It was quite a problem to know how one could take an unengaged daughter to dinner as your guest. It was somehow arranged for me, but her father would not allow me to pay for the supper, only for the wine, and there was no responsibility in seeing the lady home. It was customary, however, for two of us to escort to his lodgings one of our mutual friends from the Geodetic Institute.

Even a small amount of wine served at a dinner seemed to upset him.

As autumn came on and I had again to consider the advisability of returning to Strassburg to work for a doctor's degree, I was approached by Dr. Scheiner to see if I might not prefer to stay at Potsdam and assist him in recording his measurements of some photographs of the Great Cluster in Hercules, and then work on the reduction of the measurements. These pictures were taken with the excellent Repsold Astrographic Telescope, one of them by Scheiner and me, and the other by myself alone, and they were quite successful. The guiding of this twin telescope with its nine-inch aperture and the slow motions was so well executed that there was practically no lost motion. It was a pleasure to guide with it. Of course, even better results might have been secured by moving only the plate-holder according to Dr. Common's method which was later used on the photographic instruments at the Yerkes Observatory, but this arrangement was highly satisfactory for plates of the Astrographic Chart for which it was intended. The instrument had just been set up in the spring of my arrival and thus I had my first-hand experience in celestial photography with adequate instruments. It was a real opportunity to continue such work and to assist, however inadequately, in the reduction of the first trigonometrical survey of this large stellar cluster. The formulæ had to be developed, as the method was new. Over eight hundred stars were finally found to be on the two plates, and their position accurately given. I decided that it was more important for me to improve the opportunity for observing in the best known astrophysical observatory in the world than to go back to Strassburg for a degree. Therefore I gladly accepted the position. There was even the promise of a little salary, from eighty to one hundred marks per month, according to the amount available in the contingent fund. It was amusing to see the second assistant janitor and carpenter dressed up in his best clothes, with a revolver in his pocket going down to the treasury in the city to bring back with him the salary money in gold. My official title was in length quite out of proportion to its importance. I was to become, in fact, *Ausseretatsmässiger wissenschaftlicher Hilfsarbeiter.*

We were very much excited in the early winter over the discovery by T. Anderson of Edinburgh of a new star, *Nova Aurigae.* The news of the discovery did not reach us very promptly, in fact, not until the star had already faded to the fifth magnitude. It was not bright enough for the large Potsdam spectrograph with which the pioneer work on the velocity of stars in the line of sight had been done. Professor Vogel had the carpenter make a little wooden mounting for a small spectrograph which should be attached in place of the photographic plate on the astrographic refractor. He asked me to get this into adjustment and try it out. Dr. Scheiner being ill at this time, the duty of making all the observations fell to me. While the scale of the little plates was very small, they were sufficient to give us a good deal of information. As this was the first Nova to be recorded photographically, I secured as many photographs of the spectrum as the weather would permit until the star got too faint. Then I undertook to photograph the spectra of a number of other interesting stars for which bright lines had been reported by other observatories, chiefly in America.

There was a good deal of unnecessary skepticism among some of the German observers in regard to these spectrograms, particularly those made at the Harvard Observatory with the objective prisms. Having full confidence in the American observers, I took pains to get confirmatory spectrograms whenever possible and I readily convinced Dr. Vogel of the reality of the bright lines or components. Later a spectrograph in metal was made to replace the one of wood with which I had worked, and with this many valuable contributions were obtained by Dr. Wilsing and others. I worked hard at this observing, both early and late, and often would have gone without my supper had not Professor Vogel sent some luncheon to me from his own home. His health did not permit him to take part in any of the observations at night.

Meanwhile, I had completed arrangements with Dr. Scheiner and his publishers at Leipzig to publish an English translation of his important work which I was also to enlarge as much as was necessary to include current researches in this rapidly advancing branch of science. Ginn and Company of Boston generously agreed to publish the book with little expectation of pecuniary returns, and, if the book sold well enough, were to recompense me in three years for the money which I had advanced. There was not enough time for me to make a complete translation before my return to America the following summer. It was also not yet decided whether I should return to my position in Potsdam which was open to me for another year or whether I should remain in America.

Germany was then in the full swing of its process of emerging from the provincial group of small sovereignties. There was a great air of confidence in the future; the book by Admiral Mahan on *The Influence of Sea Power upon History* was greatly admired by the Kaiser and the leading imperial officials of Germany, and they were determined to build up a large naval force. This was not merely to make a good showing when there was a grand review of his grandmother's great fleet, but especially so that the Germans could sail away and find a place in the sun for the over-population which was beginning to be felt. The young Kaiser had plenty of sycophants, and now that he had dropped his pilot Bismarck, the Emperor did not always choose the strongest leaders to assist him; in fact, it seemed that he wished to have men of less ability than himself, and he did not underestimate his own capacity. Writers and publicists were trying to find an outlet for Germany's energy and so they conjured up the idea of the '*Drang nach Osten*' (pressure toward the East) and began to agitate the construction of the Bagdad Railroad. The Turkish Army was being trained by German officers. In due course, the Kaiser went into Jerusalem on horseback, the wall having been opened up wide enough for his imperial entrance. It was a contrast some years later when General Allenby entered the Holy City simply and on foot after its capture by the British. The Kaiser had a great variety of interests. He affected to be an expert in matters of art, music, and perhaps even of science. I remember one evening hearing the roar of eighteen splendid military bands playing the Pilgrim's Chorus while William II wielded the baton. I was probably half a mile from the royal conductor, but I was told that the effect was imposing even two miles away in Potsdam. It was a matter of course that one frequently saw the Kaiser and members of the royal family. The blue-and-white cars of the royal trains were always on the side track at the station of Wildpark near the new palace unless the Kaiser was away from home. The Empress often rode about the park accompanied by several of her young children. They frequently attended the Friedens-kirche, which was a lovely place on a Sunday morning and where there was quite an air of informality. I sat directly behind the family one Sunday morning in the spring, when the throstles were singing

cheerily along the avenues of the park. After the service, it was customary for some of the high military officers to step forward and express their homage by kissing the hand of the Empress.

Big military spectacles were not infrequent in the Lustgarten back
of the Stadtschloss when some king or potentate was being entertained. I remember a spring morning when the young Crown
Prince reached his tenth birthday and was formally entered in the
ranks of the army. There were many foreign representatives and
an array of brilliant uniforms with interesting changes of formation
by the famous First Guard Regiment and some of the cavalry. The
Crown Prince seemed to be a very nice boy at that stage, and doubtless was much occupied with the duty of getting an education, but his
future hardly justified the promise he gave at the tender age of ten.

The Kaiser and Kaiserin once paid a royal visit to the observatory
at the time of an eclipse of the moon. They were attended by a small
number of aides and there was to be no reception. The royal carriages brought up some lackeys in advance in order to prepare for a
late luncheon for the party when the eclipse was over. The chief
janitor had his quarters in the basement, and the facilities of his
kitchen were used for the preparation of the meal. The chief lackey
distributed caviar sandwiches in a grand manner to the numerous
members of the janitors' families. Presently it appeared that the
supply of caviar was insufficient for the royal party and it was therefore stricken from the menu of the imperial visitors.

The young aides in those days affected a nasal tone, not, I am sure,
an imitation of American voices. One of the naval aides was heard
to say that it was quite useless to make three observations of an
altitude with the sextant because they never would agree, so that it
was much better to be satisfied with a single observation. The Emperor Friedrich and his wife, the Princess Royal of England, had
been much interested in the equipment of the observatory. After
his death (from cancer of the throat), following his brief reign, the
Dowager Empress Friedrich sometimes came to the observatory for
an informal visit with Director Vogel. He had a hobby or *Liebhaberei*,
for the collection of beetles. In this Her Majesty had a special interest, and so, after a cup of tea, there was an examination of his rare
specimens. Professor Vogel was also musical, getting much satisfaction from a pipe organ installed in the director's house. He en-

joyed, too, the small 'American Harmonium,' as he called it, which was an Estey organ made at Brattleboro, Vermont, my birthplace. I wrote Governor Fuller, then head of the company, about the high appreciation in which this organ was held by an expert.

In the autumn, after the crops had been harvested, it was the custom for the Kaiser and his friends to put on their red coats and go hunting for wild boars in the vicinity of Potsdam. There were large areas of royal forests south of the observatory. I have an impression that these pigs were 'planted' at certain points and there may have been even a royal piggery somewhere for the purpose of breeding these 'wild' animals. On one occasion a frightened pig came dashing down the road from the observatory hill across the Schützenplatz, scattering in consternation the crowd of small children who were always playing there. The pig swam the Havel and raced over the cobblestones in the main streets of the city. Bootblacks and all sorts of common people joined in the chase, the noble hunters in their red coats departing in disgust. The next day you could buy at any restaurant a pork chop said to be from that particular animal.

CHAPTER X

BACK TO HANOVER

WHEN I took the steamer at Antwerp on my passage homeward, I found letters awaiting me regarding future positions in America. One was from the University of Minnesota, which was seeking a young man to carry on the work of astronomy, and the other was a proposition to return to Dartmouth as an assistant professor with duties in astronomy, but without responsibilities for teaching physics. I decided to return to Hanover, as I felt that this would be a satisfaction to my parents after my long absence.

After I was re-established in my home in Hanover in the autumn of 1892, I felt rather keenly the loss of the opportunity for research which had been the whole activity of the observatory at Potsdam, but looked forward with great satisfaction to teaching the classes at Dartmouth. After I had arranged for the courses which I was to give in astronomy, analytic mechanics, and meteorology, I devoted myself assiduously in my spare time to the translation and revision of Dr. Scheiner's work. It was quite a task, as the original was an octavo, with 482 pages, including extensive tables. I decided to use the Rowland system of wave-lengths instead of that employed at Potsdam. Rowland's photographic map represented such an advance in recording the solar spectrum that previous drawings could not for a moment be compared with it. It turned out some years later that the Potsdam system was nearer the absolute value than Rowland's, but the main issue for a couple of decades was to have an accurate system of relative wave-lengths. I therefore copied and published as the first tabular appendix Rowland's table of wave-lengths in the solar spectrum, which had appeared from measurements, both visual and on photographs, in the magazine *Astronomy and Astrophysics* in the year 1893. I gave the name *Astronomical Spectroscopy* to the edition in English, and the first issue bore the imprint 1894. It covered 495 pages. A final printing of a few hundred copies with some additions and alterations appeared in 1898. About ten per cent in conciseness of expression was saved in the translation into English from the

German. I had bought the original engravings and the right to use them from the German publisher, and added only a few more recent illustrations.

After the publication of my translation of Scheiner's *Astronomical Spectroscopy*, I was favored by Director E. C. Pickering of the Harvard Observatory with an opportunity to study the complicated spectrum of the variable star Beta Lyræ on the Harvard plates which he lent to me. Unfortunately, we had no adequate measuring machine at Dartmouth for this purpose, but I made quite a qualitative study of these plates and presented a paper on my results before the American Association for the Advancement of Science.

The small observatory on the crest of the hill in the college park had been established forty years before by Dr. Shattuck of Boston and had an excellent solar spectroscope with which Professor Young had made important researches until his departure for Princeton in 1877. This equipment could be used for the study of the sun and there was other apparatus adequate for teaching practical astronomy. This science needed a revival in the college, as no one had given his whole time to the department for fifteen years. I therefore undertook the rehabilitation of the observatory and the stimulation of interest in the subject in the college. The men seemed to enjoy the appointments even although they were sometimes scheduled to meet at the observatory as late as 2 A.M. At that hour the members of the class apparently aroused every dormitory, and the noise of the advancing column over the temporary board walks with the thumping of the canes which the junior class affected at that time of the year could be heard through the whole village.

Then for an hour or two the class of eighty or more men would take their turns in looking through the telescope in close marching order, and when the exercises were over the return to the different dormitories was made without regard to those who would fain sleep. These were joyous years of teaching and association with lively young men, many of whom took hold with a will. It was my good fortune to teach these classes for the next eight years.

On one occasion when exploring for apparatus which had been junked in convenient empty spaces under the roof of the observatory, I discovered a set of glassware of an interesting sort, consisting of a decanter and half a dozen glasses. It had been placed among the brass and iron junk as if to keep the possessor out of temptation. I failed to find any trace of ownership. At one time Professor T. W. D. Worthen (called 'Alphabet Worthen') roomed in the observatory, but the last time that I saw him in Hanover, when he was over eighty years of age, he could not recall that decanter. He had some vague idea on the subject, but transferred to me all rights, if any, which he might have had, and I therefore keep possession.

When President Bartlett resigned at the end of the academic year 1892, there was an interregnum while a search was being made for a new president. Meanwhile, Professor John K. Lord acted as academic head of the college, and my father, as the resident trustee, took over some of its financial and business responsibilities. It was rather a heavy addition to my father's duties as Dean of the Medical School, Professor of the Science and Practice of Medicine (including eleven months of teaching), and with a large consultation practice in New Hampshire and Vermont besides his long-established local practice in Hanover. After I began my work as assistant professor in the autumn of 1892, I relieved him as much as I could, particularly as regarded the oversight of the introduction of electricity into the college buildings. The wiring was then done in a manner which would not now be regarded as safe, as a code for the wiring of buildings had not been fully developed; but there was a vast improvement in the illumination of the classrooms even if porcelain cleats and cheap loom or insulating conduit were everywhere in evidence. We had our own house wired at this time, and this involved opening up some floors that had been laid for a century.

Dr. William Jewett Tucker, Dartmouth '61, an outstanding liberal member of the faculty of Andover Theological Seminary, had been offered the presidency in 1877, but had declined. He was now persuaded to accept the responsibilities of this post, and entered upon his duties in the autumn of 1893. It was a time of financial depression in the country, and prospects were not encouraging for the receipts of the large endowments necessary to put the college on a modern footing. Dr. Tucker had a philosophic mind and the patience to wait for results when correct foundations had been laid. He gained great popularity with the students and alumni and exhibited a wonderful power of leadership. It was very stimulating to serve on the faculty under him, although he often called upon the faculty committees for information which required much study and research. Dr. Tucker was learning how to run a modern college as well as we were.

Dr. Tucker, like many others of the Board of Trustees, saw the introduction of a water supply as one of the important needs of making a college habitable in a modern way. The question had been under discussion for some time, largely under the initiative of Professor C. H. Pettee, Dean of the State School of Agriculture, and of Professor Robert Fletcher of the Thayer School of Engineering. In the Board of Trustees, my father had a sharp controversy with Trustee C. W. Spalding of Chicago. The latter favored pumping up the water from the Connecticut River, which, of course, was infected by the sewage from the towns lying to the north, but it seemed pure to anyone used to drinking Chicago water prior to the construction of the drainage canal. The necessary legislation was finally accomplished at Concord and in the village 'so that a large drainage area in 'district number four' was taken over and made a reservoir for impounding the flow from the little streams which came down from the still higher hillsides. The level of the reservoir must have been at least two hundred feet above the village, and the distance was about three miles. The reservoir was completed and the pipe line installed in the summer of 1893, and thereafter a safe water supply was assured, and the necessary modern sanitary equipment was secured for the village and for the college.

New money began to come to the college, and Butterfield Hall for the natural sciences was erected in the block whose corners were the White Church and Webster Hall. This was an obvious forecast that the whole block would ultimately be needed by the college. The Baker Library now makes a splendid centerpiece for this block, with Sanborn Hall for English literature and the Carpenter Art Building on its Western flank. New and modern dormitories were gradually added to the equipment, and Mr. Charles T. Wilder, owner of the paper mill two miles down the river, contributed an important sum for the erection of the Wilder Laboratory of Physics, with the provision of an endowment of ten thousand dollars for the current needs of the Department of Astronomy. The Wilder gift was obtained chiefly by the suggestion of my father, who had friendly relations with Mr. Wilder, both personally and as his physician. A new Dartmouth sprang into being rather rapidly, the classes increasing greatly in size, and the men coming with much better preparation than formerly. New policies were inaugurated by Dr. Tucker, beginning with the consolidation of the Chandler School of Science with the college proper. Henceforth the college made a decided advance.

I know of no subject which can give more inspiration to student and teacher than astronomy, and I had already had experience in teaching other branches. Just at this time photography was being applied in astronomy and astrophysics, and it was a period of progress in the unfolding of the majesty of the cosmos. Every student was required to take the course in astronomy as they had been for many decades past. The presentation naturally had to be elementary and descriptive, but it gave a good field for the enthusiasm of a young teacher. There were many splendid classes in the nineties which responded with attention and interest. There was often quite a bit of humor in the classroom, and curiously enough I find that after thirty years or more, some of these jocosities are not forgotten by the men. Oddly enough the position of the men in the classroom is persistent in my memory. When I attended my forty-fifth class reunion in June, 1931, I happened to mention to President Hopkins that I remembered just where he sat — 'right over there in the corner of the classroom in Wilder Hall.' And knowing that his interest in the subject was only cultural, I added, 'I also recall that sometimes you read a book.' His retort courteous was not immediate, but came later in the evening of the same day when I reached him in the receiving line at the President's reception. 'That book, Professor Frost,' said the genial man affectionately known as 'Hoppy,' 'was, I now remember, a textbook on astronomy.'

In the winter term, the whole class was required to take the descriptive course, followed by an elective practical course in the spring. More advanced work was offered to a limited class throughout the senior year, and the men who elected this were very able. It was stimulating to work with them. I had the pleasure also of giving the descriptive course for the four winters following my departure to the Yerkes Observatory in 1898. By that time the classes had grown almost too large to be handled by one teacher, and I requested that the course be made elective. This change naturally reduced the numbers in the classroom, but there was still a large class of two sections.

At this time our system of presenting a subject was by direct recitation and assignments at the blackboard. I still argue for the advantages of this procedure which gives a contact between the professor and the student that does not occur in the lecture system and throws less stress upon final examinations. This view of mine may be regarded as odiously mid-Victorian by the younger generation, but it is based upon experience with both methods.

We had a fine group of young men joining the teaching staff at this time, and their advent enlivened the social life of the college. We young men were said to form the 'Kid Faculty.' It was an odd circumstance that my brother and I returned to the service of the college at the same time, he to a teaching position in the medical faculty and to assist Father in his general practice. My brother had taken his medical degree both at Dartmouth and Harvard and had completed his duties in the hospitals in Boston. It soon fell to him to be the first medical director of the new Mary Hitchcock Memorial Hospital. Until his marriage in 1895 our family was therefore complete at home. He then built a house just east of the old home on a portion of the property which Father gave him. This is still his home.

I had an excellent saddle horse, Jack by name, and greatly enjoyed riding about the shady roads in the vicinity of Hanover and across the river in Vermont. The many brooks added a special attraction to these country roads. It was regrettable to me that not more of my colleagues rode. However, we had some fine walks together, climbing hills and making excursions to neighboring mountains. We had an enjoyable life besides giving close attention to our college duties.

The intimate Dartmouth that I knew meant to me the rugged quality of the men. They were there to get something and usually at great sacrifice — not because they were sent. They had been touched with the spirit of the classics by some teacher in their preparatory schools, or they were stirred by the rapid discoveries of applied science. Or perhaps they still felt the old appeal of the godlike Daniel Webster and aspired to such heights in the field of law or politics. The general average came to learn and valued their opportunities. In those days not many were brought up in the lap of luxury and even those who were soon caught the spirit of thrift. Extravagance was rare. It will be very interesting after the lapse of sufficient years to find whether the plan of selective admission in effect at Dartmouth since 1921 produces a body of alumni more competent to carry on the world's work than was the case when practically every applicant was admitted if only his preparation was tolerably adequate. The 'spirit of the hills' and the rugged North probably still makes an impression upon the youth who now come from the great plains of the West or from the largest cities of the entire country. One may question somewhat, however, the application of Richard Hovey's song with the implication that 'the granite of New Hampshire' forms a part of their brain tissue.

> 'Men of Dartmouth give a rouse
> For the college on the hill!
> For the Lone Pine above her
> And the loyal men who love her —
> Give a rouse, give a rouse with a will!
> For the sons of old Dartmouth
> The sturdy sons of Dartmouth
> Tho' round the girdled earth they roam
> Her spell on them remains;
> They have the still North in their hearts,
> The hill winds in their veins,
> And the granite of New Hampshire
> In their muscles and their brains!'

Toward the end of the summer vacation in 1893, my old friend, Dr. Joseph Thompson of Amherst, joined me for a trip to the World's Fair in Chicago. The trains were very crowded in those days and we met some curious strangers. I remember an interesting cultured Russian baron who was one of our seat-mates in the Pullman. He had his American Baedecker with him, but seemed glad to find some-one who could speak German which he knew well. The scheduled time over the Grand Trunk to Chicago from the East had been materially shortened so that we no longer had to spend two nights *en route*, but arrived late in the evening of the second day. We had foolishly made no reservations and went to the old Saratoga Hotel, where we were packed into a large room with a miscellaneous company of not less than six men in nearly that number of beds. One of our roommates thought that he was a philosopher and rejoiced to find an audience. He was still expatiating at great length as we drifted off into slumber.

The Columbian Exposition at Chicago in 1893 was in itself an education in art, architecture, and the mechanical arts. To a young man who had just returned from two years in Europe, where the great masterpieces of architecture, painting, and sculpture in several of the largest cities had become somewhat familiar, this notable assembly of great works in all of these fields made an impression not to be forgotten. The art of illumination was developed and applied on the noble structures in the Court of Honor as it had never been applied before. The situation in Jackson Park on the shore of Lake Michigan, with the lagoons and bridges and the Venetian gondolas rapidly piloted through these artificial waterways, combined to produce an extraordinary effect of beauty.

I made my visit toward the end of the summer and took time enough to inspect those features which interested me most. Aside from the art treasures, there were many exhibits of a scientific and mechanical nature that must appeal to everyone interested in these fields. Important scientific congresses were held in connection with the World's Fair, one of the most notable of these being that concerned with physics and electricity. It was attended by such eminent authorities as Helmholtz of Germany, Mascart of France, and many others. Some of the important units of electricity were legally defined at this congress, and thus electricity developed in a scientific manner and under a much more definite plan than had been the case with other branches of physics. The astronomical congress was not very largely attended, but was interesting. The local committee included Professor S. W. Burnham, who had resumed his post as clerk of the United States Court in Chicago after spending several years at the Lick Observatory, and Professor George E. Hale, who had joined the staff of the University of Chicago, and had placed his private observatory on the corner of Drexel Boulevard and Forty-Sixth Street at the service of the university for research and instruction. Professor Max Wolf of Heidelberg was present, and Professor Henry A. Rowland of Baltimore came to take part in some of the discussions of an astrophysical character.

One of the striking exhibits in the great manufacturers' building was the pier and mounting of the great Yerkes telescope destined for a permanent location on the shores of Lake Geneva, Wisconsin. It was a notable engineering achievement by Messrs. Warner and Swasey of Cleveland that, after receiving the order for the construction of this telescope in the autumn of 1892, they were able to install it at the Fair in the following summer. The story of this telescope is an interesting one. I recall being in a group of men who were attending the meeting of the American Association for the Advancement of Science at Rochester, New York, in early September of 1892, when Mr. Alvan G. Clark of Cambridge suggested to Mr. Hale that the new University of Chicago, just being re-created out of the intellectual remains of the old Chicago University, should properly have a large telescope. The University of Southern California had hoped to secure such a telescope and had ordered from the glass-making firm of Parra-Mantois in Paris a pair of discs, one of flint glass and one of crown glass, nearly forty-two inches in diameter. These had turned out very well, but the plans of the University of Southern California went awry, and the discs could be bought for fifteen thousand dollars. With great energy Mr. Hale adopted Mr. Clark's suggestion and easily persuaded Dr. William R. Harper, President of the University, to attempt to realize the plan. An approach was made to Mr. Charles T. Yerkes, who was then a leading figure in developing the surface traction lines of Chicago, and who, a few years before, had introduced the system of cable transmission of power and had even carried the cable under the river by a tunnel at La Salle Street. Mr. Yerkes was intrigued by the idea of erecting the biggest telescope that had yet been constructed. His business was expanding rapidly at that time and he needed considerable credit. When he found that he would not have to advance the money for the expensive dome and building, or even for the object glass, for two or three years, he is said to have remarked to some confidant that by that time his fortune would be fully made, or else he would be completely 'busted,' and therefore he decided to take the chance. He agreed to make the necessary donation to the university, and when the announcement was made the next morning that Mr. Yerkes would erect a great observatory to house the biggest refracting telescope in the world, at a cost of several hundred thousand dollars, he found that his credit was greatly strengthened, and that he could borrow all the money he needed for his business enterprises. This is not said to belittle Mr. Yerkes's benevolent intention in behalf of science and education, but merely to illustrate how such gifts may react in favor of the donor. I am giving the story as it was once told to me by a former trustee of the university.

In the autumn of 1895 we began to have some concern about my father's health, as his heart seemed to be somewhat affected. I marvel at the amount of work which he was able to carry on at this period of his life as Dean of the Medical College, constantly teaching its classes, attending to his local practice and having a rather wide practice in which he was called in consultation with other doctors. He was a man full of humor whose presence greatly cheered his patients. I remember with some amusement a story which my father told to one of his patients. A student, who was rather older than the average, was concerned about his increasing baldness. After an examination, my father's verdict was as follows: 'I know only one way to cure your trouble. There was a man so noticeably bald that he was greatly annoyed by frequent visits trom salesmen with various nostrums for the sure cure of baldness. He resolved that he would give a lesson to the next vendor who came. When the unwelcome man appeared, he was promptly kicked out. In his hasty retreat, however, a bottle of his cure was broken on the hitching-post upon which within a few days appeared a fine growth of hair. Now,' said the Doctor, 'your only chance is to find that man.'

My father did not believe much in drugs, but was an advocate of fresh air and good nursing. He was an extraordinarily clean doctor in the days before antiseptics were much used, and I believe that his cleanliness increased his success with his patients. He was a great admirer of Pasteur when his researches became known in America, and taught the new methods of asepsis and antisepsis earlier than would have been expected. He participated actively in civic affairs and was for a time village commissioner, greatly assisting in the introduction of the first sidewalks. He was not inclined to give his sons much advice as they grew up, assuming that our actions would be gentlemanly and correct. I persuaded him to take a vacation trip of a few days with me to Washington in about 1894. He had stuck so closely to his duties in the Medical College and to his medical practice that he had not been to the capital city since he resigned as Surgeon of the Fifteenth Vermont Regiment on May 3, 1863. His Colonel, Redfield Proctor, was now Senator from Vermont, and there were many other friends in the city. On another occasion I persuaded him to go with me to Mount Moosilauke, where we spent an interesting night on the summit, a favorite resort for me. In the spring of 1896, after much hard riding over muddy roads on consultation calls, Father began to have serious trouble with his heart. This proved to be angina pectoris. He was too familiar with the symptoms not to realize the probable outcome, and he often had me read to him from the latest books on the subject. Under the careful nursing of Mother and of a trained nurse he recovered enough to be able to go out to drive in the early part of May. But the disease increased, and he died on May 24, a few days before his sixty-sixth birthday. His death brought out many expressions of deep affection from the community and from his many friends. The funeral address was given by President Tucker who had a fine appreciation of Father's qualities. It seemed to us only proper that the hearse should be drawn by old Fanny, the gray horse which was known as the Doctor's all over the countryside, and on the seat sat the man who had been his driver and had taken care of our stable and gardens during a number of years. It was a great regret to us that Father did not live to see any of his grandchildren of whom there were ultimately eight. The first of these was named for him, Carlton Pennington, and was born a few months after Father's death. Father was exceptionally fond of children and had been present at the advent of most of those born in Hanover between 1871 and 1890.

My brother carried on Father's practice, and I was able to be of some comfort to Mother in taking over the household duties which had been Father's. My mother had suffered a detachment of the retina not long before this, making it impossible for her to read. Those of us in the household took turns in reading to her, but she was a very patient woman and bore her trouble with dignity.

In January, 1896, fragments of information began to come over the cables of a striking discovery by Professor Röntgen of Würtzburg whereby penetrating rays were developed in vacuum tubes from points bombarded by cathode rays. It was reported that Röntgen was able to photograph through opaque matter by these new rays. His original paper, published late in December, had not reached this country so that the particulars of his experiment were lacking. I immediately tested the numerous vacuum tubes in our physical laboratory for their capacity to produce the mysterious rays. The results were startling. No one could ever forget the interest felt in watching the development of those first plates on that Saturday evening, February 1. It did not take long to find where the rays were most active around the tubes, and the Puluj tube proved to be the most efficient. I suspect, in fact, that it was one of the best tubes in use in America at that time. It was handled carefully and was not burned out as were many of the tubes used in other laboratories. It was attached to the secondary circuit of a large induction coil fed by Grove batteries. This tube is now preserved as a museum piece in the Wilder Laboratory.

A Hanover boy, Eddie McCarthy, had broken the ulna of his forearm on January 19, and my brother, Dr. G. D. Frost, wished me to make a test of the new method on this case. We secured quite a satisfactory photograph on February 3. The following day I reported my experiments to *Science* in an article which appeared in the issue of February 14 along with articles by Professor M. I. Pupin and Dr. Arthur Goodspeed, their articles bearing the date of February 8. A page of pictures was printed giving photographic results obtained by each of us. In the same number also appeared the first account by Röntgen himself. One of my photographs reproduced one of my own fingers as they grasped the plate-holder placed under the tube. I later obtained a photograph of a hand which shows details quite as well as the best of the present X-ray pictures.

The value of the new method to surgery was so apparent that there was a great development in the manufacture of X-ray tubes in this country, and a vast number of experiments were conducted in many laboratories and hospitals. Other photographs of broken limbs were made with the Dartmouth equipment in the spring of 1896, and as early as the autumn of that year, I was called upon to testify in a damage suit involving a broken arm. The testimony of the X-rays was accepted by the courts without question.

CHAPTER XI

ROMANCE

MY COUSIN, Mary Brant Little, always called by us 'Mary B.,' was the daughter of Dr. Arthur Little who married my father's only sister Lizzie. Dr. Little, after having two pastorates in the Middle West, including the New England Congregational Church in Chicago, was called to the old Second Church in Dorchester, Massachusetts. Mary was more like a sister to us than a cousin, as she had as a girl spent many summers in our home in Hanover after her mother's death. When, in 1894, she married Dr. John F. Thompson, Dartmouth '82, my brother and I were naturally members of the wedding party. I agreed to serve as an usher if among the bridesmaids I should be given as a partner one who would fulfill certain exacting requirements. So Miss Mary Hazard was assigned to me for the various functions connected with the wedding festivities in Dorchester.

During the next year and a half, Miss Hazard and I saw little of each other, but entered into a correspondence which promised developments. We did accept an invitation to spend two days with 'Mary B.' in Portland to attend some play in which she was interested. In those days such a trip implied more of a commitment than now when there are no longer such absurd conventionalities. At that time I was a little nervous when I entered the North Station for fear some Dartmouth boy from my classes might be there to report upon my departure to Portland with a pretty girl. Such was the case.

It befell after commencement in 1896 that four of us of the teaching staff, being aweary of our academic duties, strenuously performed, sought rest and relaxation. We were Professors D. Collin Wells, Herbert D. Foster, Frank G. Moore, and the oversigned. We started out with light equipment, and on a Saturday night reached the Asquam House (once a favorite resort of Whittier's), which lies on the shore of Squam Lake in New Hampshire and commands a fine view of Chocorua and the Sandwich Mountains. We rested for the Sabbath, some of us spending the afternoon in writing letters. I ostensibly wrote about four, but they went into the same envelope when mailed. Except for Mr. Wells, we were unmarried. Foster was to leave us at Portland and once more to go to England to try to persuade that English girl whom he had met at Sienna to take his name and come to America to live. Moore and I were not supposed to have any matrimonial intentions. Just to enliven the occasion I advanced a proposition to the effect that this was a good place to come for a wedding journey and that we should each subscribe ten dollars for a fund for the purpose to be paid to the person who should first bring his bride to this hotel. Mr. Wells, being *hors de combat,* was to hold the stakes. After securing the agreement of all parties, I took the matter up with the proprietor of the hotel, and how he did laugh! He agreed that thirty dollars would do for the first week, and a written document was drawn up, signed by us four visitors and by the proprietor, and deposited with the arbitrator, Wells. It looked as if there would be no active claimant for some time, as Foster had had no luck so far. Very likely I told the joke in my letter addressed to a young lady in Boston. We climbed various mountains, spending the night on Chocorua, and generally had a fine trip. Foster left us for his steamer and I soon went to Boston. By prearrangement Frank Moore was to call the next evening. I had much pleasure in introducing him to my fiancée, Miss Mary Elizabeth Hazard, daughter of Dr. and Mrs. Marshall Curtis Hazard of Dorchester and I proceeded to show him to my own satisfaction how he was wasting time. In Brooklyn there was a fine young woman whom he and I had both known when we were in Germany, and I had my suspicion that she would not object to a call from him. He had her picture in his room at Hanover, but did not keep it on display as much as I thought he should. I was accustomed to rummage around in his bureau drawer until I found it and displayed it on the mantel in what I thought was a proper manner. Now, strange as it may be, Frank left Boston almost immediately, and before the week was over sent back word that he and Anna White were also engaged. Thus were four people already greatly pleased with the situation regardless of how it originated. We did not write to Foster and perhaps lacked his address, but in about six weeks we got a most exultant letter from him saying that he had persuaded the lady and adding, 'I have won the pool!' When he got to Hanover just before the fall term opened, he was in a state of supreme joy, and we let him rave on for a good part of the first evening, finally telling him that we were not without experience ourselves and that it was a fair question who would win that week's stay at the Asquam House. Foster had the disadvantage of distance and well knew that he could not bring his fiancée over to America until the next summer vacation. At that moment Frank and I were not certain that any wedding bells could ring before the next June after college closed. But as time went on, it seemed useless to wait unnecessarily for the summer vacation. I coaxed my lady along first to consider Easter vacation, then Christmas vacation, and finally I worked out a scheme by which I could be away from college for a week or ten days around Thanksgiving time.

The short weeks of our engagement were busy ones for us both with only an occasional visit together. Early in November I drifted one Sunday morning into the large room of the infant class of the Second Church in Dorchester where Miss Wales was teaching a group of over two hundred and fifty little folk and where Miss Hazard presided at the piano. Miss Wales asked the children what they had to be thankful for, and added, 'Perhaps Professor Frost would be willing to write the list on the blackboard.' When my task was fairly completed, she unexpectedly turned to me and questioned, 'What are you thankful for, Mr. Frost?' I printed in large letters and with a firm hand, 'Miss Hazard.' The answer might have been a bit enigmatic to the children, but was perfectly clear to their elders who fringed the room in large numbers. I may have embarrassed the young lady somewhat, as she fled precipitately from the room, being at the moment conveniently near the door.

The nineteenth of November was a beautiful day, but how can one describe one's own wedding? I suppose that every bridegroom is nervous and impatient as he watches that slowly advancing group with his lovely bride-to-be coming down the aisle on the arm of her father. However overcome he may be, he finds his voice as the proceedings require.

Frank Moore was my best man, and Miss Hazard's sister Carolyn was maid of honor. My uncle, Dr. Little, performed the ceremony.

Anna White, Frank's fiancée, had what I called just the right spirit. She confided to my cousin that she would be perfectly ready to walk up the aisle and be married to Frank as soon as the minister was through with us.

I often recall that lovely moonlight night and our escape from rice and slippers through the back door of my bride's home after a jolly reception enlivened by the presence of many Wellesley girls and Dartmouth men. We spent that night in a hotel in Boston, planning to go on to New York the following day. As usual we flattered ourselves that we were quite 'lost in the crowd,' but as we stepped into the dining-room the next morning, I was greeted by one of the waiters with 'Good-morning, Professor, I believe you was the gentleman who was married in Dorchester last night.' When I failed to respond quickly, he added, 'I was at de weddin'.' He was one of the caterer's men.

Our wedding trip was a short one, as I had to be in Hanover immediately after Thanksgiving, but we knew that we were to have a more extended holiday in Europe the following summer. So I proudly took my bride to Hanover which she has always loved. Among the younger members of the faculty at that time there had been no recent marriages, and when an elderly second wife called upon Mrs. Frost, she was informed, 'Now you are the bride of the town. I have held that position for two years.' This was a novel idea to the younger woman. Another thing which amused Mrs. Frost, who had spent her earlier years in the Middle West, was the oft-repeated expressions of conservative New England, 'We never have' and 'We always have.' She found them final.

Frank Moore and Anna White were married in Brooklyn on January 2, about six weeks after our wedding, and they sailed away for half of a sabbatical year in Europe. We met them there the next summer and spent several pleasant days together on Lake Geneva, Switzerland. We were not able to go to England for Foster's wedding, and thus it turned out that no one could go to the Asquam House before the hotel had closed for the winter. Under the circumstances, an impartial jury awarded the prize to me, and it took the form of a mahogany chair which has been an especially valued piece of furniture in our household. Kind readers will draw their own moral from this strange true tale.

BRIDE AND GROOM, 1896

CHAPTER XII

A NEW ENGLAND WINTER AND A EUROPEAN SUMMER

I RECALL an amusing incident on a sharp evening in December soon after our return to Hanover. We had invited Foster and Moore and a few others in for a formal dinner. After dinner we were gathered around the fireplace, with a blazing fire of white birch which we always kept on hand. There was a sudden ominous roar in the chimney and I hastily left the room. Moore and Foster followed. We were putting in a hardwood floor in the room overhead and the whole floor was covered with shavings. I got there just in time to see the burning soot coming down the flue into that fireplace and some of the shavings in the room on fire. Moore attended to this while I pulled off my dress-suit and got into my outfit as a member of the volunteer fire brigade. Rushing up to the third floor, I found the chimney and thimbles at white heat. So much burning soot was falling upon the shingled roof that it seemed best to call the fire department. They sent up a stream of water which froze as it fell on the roof, leaving our friend Foster astride the ridgepole in his dress-suit, with an icy descent to safety. There were no further consequences.

One of the features of the winter in Hanover was the great blanket of snow which usually came soon after Thanksgiving and sometimes provided as much as a hundred and twenty days of good sleighing. It was always customary to have bells attached to the sleigh, presumably in order to warn other sleighs to watch for a place to turn out. It was rare for the snow to drift in this section of the country where on account of many hills the wind had little chance to gather force. The white flakes usually fell quietly and often for many hours together leaving no trace of the previous tracks along the road. I have sometimes driven in the early morning in light snow so deep that it broke over on the seat of the sleigh. I remember well the great snowfall of March 11–14, 1888. It had fallen during the previous afternoon and the whole night. I was almost afraid to go to chapel, lest the older members of the faculty would not be able to get through and thus involve me with some kind of responsibility. But the venerable president was undaunted and left his home early enough to be on hand at ten minutes of eight; in fact the senior members of the faculty seemed to make it a point of honor to overcome such obstacles presented by Nature. This particular storm was really much worse in New York and the large Eastern cities than it was in the country which could more easily adapt itself to the condition. One suburban employee in New York City telegraphed his firm, 'Cannot get to the office today; have not gotten home yesterday yet.' The full sporting value of these great snowfalls for cross-country snowshoeing and skiing was not realized by the college until about 1900 when the Outing Club developed great zest for winter sports. The young people of my day were not afraid of the cold, and engagements with a young lady for an evening sleigh-ride were not postponed because the temperature happened to be ten or fifteen degrees below zero.

The question is always raised whether the winters have not changed, becoming milder than formerly and with less snow. I investigated this matter while I was in charge of the observatory where the records went back for about forty years, but could not find evidence of any change. I was also given access to a diary kept for more than a generation by a bright old lady, who conscientiously kept the dates of the beginning and the ending of the sleighing season. These records also showed no appreciable change when averages were taken over periods of ten or twenty years. As I recall it, the snowfall at Hanover in 1888 was eight feet, but that was quite an unusual amount. Records kept at the Yerkes Observatory for the last thirty years also fail to indicate any noticeable change in the climate. It is true that wire fences prevent the choking of the roads by snow which occurred with the high board fences, and it is also true that the universal use of automobiles has made it necessary to keep the roads open as was not formerly the case. The roadways now therefore seem more free of snow.

Our trip to Europe the next summer was a happy one. We took the slender steamer *Kaiser Wilhelm II* of the North German Lloyd from New York to Genoa, with several hours' stop at Gibraltar. The weather was fine as we went up the Spanish coast and along the French Riviera where we could often see the individual buildings. One could easily recognize the observatory at Nice. There were at least a dozen other young married couples on board, and some old friends from Dorchester and from Wellesley. At Gibraltar we took on two or three Spanish grandees who thought they had the right to sit on the rail and comment in Spanish very obviously about our handsome group of young women. Some of us young husbands seriously considered throwing them overboard, but they desisted from their acts just in time to prevent a scene. It was hot in Naples for sight-seeing, but we shall not forget the refreshment we felt as we drove into the hotel garden at Sorrento after a busy inspection of the ruins of Pompeii and there found a cool breeze with the ripe oranges falling from the trees at our feet. It was the hottest summer for many years at Rome, and Mary became ill after too much climbing around Saint Peter's. So we transferred from the Italian hotel that had been recommended to us, patronized by many deputies and full of local color, to a quiet English *pension* where my wife soon recovered. Here we had the pleasure of meeting the Honorable Henry C. Ide of St. Johnsbury, Vermont, who was returning for a vacation from his duties as Chief Justice of Samoa. He had graduated at Dartmouth in the year that I was born. It was his younger daughter, who accompanied him from Samoa, who received from Robert Louis Stevenson the gift of his birthday because her own fell on December 25. Judge Ide was later Governor-General of the Philippines, and finally Ambassador to Spain. Our friends, Mr. and Mrs. Charles F. Kittredge, and their daughter Louise, traveled with us from Florence to Venice and later through the Italian lakes. He was a graduate of Dartmouth in the class of '63 and had many reminiscences to tell me of his years in college.

It was funny how small groups of travelers began to attach themselves to our nucleus. I made no pretense of speaking Italian, but knew just words enough to get along. I remember our amusement when we drove to a hotel in Milan in a pouring rain, in a company of thirteen men and women, waiting for me to go into the hotel to dicker with the proprietor for special rates for the crowd. After leaving this brisk modern city, with its beautiful cathedral, we moved on to the Italian lakes, so marvelously situated in the mountains. They impressed us deeply, and we were loath to leave that picturesque country. With the Kittredges we took the diligence over the Simplon Pass from Domodossola in Italy to Brieg in Switzerland.

It was a special delight to me to visit with my wife the places which were familiar to me from my previous visit, but in particular to call upon friends in Strassburg, Heidelberg, and Potsdam.

Our trip of thirteen weeks covered the usual routes of travel for tourists, including about ten days each in Paris and London. It had been a joyous summer, but we were glad to get home for the beginning of the new college year.

CHAPTER XIII

WINTER OF 1898–1899

IN OCTOBER, I attended the conference of astronomers held in connection with the exercises of dedication of the Yerkes Observatory at Williams Bay, Wisconsin, on the shore of Lake Geneva. As the summer camps around the lake had been closed some weeks before the date for the formal opening of the observatory, provision was made for many of the visiting scientists by placing bunks in the basement. The meridian room served as a kitchen for the caterers who provided the meals. I was hospitably entertained at the house of Professor Wadsworth, little thinking that this was to be my own home for six years, beginning in the summer of 1899. October 21 was a beautiful autumn day at Lake Geneva. A special train brought the trustees and many guests of the university. Dr. William R. Harper, the energetic organizer of the University of Chicago, was inclined to follow somewhat the English formalities in academic celebrations. The principal addresses were made on the floor of the large dome with the presentation by Mr. Yerkes and the acceptance by Mr. Martin A. Ryerson, president of the Board of Trustees. The main scientific address was by Professor James E. Keeler, Director of the Allegheny Observatory. He spoke on the subject, 'The Importance of Astrophysical Research and the Relations of Astrophysics to other Physical Sciences.' After the exercises the official party and guests returned to Chicago for a dinner in honor of the occasion. Some demonstrations were given by Professor Michelson and his associates at the new Ryerson Physical Laboratory, one of the first buildings erected on the campus for scientific research and instruction, and a gift from Mr. Ryerson.

The astronomical conference of visiting astronomers and physicists during the two or three days preceding the formal exercises of dedication on October 21 was a great success, many papers being presented and some demonstrations of apparatus and methods being given. I reported upon these meetings and upon the formal inauguration of the observatory in the issue of *Science* for November

15. A later conference was held at the observatory in 1899. It was then decided to form a National Astronomical Society. A constitution and by-laws were drawn up, chiefly by the efforts of Professor G. C. Comstock, so that this conference became the first meeting of the Astronomical and Astrophysical Society of America. Professor Simon Newcomb was elected as the first president and Professor Comstock as secretary. His health being impaired at that time, I agreed to serve as acting secretary during that first year. The rather clumsy name of the organization was simplified in 1914 and became the American Astronomical Society, meeting once a year, and at least once in four years with the American Association for the Advancement of Science.

In the winter of 1898, in order to enliven the midwinter season, my wife and I got up a play which was produced with the aid of our many friends in the young faculty group. A few of my wife's Wellesley friends came up to assist. In the previous summer I had noticed on the kiosks in Paris a poster of a play entitled *Au Nord Pol* which gave me the idea of a humorous adventure in which a scientific explorer might be commanded by the chief of an Eskimo tribe to take his daughter for his wife. The music which was worked out for the story was largely original. Mrs. Frost was in charge of this feature and acted as accompanist. Craven Laycock, now the Dean of Dartmouth College, was King of the Snows, and the King's daughter, Mrs. Herbert Foster, was Ugu. Roland Stephens was Kikwok, the Eskimo candidate for the hand of the princess. His failure to join in the chase of the bear, because of his attentions to Princess Ugu, led to his immersion and supposedly to his drowning in the cold waters. I took the part of the American professor; William Patten, Herbert Foster, Mrs. Margaret Frost, and Frank Moore were among the other leading participants. The unfortunate Kikwok after his immersion had apparently been able to swim to the royal reindeer's drinking-hole and thus make his escape. He sang, in alliteration, when he came back, bringing the American Professor,

'I was rescued by a curious chain of chances
And I wonder if I really am alive,
For a fiercer fate no futile frenzy fancies
Than to take that fearful, frightful, frigid dive.

'Then I, weary, worn and wretched, roamed in exile
Famished, 'til at last I found a frozen whale.
Quick, I crawled within the stomach of the reptile
And for weeks at ease, repeated Jonah's tale.'

Explorers found him looking out of the eye of the whale, and they
explained to him,

'We sought the hot equator,
'Twas mighty long and thin.
Then we felt a yearning to
Hear earth's axis spin.

'So we sailed up northward
Until we got icebound.
Is this the place to come
To hear the world go 'round?'

The tribe received the travelers very cordially.

'You're welcome to our winter's store —
Eat all you can, then ask for more.
For months the sun will not appear,
The light of the moon will lend you cheer.

'So eat your fill of blubber sweet,
And wrap yourselves in fur so neat
That winter's cold cannot creep in,
And then good-bye 'til spring begins.'

The professor is naturally quite horrified at the chief's proposal
that he should wed his daughter and he explains in song his devotion
to the wife awaiting him at home. His positive refusal to play the
rôle of son-in-law, coupled with gifts which the travelers had made
to the young gentleman who was rescued, releases him. Kikwok
is restored to favor and finally marries the chief's daughter. One
middle act was entirely impromptu, calling upon the inspiration
of all members of the company. We invited about two hundred
and fifty friends to the gymnasium which we were allowed to use
for this entertainment and which we entitled 'A Mid-Winter Night's
Dream.' I still have the printed program.

A form of entertainment which was in vogue toward the end of
the winter, as the maple sugar came from the farms to the local

market, was 'sugaring off.' We used the kitchen, which was of ample size and not suggestive of the modern apartment. Each guest was provided with a milkpan filled with snow. The syrup was boiling on the stove and when a little was poured on the snow, it congealed to the consistency of wax. Then with a crock of home-made doughnuts, tongues were unloosed, songs were sung, and everybody was happy.

It was in the following April, when we were rejoicing in the birth of our little daughter Katharine Brant in the old home, that I was invited to join the staff of the Yerkes Observatory of the University of Chicago. Professor Hale had been successful in obtaining a gift from Miss Catherine Bruce of New York to provide the salary of a Professor of Astrophysics for five years. It was not an easy matter for me to decide to give up my position in Dartmouth, leaving my mother, my intimate friends, and the comforts of home for the somewhat pioneering experience in an undeveloped little village in Wisconsin. For my wife, who was born in Chicago and had spent her early youth in Wheaton and Oak Park, this migration did not seem so serious, as she had many friends in this part of the country. But the opportunity for research with a great telescope and of working under the inspiring leadership of my friend Professor Hale outweighed the sacrifices involved in leaving Hanover and I accepted the appointment to be effective July 1, 1898. We were glad that we were not committed for a period of over five years, not realizing how deeply we should become attached to the new home and to the new friends.

Shortly before leaving for the West, Mrs. Frost and I were offered the opportunity of buying at a very low price three hundred and sixty acres of woodland on the side of Moose Mountain, less than ten miles from Hanover. It was a great temptation and we have sometimes regretted that we did not yield to it. We often imagine the supreme delight of tracing the course of its tinkling brook and of exploring those deeply shaded woods, hearing the ruffed grouse drumming on his hollow log; or when tired, resting upon the soft carpet of pine needles while we listened to the lovely songs of the veery and the hermit thrushes.

Let the unfortunate city dweller rightly proclaim the beauty of the city's skyline at dusk, or praise the architecture of its buildings;

let him rejoice in the opportunities which the city has to offer. As for me and mine, we like the open spaces with their sense of freedom, their beauty and their calm.

How fortunate for us then that the Yerkes Observatory, to which we were coming, had been located in the country in Wisconsin instead of in Chicago, and that we were to spend the next thirty-odd years on a beautiful hilltop overlooking the justly famous Lake Geneva.

CHAPTER XIV

LAKE GENEVA AND YERKES OBSERVATORY

IN THE first week of July, we started with our infant daughter for the new adventure. At this time, we took neither furniture nor equipment for our new home. We knew that we could find accommodation for the summer at the well-known Camp Collie which consisted of a group of some cottages and dormitory buildings and a dining-hall. This camp was picturesquely situated on the shore of the lake and about a mile from the observatory.

We spent a night in Chicago with our friends Mr. and Mrs. James H. Breasted. On arriving at the station of Williams Bay, we were met by Mr. Hale and were taken on the handsome yacht of Mr. E. E. Ayer to the pier at Camp Collie. There were many pleasant people and some queer ones at the camp. I remember one woman who walked on her toes and with her arms outspread like the wings of a bird. She alleged that in her previous incarnation she had been either a bird or a squirrel, and she still lived largely on nuts. The camp had been used earlier by its owner, Dr. Joseph Collie, for forty years minister of the Congregational Church at Delavan, as a gathering-place for religious conferences. In fact, Dr. M. C. Hazard, Mrs. Frost's father, had been accustomed to come to the camp for such purposes in the seventies. Mr. and Mrs. Tracy Drake of Chicago had rented for the summer the country home of Mr. and Mrs. William J. Chalmers, which was situated close to Camp Collie. We were fortunate in having these delightful neighbors whose lasting friendship has been a great joy to us. Tracy and I are brothers of the D. K. E. Fraternity and for some years the Northwest Association has made an annual pilgrimage to Lake Geneva for golf, trips on the lake, and a visit to the observatory.

On the morning after my arrival at Camp Collie, I was addressed in a friendly manner by a man who was engaged in raking the walks and who appeared to be a gardener. He evinced a considerable interest in knowing from whence I came. With my normal New England chill, I replied, 'I came from the East.' He pressed me for more definite information. 'The Connecticut River Valley,' said I. That was not enough. 'What part of the valley?' he inquired further. When I explained that I came from Hanover, New Hampshire, he admitted that he had some knowledge of my forbears, who they were, and where they lived in Vermont. In fact, he seemed to have a complete biography of my Frost connections. I later learned that he was brought up in the very part of Vermont most familiar to me, that he was a guest at the camp, and an active member of the Chicago Historical Society.

A stellar spectrograph for the forty-inch telescope had been included in Mr. Yerkes's gift and had been constructed by Mr. Brashear. With the efficient assistance of Mr. Ferdinand Ellerman, who had for several weeks been getting the instrument into working condition, I began to photograph the spectra of the stars for the purpose of measuring their speed in the line of sight according to the methods inaugurated at Potsdam ten years before. The technique had been greatly improved by other observers, chiefly by W. W. Campbell of the Lick Observatory, who had constructed a spectrograph of much greater stability and with greater freedom from flexure. New methods for the measurement of the plates and their reduction had also been worked out by Campbell and published in the *Astrophysical Journal*. I desired to take advantage of all these improvements and to see if other perfections could be introduced. A measuring machine was received from the Zeiss Company in the autumn, and much time was spent in testing the accuracy of the results which could be obtained. It soon appeared that the spectrograph was insufficiently protected from flexure and from changes of temperature during the exposure. Efforts were made to overcome these difficulties, but they were more serious than we realized at first. Professor Hale therefore discussed plans with me for the design of a new spectrograph which would eliminate these difficulties as far as possible, but they could not be carried out until a gift of three thousand dollars was received from Miss Bruce for the purpose. Then the attempt was made to secure the finest and best prisms which could be manufactured at the works of Parra-Mantois in Paris. Tests of the new prisms were made while the instrument was being built in our shop, but it was finally decided that the prisms were not sufficiently homogeneous, and a new set was ordered from the Jena glassworks. Thus it was not until the summer of 1901 that the Bruce spectrograph could be put into regular operation and highly satisfactory results could be secured.

The observatory was at first really meagerly equipped, and Director Hale had his serious problems in starting the new institution on its career. He had a real genius for organization and was resourceful in securing support from Dr. Harper and the university authorities. He had great imagination in outlining the future development of the observatory and in planning programs for research. His enthusiasm was contagious and has played a large part in his successful organization of large scientific undertakings. Our life and work together was not only most cordial and interesting, but he has always been an understanding and devoted friend.

Edward E. Barnard had been appointed Professor of Practical Astronomy, and had come to Chicago from the Lick Observatory long before the observatory building was ready or the telescope could be mounted. Mr. Barnard continued the pioneer work he had begun at the Lick Observatory, of photographing the Milky Way and comets with portrait lenses carried on the mounting of an equatorial telescope. Miss Catherine W. Bruce, recognizing the value of this photographic study of the heavens, made a gift of seven thousand dollars for the erection of a special telescope to be provided with the best possible lenses for this class of work. Many opticians in America and abroad tried to fulfill the exacting requirements, but it was not until 1904 that a satisfactory doublet lens of ten inches aperture and fifty inches focal length was produced, and a new type of mounting was built for it by Warner and Swasey. The accumulated interest on Miss Bruce's gift during these years of waiting was enough to provide a simple wooden building with a fifteen-foot dome, which was erected about three hundred and fifty feet southwest of the great ninety-foot dome which housed the forty-inch telescope.

Mr. S. W. Burnham of Chicago had been invited to join the staff at the beginning and continued his remarkable observations of double stars which had brought him distinction many years before as an amateur. Without giving up his work as clerk of the United States Court, Mr. Burnham came to the observatory on Saturday afternoons and worked with great speed and skill in observing throughout Saturday and Sunday nights when the weather permitted, returning to the city on the early Monday morning train. It was not until he had retired from the service of the courts, a number of years later, that he received a salary from the university for his services as a member of the staff.

At the end of our first summer at Camp Collie, we had to search about for a place to live and temporarily rented a small house on the main road about a quarter of a mile north of the observatory. We called this house the 'Cracker Box.' The entire plumbing system consisted of a pump from the cistern and a bucket under the sink. We were unable to get our bedstead up the stairway to the second floor and therefore installed it in what was meant to be the parlor. We acquired one of those base-burner stoves which was fed from the top and proved very satisfactory. Our conditions of life in the 'Cracker Box' during that autumn and following spring were decidedly rural. The cowbells in the pasture across the street lulled us to sleep in the evening. The traffic on this road was light, in very marked contrast to conditions at the end of 1931, when the paving of this section of State Highway 36 was completed after the municipal sewers and water supply had been introduced along the whole length of this street. In 1898 there were but five houses on the plain in which was situated Yerkes Observatory, with the exception of the five occupied by the university families.

Across the street dwelt old Mrs. Bailey on the eighty-acre farm in which she had a widow's rights. She was rather a bright woman and had been a school-teacher before she married Mr. Bailey, whose title to this farm came direct from the Government. She had lived alone so long that her personal eccentricities had become somewhat highly developed, and it would not have been safe for her to have dwelt in Salem, Massachusetts, in the days of witchcraft. Not much that went on in the neighborhood escaped her observation, and she often made a friendly call while she appraised the furniture or other possessions in the house. It was one of her specialties to recite Poe's 'Raven,' and she was in some demand amongst the summer residents for this performance. One of her most famous remarks was made a few years later to Mr. and Mrs. Parkhurst when they were inquiring about rooming in her house while their own home was being built in the vicinity. 'Yes, I can rent you the kitchen and half of a double bedroom.' This arrangement was not consummated. She had an obsession that Professor Barnard had been one of her pupils during her teaching days, but this was of course entirely incorrect.

The other neighbor on this street was appropriately named Mr. Moon, but we never got acquainted with his phases, and his house and land soon passed into the possession of Mr. M. whose specialty was lathing when new houses were erected within accessible distances. Mr. M. was firm in his convictions on all matters of politics and current history and could be induced to express himself without much difficulty. He had periodical obsessions that the university was cheating him in respect to a few feet of land at his southern boundary, and when his wrath was hot at this imaginary injustice he would tear up the fence for a considerable distance. In the dispute, Mr. M. asserted with great positiveness that he must be right because his line was 'square with the world.' The testimony of surveyors could have no weight as against this application of the law of Pythagoras. After being again convinced of the correctness of the survey, he would allow the posts to be reset. His house and three acres of land were finally purchased from him by the university.

In those days communication among the summer residents was almost entirely by water, and it was a pretty sight to see the steamers and small yachts which came to the piers at Williams Bay for the arrival of the express train at five-thirty in the afternoon. For travel by land the bicycle was still popular, and many men and women toiled at the pedals over dirt roads which were ill-adapted to this mode of transit. The mail-carrier drove daily through the observatory grounds in keeping the contract for the 'star route' between Harvard, Illinois, and Elkhorn, a round trip of about forty miles. Native pedestrians walking through our grounds spoke of it as 'going through the telescope.' Fresh meat came twice a week if ordered in advance from the Elkhorn market, and bread and groceries were delivered by the storekeeper at Fontana, who daily met the eleven o'clock train at Williams Bay for this humane purpose. It was sometimes difficult to decide what kind of protein would be best adapted to the needs of the family seven days later. In those days, too, the unexpected guest might find a shortage of lamb chops. There is a record of an early incident in an astronomer's family where a simple evening meal was being served, the *pièce de résistance* being creamed codfish. The unexpected guest, an Englishman, startled and embarrassed his hostess by announcing, 'Thank you, I don't care for the fish course.' We cannot forget in those pioneer days the invaluable services to the observatory and its community of Otis Dodge. He was the optimist *par excellence*. There was nothing which he could not in some way bring to pass. Most of his time was occupied in taking care of the stable and the garden at the Hale house, but he was always willing to undertake some service out of hours for those needing him, and we were all, in fact, greatly dependent upon him. He was a natural-born trader, on the side, and used to say, 'I'll sell the hat off my head if I can get my price.' He always knew of some maid who was ready for employment, or could buy or rent a cow or a pony if the need arose. After Mr. Hale left in the autumn of 1903, Dodge worked for us for several years, always cheerfully, and always at a reasonable price.

On the street nearer the village, Mrs. Z. V. Sawyer was another good angel for us in the community. She gave room and board to unmarried members of our staff and cared for those who came to work at the observatory in the summer. She could also find time to give needed help in the households, and we certainly appreciated her assistance and friendship.

The educational opportunities in Williams Bay in 1898 were not all that could be desired. The only institution therefor was the district school one and a half miles west of the post-office, or nearly a mile west of the observatory. Mr. and Mrs. Ritchey had growing children of school age, and they made a determined effort to secure an adequate school in Williams Bay. The crucial school meeting for debating the subject was held on a sultry night in July, 1899, at the brick schoolhouse. It was an interesting occasion. The officers of the meeting were familiar with their task and were venerable men who had received their own education within those very walls. The windows were open, and it was wonderful to see how accurately these veterans could calculate the parabola needed for conveying the tobacco juice through the window from the center of the room. It was hard for many of these farmers to see why that which was good enough for them and for their children was not adequate for their grandchildren and for the newcomers in the village. The modernists finally prevailed, and the necessary steps were voted for the formation of another school near the center of the village. A tremendous thunderstorm cleared the air, and we walked home through endless mud and water, but the cause of education had been advanced.

It was arranged when I came to the observatory that I was to take the winter quarter as vacation, and go back to Hanover to teach a general course in astronomy until my successor had completed his graduate study and could take over the work at Dartmouth. After Thanksgiving, Mr. and Mrs. Hale very kindly placed the director's house at our disposal for a few weeks, and we left in time to reach Hanover by Christmas. The following summer we moved from the 'Cracker Box' to the professor's residence which was somewhat enlarged for our convenience. The new house was quite comfortable, and commanded a fine view of the lake. We occupied its spacious porch much in the summer, and had pleasure in planting trees and in developing a lawn and a small garden.

The gradual erection of houses north of the observatory grounds involved a sacrifice of something of the woodsy simplicity, for many yellow warblers and indigo birds had nested in the hazel bushes through which led the path out to the highway. We had wandered through this underbrush in the spring, watching day by day the success or the tragedies of the bird life, counting the eggs, throwing out those of the cowbird (the lazy mother whose inheritance urges her to lay her eggs in the nests of other birds), scratching on the oak tree where we hoped to see that little batlike flying squirrel thrust his charming and inquisitive head out of the woodpecker's abandoned hole, and by a little persistence encouraging him to take his glider flight to a neighboring tree where we could photograph him. Then there was the beautiful carpet of wild flowers, hepaticas, violets, bloodroot, and so forth, in profusion. We hated to give them up for home sites, but the addition of these houses by members of the staff added the element of sociability to our residence on the hill, and the life has been attractive even if somewhat isolated. It is a friendly and tempting road that has now for many happy years led me to the doors of my neighbors — neighbors among whom we have lived in the intimacy of congenial thought and satisfying informality. We have walked and talked together, even fought, have walked four

THE YERKES OBSERVATORY OF THE UNIVERSITY OF CHICAGO

miles to cast opposing votes, have shared each other's joys and sorrows, welcomed new life and buried our dead, but fortunate that feet of lead are reshod by human optimism, that the dark hours of sadness and discouragement and depression give way to the light of new and happier experiences. We forget our aches and pains and broken bones and laugh again.

In Chicago the university was expanding greatly in many directions in 1900, and it was with the greatest difficulty that the president and trustees could increase the budget and provide for the necessary enlargement of the staff. By securing appropriations for scientific research from learned societies and similar organizations, Director Hale was able to finance the new members of the staff. In 1902, when Andrew Carnegie created the new foundation which was to assist the exceptional men in science, Mr. Hale received grants from this institution, making possible the inauguration of certain long-planned investigations. We were especially anxious to study the development of the photographic method of finding the distances of the stars from the exceedingly minute oscillation of the star's image due to the annual circuit of the earth around the sun and the consequent change at different seasons of the point from which the observations were made. Dr. Frank Schlesinger had proposed a trial of this method some years before, and meanwhile the use of the great telescope as a camera with the intervention of a yellow filter to exclude the violet rays not in focus had been successfully developed by our optician, Mr. G. W. Ritchey. He had secured some of the best photographs thus far obtained of the moon, star clusters, and other sidereal objects. With the attainment of such sharp images, it became possible for Schlesinger to make very accurate measurements, and in two or three years the new method had proved its value and the distances of some of the nearer stars were determined with a greater precision than had been reached in a period of almost a century preceding.

In the class of 1898 at Dartmouth, there had been a brilliant scholar, Walter S. Adams, who had taken all the courses offered in astronomy, and was intending to do graduate work. I induced Dr. Harper to offer him a fellowship at the observatory, and he worked in close co-operation with me for the next few years. When Dr. Hale retired from the directorship of the Mount Wilson Observatory in

1923 on account of ill-health, Dr. Adams became his successor and has done a great piece of work both in research and administration.

Solar observations were also in full swing with the use of the large spectroheliograph of Dr. Hale's design. In 1903 the university was ten years old and Dr. Harper secured the assent of the trustees to his plan of publishing a dozen or more quarto volumes covering research that had been accomplished in the decade by members of the faculty of the university. Volume VIII was assigned to the Department of Astronomy. It was a much-needed outlet. We were not restricted at first as to the size of the volume, and it reached 413 pages, covering a wide variety of subjects and being amply illustrated. This volume was also issued under a different title-page as Volume II of the Publications of the Yerkes Observatory. My contribution to this volume appeared under the title 'The Determination of the Speed in the Line of Sight of Twenty Stars of the Orion Type.' These stars are characterized by the presence of many lines of helium, the gaseous element first discovered in the sun in 1868 and finally detected as it lay locked up in certain crystals on the earth. I had been working on the stars of this variety for two years past with the able co-operation of Mr. Adams, and we found it quite possible to get satisfactorily accurate results for many stars of this type. This first paper brought out the peculiarity of these stars that on the average their speed is slow as compared with that of the yellow stars like the sun, and that they showed a distinct tendency to move away from us. These findings were later more fully developed by Dr. W. W. Campbell in his paper dealing with the radial velocities of about two hundred and twenty-five helium stars, and he introduced the expression known as the K-term, which resulted from the solution of his equations and amounted to about four kilometers per second.

CHAPTER XV

INFLUENCES AND PROGRESS

THE period covered by this narrative happens to be almost exactly the last third of the nineteenth century and the first third of the twentieth, or what would be called one generation in each of the centuries. This was an era of extraordinary change in every phase of human life on this planet. It was quite the proper thing in 1901, at the turn of the century, for academic persons to try to make a just assessment of the wonderful progress in the century just closed, and there was much insistence on the part of newspapers and magazines that this should be done. It then seemed scarcely possible that another thirty years could be so fruitful in change as had been the last thirty years, representing quite accurately the last half of the reign of Queen Victoria. That was truly a Victorian age drawn to a close with the end of the century. Young people may underestimate the influence of England upon life in America, particularly in its eastern portion. We were just beginning to develop authors, painters, sculptors, and even engineers. When I was a small boy my colored picture-books were printed in England. It was hard for me to understand why the locomotive engines looked so strange with the engineer and fireman standing behind the boiler unprotected by a cab. The slender smokestack for engines using coal was quite different from the flaring ones which I was accustomed to see, and the exposed machinery of cylinders and around the driving wheels was quite different from the colored pictures in my London story-book of the alphabetic sort.

My little velvet suit came from England, and I was very glad when I outgrew both my own and my brother's. Our parents still thought in terms of Thackeray and Dickens, of Tennyson, Wordsworth, and Scott. It was customary to strew over the parlor tables all the miscellaneous bric-à-brac which the household possessed. 'Whatnots' stood in convenient corners covered with products of the English porcelain factories and with decanters that were never used. Magazines, it is true, had become much more highly developed in America than in England. *Harper's Monthly Magazine* had been published continuously since 1850, but in our house we had a long file of the English *Eclectic Magazine*, each with a fine steel engraving as a frontispiece. A young man would spend his hard-earned savings, if he were of an academic turn of mind, for such possessions, which were by no means inexpensive. Thus did my Uncle Edwin Brant Frost, even while he was a medical student, spend some of his meager income. The Prince Consort Albert figured in America, as in England, as a model husband as well as a thoroughly useful prince.

In the seventies it was the ambition of the well-dressed woman to wear a cashmere shawl when she went to church. They came *via* England, and I remember well how carefully such a shawl must be packed away during week-days. There was a period about 1870 when men went about wrapped in long capes, which blew in the wind and covered the arms so as to make the wearer more or less a prisoner of his garb. How my brother and I did hate the small edition of these capes which we had to wear, gifts probably, from someone who had brought them from England. With them we wore under protest one of those little Scotch caps with its floating ribbon. There was, of course, a flare-up of French influence during the reign of Louis Napoleon and the handsome Eugénie, but it did not seriously lessen the influence of England. Toys and games also came from England, and there were always strange pictures of a robin redbreast hopping about in a light snow, and having no resemblance to our American robin. Even steel rails for the trunk-lines were imported from Britain as late as my college days. Then Andrew Carnegie and others found that rails could be made better and cheaper in America. The dominant political party let the American ironmasters decide on how much duty would be satisfactory to them to protect their 'infant industry,' but it was hard for them to admit that the child was rapidly getting out of its infancy. I do not know where a better picture can be found of the closing of the Victorian era than in E. F. Benson's book, *As We Were*. Of course it contains no reference to America, but by reading it one can recognize the numberless ways in which English thought, manners, and habits were influencing American life, especially along the Atlantic littoral.

The comforts of life were greatly influenced by American discoveries and inventions. Thus, kerosene oil began to be used for illumination only a little before the beginning of the period of which I am speaking. Big fortunes were made in its exploitation. Hard coal began to be sent up into New England from Pennsylvania, and this tended to eliminate the building of big woodsheds connected at the rear of houses in the country. Gas began to be introduced into the larger towns, sometimes being piped through long wooden logs with much consequent waste and often serious damage or death to the shade trees along the sidewalks. Hot-air furnaces and bathrooms began to be installed even in country towns. Our house was thus equipped in 1875, but this was an exception. There was no very great improvement in the highways until the advent of the automobile. In the North country it was always desired that there should be an early heavy fall of snow in order that there should be 'good traveling.' The mud season about the time of town meeting, or at the end of March, was very trying on horses and drivers.

Horseless carriages began in a few years to make a hesitating and dubious appearance on the highways. At the end of the first decade of this century they were quite numerous and more dependable. But in the early days it might well be necessary for a motorist to take out the manifold and heat it on someone's kitchen stove in order to revive the carburetor. If no kitchen fire was available, a small one could be built with paper and sticks on the roadside.

I remember coming up from Chicago on a summer day with my friend Tracy Drake in his open 'Auto Car.' We started about the middle of the morning, stopping at Highland Park, twenty miles north, for lunch. The drive across the country from there was broken by repeated stops in order to help the drivers of restless horses. The radiator had to be filled repeatedly and attention had to be given constantly to the oil falling drop by drop in the gauge on the dashboard. A few miles from home, it seemed wise for me to take the train for Williams Bay. We had enjoyed the trip, however, and fifteen miles an hour on the open highway was considered pretty speedy.

In astronomy at this time there was considerable interest in the horizontal type of telescope which used a cœlostat with silvered mirrors and driven by clockwork to keep stationary the image of the object under study. The convenience of changing from one attachment to another by merely sliding them into place on a pair of rails was very great as compared with the labor and even risk involved in changing from one spectrograph or spectroheliograph to another at the eye end of the great telescope which had to be balanced most carefully after every such change. This meant the shifting of hundreds of pounds of weights. A special grant to Director Hale from the Carnegie Institution made possible the testing of the cœlostat type of telescope and the optical parts were made in our own shop. To house this telescope, a temporary structure of wood and paper some eighty feet long was set up on the ground just south of the main observatory building. Unfortunately, a spark from the induction coil set the flimsy structure on fire as tests were being made on a December morning, and in a few moments the whole equipment had been destroyed.

By the efforts of our good friend and summer resident at Lake Geneva, Dr. George S. Isham, his aunt, Miss Helen Snow, gave ten thousand dollars for the erection of a more permanent building six hundred feet north of the observatory, and for the construction of a large horizontal instrument which has since been known as the Snow Telescope. The ceremony of inaugurating this telescope took place in the autumn of 1903, and its completion involved much work for both our machine and optical shops.

In the summer of 1900, as a guest of the observatory, Professor Ernest F. Nichols of Dartmouth was making the first successful experiments in detecting the heat from the stars. He employed the radiometer which he had improved and developed in previous work. Mr. Nichols was the first one to obtain a definite measure of this form of stellar radiation. The delicacy of the instrument had to be such that it would detect the heat of a candle at a distance of sixteen miles. That, of course, referred to a theoretically pure atmosphere, but a tent was set up in a field nearly a mile away and the heat of the candle-flame was actually measured despite the absorption of the lower layers of the atmosphere. On one occasion the assistant in the tent substituted his head for the candle and a measurable heat was definitely indicated at the instrument.

Nichols found a measurable difference between the radiation of Arcturus and Vega, that of the former, the yellow star, being nearly twice as great as that of Vega, the bluish-white star. This indicated that much of the heat must come from the invisible heat-waves longer than the red rays. Very great improvements have been made in recent years in apparatus for the measurement of stellar radiation and important results have been obtained at Mount Wilson and the Lowell Observatory and by Dr. C. G. Abbot of the Smithsonian Observatory.

It was an especial pleasure for us to have Mr. and Mrs. Nichols and their young daughter spend the summer with us in our home. Mrs. Nichols was annoyed by the noisy monotony of a katydid who had taken up his habitation in a tree near her window. I therefore made a regular practice of beating the trunk of the tree so that the katydid would keep quiet for half an hour or more and thus allow her to get to sleep. I set a ladder up against the tree and made repeated searches for the offender. On the day after they left, I found him, and without other letter of transmission mailed him in a small aerated box to Mrs. Nichols at Hanover, New Hampshire. When they opened the mail at the supper-table, the katydid hopped out and gave a solemn announcement of his presence in the tones that he had used during the summer.

Visits for shopping in neighboring towns were occasionally made over rather poor roads in a carriage supplied from the local livery stable, but a shopping trip to Delavan, seven miles away, absorbed the whole afternoon.

Golf was beginning to be popular in all parts of the country, and Mr. Hale, Mr. Ellerman, and I began to get some exercise in driving a ball over the rough ground near the observatory. We started with two holes about four hundred yards apart, and by mowing succeeded in getting some tolerable putting greens. When others began to be interested, we laid out a course of six holes, partly on the adjacent land of the Y.M.C.A. athletic field and partly on that of the observatory. We tried to stimulate some rivalry between the members of the observatory staff and the officers and guests of the Y.M.C.A., whose Mid-Western summer camp is located on the shore just below and adjoining the observatory property. Tournaments were held in July and August, and the observatory was fairly successful in these events. For some years it fell to me to defend the honor of our group and I received the silver cup as the winner for three successive years. Some of my city friends were amused at my driver with its double spinal curvature. I nevertheless used it with some success and still possess it. It became necessary for the golf club to mow quite a large area with a horse-drawn lawnmower, incidentally improving very much the appearance of the observatory grounds. In later years this course was developed by the addition of nine holes in a forty-acre lot west of the athletic field, bought and presented to the Y.M.C.A. by Mr. S. B. Chapin. Water was brought to the greens from the storage tank of the Y.M.C.A., and the Kishwauketoc Golf Club, bearing the Indian name for Bigfoot, an early chieftain of the Pottawatomies, became quite a flourishing institution. In 1929 it was even possible, again through the generosity of Mr. Chapin, to add a simple field house to the equipment, with lockers and other conveniences and an opportunity for players to get light refreshments or to rest on the porch.

A total solar eclipse is one of the most dramatic events of Nature and gives us the only opportunity thus far devised to see and photograph the solar corona. It occurs, on the average, only once in about three hundred years at any particular place, and the duration of totality is usually not over two or three minutes. It is estimated that astronomers have only about an hour and a half in a century to observe the corona if they travel to all possible eclipses. Thus it is important that every effort should be made to send expeditions to study these interesting phenomena. There is a brief interval of about two seconds at the beginning and end of totality when the moon has covered everything but the slender rim of gaseous solar atmosphere called the reversing layer.

On May 28, 1900, there was a fine opportunity to observe a total eclipse in America. The track of totality passed through the Southern States and went out to sea in the northern part of Virginia. The Yerkes Observatory, under Director Hale, sent a party to Wadesboro, North Carolina, where we occupied a station for a couple of weeks with a party from the Smithsonian Institution under the direction of Professor S. P. Langley.

A party from Princeton University, under Professor Young, also chose a location at Wadesboro as did several foreign astronomers. We, therefore, had quite a gathering at the little hotel in this Southern town and there was much discussion and interchange of opinion. Professor Hale and Mr. Ellerman had attempted the difficult problem of measuring the heat of the corona, but this could not be accomplished with the apparatus available.

It was my part to obtain photographs of the so-called 'flash spectrum' at the beginning and end of totality; also to secure if possible photographs of the spectrum of the corona. I planned to use prismatic cameras, and Dr. Isham assisted me in making the exposures. The light came to our apparatus in a horizontal beam reflected from mirrors which were driven by clockwork, being a portable form of the cœlostat. Other mirrors on the apparatus threw a beam into a dark room where the corona could be photographed directly by Professors Barnard and Ritchey who secured excellent pictures on a large scale. It was also my duty to watch the progress of the transformation of the spectral lines and to give the signal to begin and end the exposures for the flash. These are tense moments and occasionally a man is so panic-stricken as to forget to give the signal! This eclipse was about eighty-seven seconds in duration, and while the long exposure of sixty seconds was being made on the corona, I was able to turn for just a moment and see it for the first time visually. It was amusing to see the reaction of the naturally superstitious Southern Negro to the mysteries of an eclipse. There were many colored folk in a large crowd gathered just outside the field where our equipment was located. When the sun reappeared, there was a tremendous and audible sigh of relief.

Dr. Isham left for home as soon as the eclipse was over, but telegraphed me that he had forgotten to check his trunk. My reply to him amused his wife who for some time thought that it was a case of the absent-minded professor instead of the thrifty Vermonter who wanted his money's worth. To complete my ten-word allowance, I had signed myself 'Yours truly.'

At the close of a very hot day on the trip North, I had just time to get a cooling drink in the station at Atlanta and there had visions of a quenched thirst from the steins standing '*mit einer Blume darauf.*' I picked up one with great anticipation and took a long draught, but was horrified when as I saw the bottom I got my first taste of buttermilk. I never did like buttermilk, anyway!

Our photographs of the spectrum were quite successful, and I spent several weeks in measuring the positions of the lines upon them, later publishing an extensive paper in the *Astrophysical Journal* of December, 1900.

I take off my hat to the early Sumerians who learned to predict the recurrence of eclipses. Nearly thirty centuries ago, they found that an eclipse of the sun repeated itself at intervals of eighteen years and ten and one third or eleven and one third days according to the number of leap years intervening. I think that they must have found this repetition at first from the triple period of fifty-four years and thirty-two days at which the eclipse would happen in the same general region of the earth. The two intervening repetitions would fall at points one third and two thirds of the circumference of the earth distant from the point of their first observation. How could they know what was going on at a point some eight thousand or sixteen thousand miles away from the temple or astronomical bureau? They just couldn't! It suggests that they must have had a suspicion that the earth was spherical.

I think that I ought to give a modern illustration of this ancient cycle. A fine total solar eclipse swept eastward across the American continent on July 29, 1878, and included the city of Denver. Eighteen years and eleven and one third days later, on August 9, 1896, a repetition of this eclipse crossed Japan. Eighteen more years bring us to August 21, 1914, when the track of the eclipse crossed the Crimea. (Incidentally several German astronomers were marooned there by the Great War and their instruments were not recovered until after the war was over.) But another cycle of eighteen years and ten and one third days brings us to the eclipse of August 31, 1932, which occurred on the same continent as the one of 1878, although this time in New England some fifteen hundred miles farther east, thus completing the triple cycle of fifty-four years.

The summer of 1901 was excessively hot, and on one day the temperature at my house read 104°. The hot wind from the Western plains dried the leaves of our young elm trees to a crisp, and they soon fell off. At the end of the summer a new set of small leaves developed to take their place. Such extremely hot weather has not been experienced since.

In September, 1901, we went to Hanover for the Daniel Webster Centenary at Dartmouth, and Mrs. Frost and Katharine remained there for the autumn, while I returned to my work at the observatory. When I left Hanover, little daughter asked her mother, 'Why does my Daddy have to go back to Williams Bay to work? — the stars are here too.' We invited Mr. and Mrs. Parkhurst to occupy our house and to take care of me, which was a very satisfactory arrangement, but in spite of their kindly ministrations, it was a lonely autumn, and at Christmas I joined my family for the winter. Our first son, Frederick Hazard, was born in the old house in Hanover on January 11, 1902.

We returned to Williams Bay with our two children at the beginning of April, and life was very pleasant with the addition of a baby in the home.

CHAPTER XVI

POLITICS

THE political situation in 1884 was interesting, particularly to a young person who was of college age and was brought up on the *Springfield Republican*. Despite the rugged honesty of President Grant, abuses had crept into the Federal Government by the connivance of some of his appointees. The situation had not been thoroughly remedied by President Hayes or by President Garfield. The bargaining power of the tariff had reacted upon the party in office. The *Boston Journal* was gospel to a great part of New England, especially to Vermont, and it espoused the cause of James G. Blaine, 'the plumed Knight' of that day. While I am speaking of Vermont, I may mention that it took a fine-toothed comb to find a Democrat in that State. There were, of course, a few hereditary ones, among them my Uncle Willard Gay. It befell that in one year his party nominated him as candidate for State Treasurer to oppose his Republican brother-in-law, my Uncle William H. DuBois. It was a great joke in the family. The *Springfield Republican* was anathema to the latter, who still regarded the Democratic Party as in league with the Devil.

Grover Cleveland had attracted attention by his fight against corruption in Buffalo and by his vigorous efforts for simple governmental honesty as Governor of New York. My father was a 'Mugwump,' the name given to one who did not have faith in the entrenched Republican Party to reform itself. Although I lacked three years and my brother lacked one of being old enough to vote, we were enthusiastic in supporting the revolt. Cleveland was elected and my Republican relatives in Vermont felt sure that the country would go to the 'demnition bowwows.' Cleveland's appointees to the Cabinet were for the most part outstanding men with deep faith in Jeffersonian principles, and an era of reform government set in at Washington. Cleveland was defeated for re-election in 1888 by Benjamin Harrison of Indiana; but the tables were turned in 1892 when Cleveland was re-elected and served efficiently without the lure of a third term in the White House. Mr. Cleveland had married at the White

House a charming young woman who was his ward, and her popularity with the whole people meant much to his administration.

McKinley succeeded Cleveland, and a high tariff wall was re-erected around the land. It was a shock to the whole country when, shortly after his election for a second term, a fanatic shot him. He was dramatically succeeded by Theodore Roosevelt, whom Senator Platt of New York and other political managers of the day had shelved by inducing him to run as Vice-President. Roosevelt's services as a Colonel in the Spanish War and as Assistant Secretary of the Navy had made him conspicuous and highly popular, and his strong intellectual ability and the virility of his personality gave him a fine start in the White House. Toward the end of his second term he began to be too dogmatic toward Congress, and the majority in the House went against him so that the last years of his administration were not so efficient, and there was a good deal of scolding between the White House and Congress. Such men may have an excess of confidence in their own judgment, and it is not surprising that Congress was considerably restive toward the end of his administration. I am sorry that I never had an opportunity to become acquainted with Mr. Roosevelt in a personal way. I am sure that I should have found many interesting things to discuss with him. His friendship with Sir Edward Grey of England was a natural one. Here was another man that one would have liked to know, a great leader with a genuine interest in world peace. Roosevelt gave a fine description in a magazine article of his interesting walk with Grey across the fields and through the brooks on a summer day in England as they studied the birds and the features of nature. I do not know how much Roosevelt cared for the stars, but Sir Edward Grey certainly did, as is seen in his memoirs.

The genial Taft, who had performed a very fine service as mediator with the Vatican regarding the position of the Roman Church in the Philippines and later as Governor-General of the Islands, was swept into office with the support of President Roosevelt. But while he was a man of the strictest integrity, he was not quite firm enough to suppress the tendency to corruption in a party now long in power. Taft's real place was as Chief Justice, and he seems to have filled the position to perfection.

When Taft in his candidacy for a second term was opposed by his former friend and supporter, Roosevelt, with his Bull Moose Party, the opportunity came for the Democrats with their nomination of Woodrow Wilson. I voted for Wilson for whom I had held great esteem. He was a character to be remembered. I had occasionally met him at Princeton as a professor and president, and much respected his knowledge of political history and jurisprudence. It was a great pity that he did not choose bigger men for his official family, but he seemed too dominant to work with his equals. While some of his acts in the first year of his administration in the difficulties with Mexico appeared rather dubious, he certainly wrote some state papers of the first rank. I believe that they will be even better appreciated in the future. His efforts to end the war long before we entered it, and afterward, impressed me greatly. I also admired the way in which he let Newton D. Baker act effectively as Secretary of War, and both of them gave a worthy support to the earnest efforts made by Pershing against all kinds of European intrigue. It was really regrettable that Wilson himself went to Europe to participate in the Treaty of Versailles. I think that he should have sent the greatest leaders in international law in our country, regardless of party, and that he would have done better by staying in Washington as President. His great fight to secure our entry into the League of Nations was heroic, and the petty politics practiced by some men who were supposed to be national leaders was disheartening. I was always strong for the Hague Court and also for the League of Nations. If we had gone into it at first, we could have helped the world's peace. The action of Japan in 1932 in attacking Shanghai and in seizing Manchuria has put the League in a very difficult position, but we shall probably see in future years that it did accomplish some significant results.

It may have been a political necessity to appoint Bryan Secretary of State in Wilson's Cabinet, but the qualification of fitness was not assured. I first heard Bryan in his initial campaign. He was speaking from the tail of a cart, as it were, at Buffalo in 1901. I did not get an impression of oratorical skill and certainly was not moved by his views on free silver.

I have recently heard a story which is well worth repeating. Bryan had a very good friend in a well-known university professor who was an authority in botany. These two used to meet frequently

and amicably during the years at the various sessions of the Presby-
terian Assembly. As long as the subject of evolution was avoided,
all went well. The men also corresponded occasionally, but one
day, the professor was surprised to receive a letter from Bryan in
which he is alleged to have said, 'I am very much hurt by your reference to me in your radio lecture last evening.' The professor
couldn't recall the reference and wrote to him to that effect. But
Bryan's reply, as it was told to me, said, 'You spoke of "eloquent
ignorance" and you must have meant me.' In this case, Mr. Bryan
did himself some injustice, for he was more stubborn than ignorant
and he did possess certain forensic ability. But I never understood
how he could be seriously considered as a candidate for the Presidency of the Unites States. It was surprising to me to be told, when
I was in Florida a few years ago, that he had been persuaded to sit
at one hundred dollars an hour in a bathing-suit under a big umbrella on a raft in the middle of a little pool in Coral Gables to sell
lots to the public. But at least there was nothing immoral about it!
I don't remember whether it was during a time of depression, but if
so, and if it could in any way compare with this one of 1932, he could
surely be excused.

Although Mr. Coolidge was slow in uncovering and clearing up the
mess created by the Harding régime, we all had confidence in his
strict integrity. To me he seemed to understand very cleverly how to
be carried along by the tide of public opinion rather than to lead it.
His constant insistence upon thrift during the extravagant era while
he was President was salutary. He did not have at all the intellect of
Wilson, but was well supplied with Yankee common sense for most
emergencies.

The splendid services of Herbert Hoover during and after the
Great War in behalf of civilian relief in many countries seemed to
me extraordinarily worthy of admiration. I had hoped that Hoover
would be nominated in 1920, and I strongly supported him when at
last he had an opportunity to be a candidate for the Presidency. It
was disappointing that he should have let the politicians control his
actions as much as they seemed to, in respect to the unfortunate
raising of the tariff and his insistence that prosperity could only be
maintained by the Republican Party. In recent years no man has
had a more severe ordeal as President than Mr. Hoover, and he has

used his great ability in a constructive way. He seems to lack the knack of handling Congress. He has always sought advice from the best-known leaders of betterment in every movement he had started, but his unceasing labors for progress have often been retarded by the politicians. It is evident that a man may be a great administrator, as Hoover has been when he can choose his own assistants and create his own organization, as he did in his relief work in Belgium and elsewhere. But when Congress is critical of every recommendation, the struggle must be a very hard one for so conscientious and disinterested a man as Mr. Hoover. It was probably inevitable that in a time of such a depression as that of 1930–1933 the party in power should suffer defeat, but I felt that Mr. Hoover made a splendid effort in his campaigning and made some very clear statements of his attempts to keep the country from financial ruin during its most critical period. It is gratifying that Mr. Franklin D. Roosevelt is a gentleman and a scholar with considerable experience in public affairs and will worthily represent our country in the White House. We may hope that his efforts to hasten the recovery from the great depression, especially in accomplishing effective relief to the farmer and in settling the troublesome problems of the debts of European countries, may be even more successful than the valiant endeavors of Mr. Hoover.

I cordially supported the passage of the Eighteenth Amendment in 1920. I had been used to prohibition in Vermont and New Hampshire, but my real belief was that in such matters local option should be the fundamental principle where 'local' might well include the whole State. However, the difficulties of controlling the sale of hard liquor along the boundaries of States having different laws made any such situation unworkable. The lack of respect for law among the rising generation has seemed to be almost calamitous, but I believe with Professor Irving Fisher that the country as a whole has benefited more than we suspect under prohibition. I am not a rabid teetotaler because I have lived three years in Europe and know the quality of good German beer and Continental light wines. It is evident, however, that the annoyance on the part of many good citizens from the intrusion of federal regulation on personal habits has prejudiced many people against the Amendment. No doubt some modification will have to be made soon because the gangs have come into terrible power from the money to be made in selling liquor in spite of the law. After the Presidential election in November, 1932, the wild rush of many public officials to secure the repeal of the Prohibition Amendment seemed to me undignified and petty at a time when so many more important issues were before them.

CHAPTER XVII

INCREASING RESPONSIBILITIES

In November, 1903, the observatory had the honor of a visit from the members of the National Academy of Sciences who were holding their autumn session for the first time in Chicago. After this meeting was over, Professor Hale closed his house and went to Pasadena for the winter. His object was primarily to investigate the advantages of Mount Wilson (an elevation of six thousand feet) for carrying on special problems of solar research. With the assistance of Mr. Ellerman he made this reconnaissance and satisfied himself of the desirability of a permanent establishment on Mount Wilson. The advantages of this particular place had been previously indicated by Professor William H. Pickering of Harvard and later by Professor W. J. Hussey of Ann Arbor, who had been examining various sites in different parts of the world under a grant from the Carnegie Institution.

At this time Mr. Hale was not in good health and thereafter returned to the observatory only occasionally. The duties of administration fell to me in accordance with an appointment previously made by Dr. Harper that I was to serve as acting director in Mr. Hale's absences.

The figuring of the sixty-inch reflector had proceeded slowly in the optical shop for more than three years. The expense of this work had thus far been borne by Mr. Hale's father, Mr. William E. Hale, who had offered the mirror, valued at twenty-five thousand dollars, to the University of Chicago under the condition that a mounting and a building should be provided for it and that its maintenance should be assured. Dr. Harper had so many projects of expansion in mind and under way that it seemed impossible for the university to meet these conditions. Meanwhile, the Carnegie Institution increased the grant to Mr. Hale for an expedition to Mount Wilson, and the erection of the sixty-inch reflector at that station began to be a possibility. The Carnegie Institution at this time changed its policy of making small separate grants to many individuals and concentrated on a number of major projects, one of which developed into the Mount Wilson Observatory. The trustees of the university assented to the removal of the Snow telescope to Mount Wilson, and the work of finishing that equipment was hastened in the shops of our observatory. By the end of 1904 it was clear that the expedition was to develop into a permanent institution.

Preparations were in progress for a scientific congress to be held in connection with the World's Fair at St. Louis during that summer with quite an elaborate program for the participation of distinguished scientists, including many from abroad. We thus had the pleasure of visits from Professor and Mrs. Turner of Oxford and Professor and Mrs. Kapteyn of Holland, as well as many others. Mrs. Frost and I with Professor Barnard went to St. Louis for the scientific meetings, which were of a high order of importance. Professor Kapteyn at this time made his proposal for international co-operation in the thorough study of selected areas in the sky and soon thereafter many observatories like our own joined in this great undertaking.

The director's house was rented by President Harper from July, 1904, until the end of the year, and I was able to provide him with a spacious office in the observatory where he could carry on his writing and administrative duties without disturbance. He greatly enjoyed this six months in the country and entertained many of his friends and official visitors during the period, although he was already beginning to feel the encroachment of the disease which so prematurely ended his brilliant career. He took great pride in having his guests see the observatory and its telescope. He brought with him his own secretary and Dr. J. M. P. Smith who was collaborating with him on important work. In my official relations with him we corresponded just as if he were in the president's office at the university, but out of office hours our relations were very informal and cordial. He learned to play golf on our small course and felt great relief in the quiet and the opportunity for working without interruptions, inevitable in his office in Chicago. His presence in the observatory colony was a great advantage for our institution because it must have shown him plainly how much we lacked in the way of adequate support for our work. When he had to use a lantern in threading his way through the tall grass to pass between the house and the office on dewy summer nights, he realized why I was asking for some improvements of the grounds and the establishment of sidewalks between the buildings. On Christmas Eve, Dr. and Mrs. Harper and their guests came to the house to serenade us — and I well remember his clear voice singing with some gusto, 'Chicago — Chicago — Chicago — go —' until Mrs. Harper said, 'William — not so loud.' The next day they helped us in the celebration of our Christmas party, which that year we held in the library of the observatory, and which later became an annual event in our home.

In April came the departure from the observatory of those who were to assist Mr. Hale in the new undertaking, including Mr. Ritchey, Mr. Ellerman, Mr. Adams, and Mr. Pease, together with a good deal of equipment besides the Snow Telescope. My formal appointment as director came at this time, and in June, 1905, we moved into the Director's residence. The observatory, however, was left in a most difficult position. The new and probably wise policy of the Carnegie Institution discontinued the smaller grants which had been used for salaries of assistants in working on astrophysical problems. The university was not able to fill our vacancies from the existing budget. I was therefore authorized and assisted by the resident trustees to raise a fund for the temporary maintenance of our staff until the budget could be enlarged to cover these requirements. It was several years before the staff could be called at all adequate for the continuation of the work. The observatory was fortunate in keeping at this time Mr. S. B. Barrett as secretary and librarian. I have been greatly indebted to him for his friendly co-operation in the administrative work of the observatory, and I greatly valued his advice on quasi-legal affairs and his faithful and valuable observational work with the stellar spectrograph.

The senior members of the observatory staff at this time were Professors S. W. Burnham and Edward E. Barnard, who were both remarkable men and to a large extent self-made as astronomers. Mr. Burnham was a wiry little Vermonter, born a few miles south of my great-grandfather's house on Thetford Hill, and I suppose that after he left the district school, young Burnham walked up the hill for his studies at Thetford Academy. He early became an expert in shorthand, and during the Civil War was attached to the army headquarters when General Butler was at New Orleans. After the war he became a court reporter at Chicago and later clerk of the United States Court where his services were greatly appreciated by the distinguished jurists in that tribunal. Mr. Burnham had a remarkably keen eye and soon began to discover as double stars many which had been missed by the professional astronomers. He set up a telescope, small, but of excellent optical quality, in his yard in the Douglas district of Chicago not far from the site of the old Chicago University. His abilities as an observer soon brought him opportunities to use larger telescopes, in particular the excellent eighteen-inch of the Dearborn Observatory, then located at the old university. He became a professional astronomer when he went to the Lick Observatory upon its opening in 1888, but returned to Chicago after about five years and resumed work in the courts. During all the time of his fruitful labors at the Yerkes Observatory from 1897 to 1921, he employed any spare time in forming a great catalogue of all known double stars. This was published under the auspices of the Carnegie Institution in Washington in two large volumes which appeared in 1907. He also published at least three other volumes of his observational work, one of these being Volume I of the Publications of the Yerkes Observatory, issued in 1900, in which appeared his measures of the so-called 'Proper Motion Stars.' This means that he accurately measured with the micrometer the positions of many small stars surrounding the double stars to which he was giving his principal attention. His repetition of these observations after an interval of some years yielded the relative drift or proper motions of many of these stars. It is highly remarkable how he could become one of the world's leading experts in the special branch of astronomy without the college training which usually must precede such specialization. He was a tireless worker and very social with his friends. I regarded it as a privilege as Director to do everything possible to assist him in his work by providing any instrumental improvements which he might desire, but his greatest restriction was due to cloudy skies or those which, though clear, gave unsteady stellar images and made it impossible for him to utilize the splendid power of the forty-inch telescope which he always used for his observations. Nothing but the infirmities of old age could slacken Mr. Burnham's keenness for work at the telescope, and he was seventy-six years old when he gave up his trips to the observatory. After Mr. Burnham's retirement, I was fortunately able to secure as his successor Dr. George Van Biesbroeck of the Royal Observatory of Belgium, who had already established a reputation as an observer of double stars.

Mr. Barnard had been employed when a mere lad in a photographic studio in his home city of Nashville, Tennessee. Part of his duty on sunny days was to keep the sunlight reflected into the studio below, but he ultimately learned all the arts of photography. At night he watched the skies attentively, learning about the constellations from a book which had fallen into his hands. His remarkable vision and persistence soon brought him the opportunity of using the telescope of the Vanderbilt University, and he found some time to study there. He developed great ability as a discoverer of comets and so it was not unnatural that he was invited to become a member of the Lick Observatory staff. He applied there his knowledge of photography in photographing the Milky Way and remarkable comets, becoming a leading pioneer in this field. When he became Professor of Practical Astronomy at the Yerkes Observatory at its opening, he made one of the major items of his program the observation of some of the great globular clusters of stars, hoping to be able to detect motions among them from his skillful observations with a micrometer. The motions sought for were not found, showing that the clusters were much farther from us and objects much larger than was supposed. He could not bring himself to the completion of this work for publication before his death in 1923, and it fell to me thereafter to prepare his observations for the press as Volume VI of our Publications. In this work I had the collaboration of Professor Van Biesbroeck and Miss Calvert.

About 1905, Mr. Barnard also started on the preparation of an atlas of the Milky Way in extension of his similar work at the Lick Observatory. Over a period of several years, experiments were made in discovering the best form of reproducing these remarkable pictures taken with our Bruce photographic telescope. I finally persuaded him that actual photographic prints from the negatives would most faithfully reproduce the marvels of the original pictures. The Carnegie Institution of Washington assumed the expense of publishing this atlas, and Mr. Barnard himself inspected the quality of thirty-five thousand prints made under his supervision by a commercial photographer in Chicago. Mr. Barnard, however, did not live to finish the text, or to complete the tables which form Part II of the atlas, and this task fell to me with the able collaboration of Miss Calvert. Seven hundred copies of the work were published in 1927, forming two large volumes, and I now learn with regret that the edition is already exhausted within four years after publication. Mr. Barnard being to a certain extent a self-trained expert, naturally had his peculiarities, along with a most genial personality. Part of his unusual charm lay in his detachment from the affairs of the mundane world. He might be looked upon as a surviving example of the professor of the earlier days whose contacts with the business world were few. In the seventies they studied and taught, and like Daniel Webster were expected to serve as orators at county fairs, expatiating principally upon the joys of agriculture and the possibilities of its development.

Nowadays industry is quick to seize upon the application of pure science like chemistry and physics and in fact practically all other branches, and not only calls into the business field experts in these lines, but offers contributions through various foundations or directly to universities for the study of diverse problems which might be of advantage to its own interests.

The absent-minded professor is no doubt still with us, although he is now expected to be thoroughly a man of the world. I remember that Professor Charles Young told me that in the seventies, when he was passing through Chicago, he rang the doorbell at the house of an acquaintance, but fled because he couldn't remember his own name. And now, not long ago, a story was told at the Quadrangle Club that one of our most distinguished professors after leaving the building had returned arrayed in an overcoat which nearly touched the ground and which was much too large for him, and said, 'These gloves which I found in my pocket do not seem to be mine.'

As director I co-operated with Mr. Barnard constantly to make his indefatigable labors efficient and fruitful to the utmost extent possible. He shared with me a keen interest in trees, both ornamental and fruit-bearing, and he enjoyed as I did the progress of developing the landscape architecture for the observatory grounds and his own home. We often traveled together to attend scientific meetings, and always enjoyed such trips as well as the expedition to Wyoming for the observation of the eclipse of June 8, 1918, and our reconnaissance in the previous year in that region for selecting the site for our eclipse station.

After Mr. Barnard's death in 1923, I wrote a biography of him for the *Memoirs* of the National Academy of Sciences.

After the loss of Professor Barnard, I studied carefully the question of his successor and secured the appointment of Dr. F. E. Ross, then an expert at the Eastman Kodak Company. His work there was on the design of new types of photographic lenses and on the physics of the photographic plate. Being an expert photographer he soon began a repetition of the photographs of areas of the Milky Way which Professor Barnard had made during the twenty years preceding. By carefully comparing the new and old photographs under the Zeiss Blink Comparator, Professor Ross brought to light nearly a thousand stars having appreciable proper motions besides several hundred new variable stars.

More attention was given to the intensive study of the sun during the next few years than to any other celestial object. The International Solar Union had its first conference in connection with the scientific congress under the auspices of the St. Louis Exposition in 1904, and various committees were appointed for the development of solar research along special lines. The important discovery by Professor Zeeman of Holland that when light was passed through a strong magnetic field, as between the poles of a powerful electro-magnet, the lines of the spectrum, instead of being single, were broken up into a large number of component lines. The spectra of sun-spots revealed similar changes and suggested that an electro-magnetic field might exist in them. In order to investigate these relations, certain portions of the spectrum were assigned to different observatories and the changes in the lines within the areas of large spots were carefully studied. Fortunately, there was a period of maximum activity of sun-spots about this time and it was more prolonged than usual, so that important confirmations were obtained of the electro-magnetic theory.

The application of the interferometer of Dr. A. A. Michelson to the most precise study of the wave-lengths of the lines in the solar spectrum showed inconsistencies in Rowland's values. These had not been of importance heretofore, but now precision was being carried to one more decimal point. Primary and secondary standards of wave-lengths were agreed upon and in the laboratories during the following years new measurements of spectral lines were being made.[1]

Toward the end of the lovely day of June 5, 1906, a little brown-eyed boy came to us. We named him Benjamin DuBois Frost. He had an unusually happy babyhood and it was not many weeks before he was appropriately called 'Smiler.' For years his bed was next to mine, and as soon as he was able to climb over the side of his crib, he snuggled in beside me and therewith was content for the rest of the night.

His older brother soon adopted him as a playfellow. Ben rather inherited my love of nature and the out-of-doors. When we found that he was collecting caterpillars in his pockets, we suggested that perhaps a paper bag might be better, and I often recall what a funny little figure he was with his paper bag in his hand and a coon's tail which he adopted pinned at the back of his little coat-like suit. In 1914 we nearly lost Ben as a result of a ruptured appendix which demanded a quick operation.

When he was a lad of ten or so, he began to feel the need of pocket money. He and his friend Anthony Michel entered into a partnership to produce lamb's wool from two sheep which they purchased for the purpose. These were pastured in an unobtrusive place on the grounds or tethered on a line in the yard. On one unfortunate occasion, the lambs reached a bed of asters which Dr. Crump was raising during a summer's stay at the observatory. Being good grazers, the pets quickly disposed of the asters and then began on Dr. Crump's new bathing-suit.

In earlier days the children had a scraggly little Indian pony, 'Zippy.' They rode him bareback — often all three of them together. The ample grounds of the observatory, with their thirty acres and a good bit of lake shore, made an ideal playground for the children.

Owing to our rather isolated hilltop and to the fact that Katharine had by her own initiative learned to read early, we rather disregarded the school question for a time. Katharine read a primer

[1] A complete revision of Rowland's tables for the solar spectrum was published in 1928.

before she was four years of age, and at six was poring over *Ivanhoe* and *The Alhambra*. Perhaps, too, my own lack of a schoolroom education made us feel that there need be no haste in placing our children in the public schools. Beginning at eight years of age, Katharine was taught at home rather intermittently, but under expert teachers, for two hours a day, covering a period of two years. She then entered the public school in Lake Geneva from which she graduated at ten and a half after her first year in school, and then attended the high school for three years. For four years right after an early breakfast I used to drive her a mile to the station, and we never missed the train. Frederick entered the Williams Bay school at the age of eleven, but Ben started in more in the usual way when he was seven years old.

During his high school days Frederick carried on a printing business in the attic of our home, thereby earning his spending money. This seemed to me to give an excellent training in many ways, but it was a bit hard on the family. Ben fell heir to the business, but we were glad when the press was finally sold.

By rights our daughter should have gone to Wellesley and our sons to Dartmouth. Unfortunately, the public schools of Wisconsin did not give a preparation which admitted students to Dartmouth, and the University of Chicago was not only excellent but convenient, so that we finally decided to keep them nearer home. I feel sure that the children have never regretted this choice, for incidentally it gave them the opportunity to spend many week-ends at home, and they had the pleasure of bringing many of their friends with them. The number of these guests at one time developed into house-parties of thirty boys and thirty girls, the boys being members of the Chi Psi Fraternity. It was a strenuous time, but we enjoyed the young people and still keep in touch with many of them.

In 1910 the International Solar Union was invited to have its meeting at the Mount Wilson Observatory. Many foreign delegates attended, first going to the meeting of the American Astronomical Society at Cambridge and then proceeding to Chicago, where they were entertained at the university and given an opportunity to see something of the city. We traveled westward in a group of over forty, occupying two Pullmans which were laid over at Flagstaff for one night and at the Grand Canyon for two nights. In the party were representatives of England, France, Germany, Scandinavia, Russia, Switzerland, Austria, and Italy, with numerous Americans. The trip of four or five days was most entertaining and gave us a splendid opportunity to have discussions in regard to special problems. On some days when the temperature in the car ran as high as 110°, the sessions of committees were nevertheless held, but were decidedly informal. Some of the foreign astronomers who had preceded us by different routes joined us from time to time so that we were well acquainted and quite fully prepared for the four or five sessions which took place on the three days of the formal meetings at the hotel at the top of Mount Wilson not far from the observatory. The trip, with the visit to the observatory was a novel one for most of the foreigners as well as for many of the Americans and was thoroughly enjoyed in spite of the unavoidable heat of August. Over the first formal session Professor E. C. Pickering presided; over the second, Professor W. W. Campbell; and that duty fell to me on the third and fourth sessions. We had English, French, and German secretaries, and the three languages were employed at the convenience of the speakers. Owing to ill-health, Mr. Hale was unable to participate directly in the meetings which had been inspired largely by him.

I must relate here a somewhat amusing incident which showed the wit of a member of the French delegation. In riding up Mount Wilson with the slow horse-drawn wagons (the mountain road had not been built for automobiles), I had joined a group consisting chiefly of the French delegates, attempting to explain to them some of the features of the ride. We stopped at one point at a spring for a drink of water. One of the French delegates, who was always rather difficult at international meetings and quite opinionated, corrected my pronunciation of the word water, saying that it should be pronounced 'waiter.' I took the matter humorously. The objector was beginning to get out his dictionary to prove his point when his French colleague, who had been studying English intensively for six weeks, said, 'No, remember that in English they say, "Waiter, water!"'

We scattered after the meeting, but quite a company went north to San Francisco to visit that city and then to make the trip to the Lick Observatory on Mount Hamilton. I tried to be of service to this fine group of foreign representatives, many of whom I had met

in Europe and to whom America was new. It was a jolly international company, and it was an especial pleasure for me to have as
a roommate in San Francisco the newly appointed Astronomer
Royal, Sir Frank Dyson, who was a most delightful companion.

On one occasion on the trip eastward as we were studying the
menu-card in the dining-car, an Italian asked me the meaning of
'duck,' which he pronounced 'dook.' I gave him the equivalent
in German and French, and then, as I tried to explain the English
pronunciation of the word, the witty French delegate added, 'Yes,
we must remember that in English the "Duck of Bookingham" is
called the "Duke of Buckingham." '

On the return trip we went over the Sierras on the Southern
Pacific and from Ogden to Denver on the Denver and Rio Grande,
giving our delegates a chance to enjoy some of our finest scenery.
A Dartmouth classmate who called upon me while we were waiting
for our train at Denver later reported to the class in an amusing
way on my duties as interpreter and guide to this polyglot group.
Most of the delegates came to the Yerkes Observatory, some before
and others after the meetings, and we were delighted to have the
pleasure of entertaining them in our home. The international relations were most cordial and friendly and increasingly so, as I
have mentioned elsewhere in respect to the gathering of 1912 in
London in honor of the quarter-millennium of the Royal Society.
It was a great tragedy that the war brought a sudden end to the
general relation of friendship, breaking the previously harmonious
group into two, the Allies on the one hand and the Central Powers
on the other. However, although personal friendships between
Americans and Germans and Austrians were necessarily suspended
during the years 1917 to 1918, they were not broken. The English
censor permitted the interchange of scientific periodicals between
Germany and England, even when the war was most bitter. The
trustees of the University of Chicago permitted me to have the
regular edition of the *Astrophysical Journal* printed in anticipation
of the time when the seventy-five copies required for scientific institutions in the Central Empires should be desired to complete their
files. In the hard times following the war, the university also recognized the difficulty of the immediate payment of subscriptions by
Continental subscribers, allowing deferred payments, a courtesy

which was greatly appreciated by the astronomers in several European observatories.

Great progress was made during the period of which we have been speaking in the development of the electronic theory. There were many points, however, for which the astrophysicists could bring to their colleagues in the laboratories further evidence from the stars in which conditions of temperature were beyond anything possible in terrestrial experiments.

Studies of the radiation of the elements in the far ultra-violet region of the spectrum by the German, Victor Schumann, and the American, Theodore Lyman, contributed much to the correlation of spectral relationships. The apparatus had to be entirely in a vacuum because the narrow stratum of air absorbed the rays sought for. It was not long thereafter that these researches were extended to fill the gap between the region just mentioned and that of the spectrum of X-rays, the wave-length of the lines in the X-ray spectrum being less than one one-thousandth that of the deepest violet end of the spectrum visible to the eye.

It was interesting to watch the gradual building-up of the electronic theory from the point of view of an editor to whom manuscripts were constantly coming. A few years before came the development of the theory of radiation by Max Planck, W. Wien, and others. This was equally interesting to me. The Germans had had a leading part in this theory, and I had translated many of the papers from the *Proceedings* of the Prussian Academy, so that they should be available to the readers of our journal.

CHAPTER XVIII

A YEAR IN EUROPE

MRS. FROST and I attended the meeting of the American Association at Washington just after Christmas, 1911. I was quite occupied with my duties as chairman of the Section and on committees, and then went to New York, where I lectured at the Brooklyn Institute. We made calls at Buffalo and Cleveland on our way westward, and I was rather weary when I reached home. I then had to keep a lecture engagement in Chicago and upon my return from that lecture went to bed with pneumonia. That was a very cold January, but our excellent physician, Dr. W. H. Macdonald from Lake Geneva, so kindly and generously assisted by our good friend Dr. Frank Johnson of Chicago, was not prevented from his attendance on my needs by snow or cold, and under my wife's careful nursing, in addition to a trained nurse, I was able to go downstairs in about three weeks. One's strength, however, returns slowly after such an attack. I was therefore glad to receive from the trustees a grant of a vacation for a year's trip to Europe. I had not as a matter of fact availed myself of the vacation of one quarter of a year for ten years nor have I done so since. The conduct of the *Astrophysical Journal* during my absence was assumed chiefly by Professor Henry G. Gale of the Ryerson Physical Laboratory, and the duties of the Director were distributed among the staff, Mr. S. B. Barrett, secretary and librarian of the observatory, taking charge of the official correspondence. Professor S. A. Mitchell, then of Columbia University, also joined the staff for that year and took over a considerable part of the observing with the spectrograph. Our house was rented to a Chicago family for the summer and then closed for the winter and spring. Several friends desired to join our party, including Mrs. Frost's cousin, Miss Edith Hazard, and my niece, Elizabeth Frost of Hanover, together with two ladies, the Misses Hill who lived near us on Observatory Hill. We sailed from Montreal on the steamer *Teutonic* in the middle of June. In the meantime I had been appointed as the delegate to represent the University of Chicago at the celebration of the two hundred and fiftieth anniversary of the foundation of the Royal Society which was meeting at London before the end of June. We regretted the necessity of this early departure because the golden wedding anniversary of Mrs. Frost's father and mother, Dr. and Mrs. Hazard of Boston, was to occur on June 28. However, we arranged for the matter in rather a novel way by having the wedding breakfast on the steamer as we sailed from Montreal to Quebec. Mr. and Mrs. Hazard came up from Boston to Montreal, and my brother and his wife brought their daughter Elizabeth to Montreal from Hanover, together with three or four other friends from Dartmouth, all of whom accompanied us as far as Quebec. Thus we had a party of more than a dozen for the special breakfast which the steward served for us as the steamer followed the curving path of the majestic St. Lawrence. We arrived at Quebec early on the next afternoon and had several hours to visit the points of interest in that famous old city. Then we resumed our voyage down the river with our original party of nine. The passage to England seems materially shortened by the St. Lawrence route. We had our last sight of land on Tuesday morning, beyond Farther Point, and late in the evening of Friday we could already see some of the lighthouses of Ireland. We rounded the north coast of the island on Saturday, and we reached Liverpool on Sunday morning.

It is rather surprising how small boys adapt themselves to situations which are novel to them. Our lads soon got acquainted with all parts of the ship and established friendly relations with the stewards and other employees. The boys made acquaintance with the culinary department rather early so as to have the advantage of a little extra lunch when they felt the necessity of it. Ben never missed a meal and was always the first one to enter the dining-room. There were quite a number of young Americans and Canadians on board who were on their way to take part in the Olympic Games to be held that summer at Stockholm. They went through all sorts of exercises to keep themselves fit, and this helped to entertain the other guests on the ship. This trip was made less than two months after the tragic sinking of the *Titanic*, and a sharp watch was kept for ice, which delayed us at times during foggy weather. We were told that some of the passengers had thrown flowers overboard when they passed the point where the great *Titanic* was supposed to have been sunk.

We did not stay in Liverpool longer than was necessary to check the baggage for our party of nine and then made the short trip by train to Old Chester. This quaint ancient city full of the evidence of the Roman occupation had been to me one of the most interesting towns in England, with its sharp contrasts of the old and new. We especially enjoyed a visit to the famous gardens at Eaton Hall, seat of the Duke of Westminster. We had the advantage of the guidance of a very competent gardener who gave us the benefit of his careful attention as he soon found that we knew something about roses. Two members of our party were relatives of an American specialist who had produced the Richmond, the Hoosier Beauty, and some other fine specimens of American hybridizing. England was lovely in June, although it had had rather an excess of rain. It would surprise many, as it did me, to learn that the rainfall at Greenwich (the same as for London), is only about twenty-four inches, or three quarters of what we have in southern Wisconsin, and not much more than half of that which normally falls along the coast of New England. We get the idea that England is very wet because the showers are frequent, although light. Of course there are many points in the northern part where the rain is very heavy indeed.

I spent a pleasant day with Sir Arthur Schuster at his home in Victoria Park, Manchester, and joined my family when they passed by next day *en route* to London. One of the first striking spectacles in the city to attract the attention of our small boys was the passing down Tottenham Court Road of the funeral procession of a high military officer.

The members of our party enjoyed themselves in their visits to the many points of interest in the great city. The bus service had not yet been motorized very fully and it certainly was difficult to find a better place to see the busy life of the city than from the top of a horse-drawn bus threading its way down High Holborn, Cheapside, Poultry, and the other sections of this main thoroughfare to the bank, 'the Little Old Lady of Threadneedle Street.'

We spent a delightful afternoon at the Royal Observatory at Greenwich, where our whole party had been invited by Sir Frank and Lady Dyson. They had a family of six children, with a couple of small boys, and tea was served on their beautiful green lawn.

Inasmuch as the many social engagements in connection with the celebration of the Royal Society were to occupy all the time of Mrs. Frost and myself, we had arranged in advance to take the children and the rest of the party to Bournemouth, a delightful watering-place near Southampton, about a hundred miles from London. There, our long-time friend, Miss Lowater, who had been teaching physics in American colleges for some years, had rented us spacious rooms in a house overlooking the sea. Bournemouth was Miss Lowater's home and our party was frequently entertained at tea by her mother. We now had the experience of the English system of boarding at a summer resort. There were no visitors in the house other than our party. The meals were served in a large living-room and the service was excellent. Each morning Mrs. Frost selected the menu for the day in consultation with the manager, and the marketing and cooking were done for us, while we received and paid the original bills for the supplies. Everything was delightfully fresh, particularly the berries; the roasts were well-cooked and greatly enjoyed, and we found this an excellent way for a large party to live in practical privacy with most of the advantages of home.

This part of the town is situated on a high bluff, with many valleys cut down by erosion. These were called chynes, and driveways and parks had been arranged along these sloping valleys. The bathing was very fine, and there was still practiced the old custom of using bathhouses on wheels which were drawn back and forth over the beach by stout horses as the tide advanced or receded. It was even then regarded as improper for young persons of opposite sex to bathe at the same point, but there was an intermediate region in which bathing by families was permitted. Therefore those who did not like segregation could easily meet in the section for families, and the system suggested some prudishness. Everything was well managed by the municipality so that fresh bathing-suits and towels could be rented at a low price, and the laundries seemed to be maintained at the beach itself.

After a few days at Bournemouth, Mrs. Frost and I returned to London for the festivities. We were to be the guests at Greenwich of Sir Frank and Lady Dyson for two or three days. The home of the Astronomer Royal at Greenwich was an interesting one. It had been built by Sir Christopher Wren about two hundred and fifty years ago in direct connection with the famous Octagon Room which must have originally served for observing. This room is now more of a museum and reception room for official occasions. All of the domes, meridian houses, and the computing and business offices are separately built on the grounds. The problem of making the house suitable for occupancy by a large family and provided with guest-rooms was skillfully accomplished by modern English architects. The location on the edge of a steep hill made it possible to extend the house downward instead of upward or laterally, and thus the appearance of the original building was maintained, while handsome modern quarters were provided one or two stories below the original level of the house, the new rooms having an outlook on Greenwich Park.

We attended the various functions of the Royal Society with Sir Frank and Lady Dyson. There was a gala meeting of the Society on one of the first evenings, attended by many of the lights of England, and among them some of the Indian princes. I recall especially the Maharajah of Gwalior who sat quite near me. There was an opportunity to meet many of the distinguished men of science, whose names had long been familiar and whom it was a great honor to meet. I think in this connection particularly of Sir William Crookes, the great chemist, whose remarkable discoveries had formed an epoch in the eighties and onward. Some men, like Sir Robert Ball and Sir William Ramsay, had been guests at our observatory. Our astronomical friends were solicitous in their efforts to have us meet other members of the Royal Society. The president on this occasion was Sir Archibald Geikie, the celebrated geologist. How resplendent he was in his scarlet suit at official functions! There were delegates from all of the principal universities of the Continent, making it a most notable gathering. One of the stately ceremonies was a commemorative service in Westminster Abbey which was attended by the delegates and the flower of English society. A special sermon was preached by the Dean of Winchester, a prelate with scientific leanings, and special music was written for the occasion by Sir Edward Elgar who also played the organ. During this service we scientists wore our academic robes of great variety among the different delegates and were seated not far from Balfour and other high officers of the Government.

The ladies had a luncheon and a visit to Hampton Court with Lady Lockyer while the men were entertained at the rooms of the Society in Burlington House. There was a visit to the National Physical Laboratory at Teddington followed by a lawn party at the house of the Duke of Northumberland. This was an unpretentious old mansion secluded among the trees with a branch of the Thames running peacefully through the estate and a fine herd of cows grazing not far from the lawn where the luncheon was served. It was hard to imagine that we were only a few miles from the center of the greatest city in the world. The Duke and Duchess were very simply dressed and might easily have passed for a Methodist minister and his wife.

A stately dinner was given in the Guild Hall, lent to the Society for the occasion. Here were assembled the leaders of art, science, and literature, and of politics of the British Empire. The seating was arranged with great care, and a printed sketch showed where everyone was located. From my seat I had a fine chance to observe the Prime Minister, Mr. Asquith, the Archbishop of Canterbury, and other notables at the speakers' table. Sir Archibald Geikie was small of stature and seemed especially so in the great chair in which he sat. Behind him stood an official announcer, a large man with a powerful voice, who called out in stentorian tones, 'My lords, ladies, and gentlemen, pray have silence while grace is said by the Archbishop of Canterbury.' This man also announced the speakers, as Sir Archibald's voice could hardly carry through the great hall. On brackets at the side of the hall, arranged somewhat like pulpits, stood men dressed as cooks carving, in old English style, whole 'barons' of beef for the guests. This was an occasion not to be forgotten.

It was understood that the delegates were to be divided in making their visits to the universities. Some were going to Cambridge and others to Oxford. Some of my English friends in the Society seemed to know before word came to me that I was to go to Cambridge to receive a degree. I myself was greatly surprised to find in my mail one morning during the week a letter which had been forwarded to me from the Yerkes Observatory containing a note from the Vice-Chancellor of the University of Cambridge to the effect that

I was to be given the degree of Doctor of Science. I hastened to telegraph my acceptance to the Vice-Chancellor and then learned the details of the plan for the visit.

Before we went to Cambridge we attended the garden party of the King and Queen at Windsor. It was a lovely summer's day without a cloud in the sky. All the details of this party were carried out with the greatest perfection. A note from the Lord Chamberlain had told us just what to wear and when the special trains would leave for Windsor. Centuries of experience have given the British officials great skill in handling all of these functions. The official delegates were given an opportunity to look through the King's library under the guidance of the Royal Librarian and Sir George Darwin, and then about sixty of us were presented to the King and Queen on the lawn near the family entrance to the castle. Thereafter we joined the ladies, and refreshments were served on long tables under huge tents. It was a gay sight. The ladies were dressed in their brightest gowns, and the gorgeously robed Indian princes were much in evidence, keeping their wives in marquees of brilliant tapestries. The members of Parliament were present, but the spacious lawns were not at all crowded even with several thousand guests.

It seemed incredible to me at that time that a terrible European upheaval was imminent. Everyone knew, of course, that there was a feeling of tension in Europe, but to my surprise I heard here perfectly free discussions of possible methods of attack on England. During the afternoon when a dirigible lazily floated overhead, we heard not a few remark, 'How easy it would be to drop a bomb.' In that setting, such suggestions gave the impression of being hysterical, but little did England then dream that she would be passing through the most awful tragedy of our times within two years.

At the end of this brilliant day we took the train for Cambridge with Professor and Mrs. Newall with whom we stayed as guests in their country home, 'Madingley Rise,' a couple of miles out of Cambridge. The Solar Physics Observatory was located here, and the great refractor had been given by Mr. Newall's father. The Newalls maintained an English rural estate. Aside from a fine dairy, they specialized in horses, and it was a pretty sight to see them come galloping across the field to greet their mistress. It was the custom to give to the colts foaled in a given year names beginning

with the same letter of the alphabet. I recall that 'P' was the letter
that began the name of each colt in 1912.

The ceremonial of granting degrees in the Senate House was
highly formal. Lord Rayleigh was the Chancellor, and before him
went two of the Esquire Bedells, one bearing the mace of the university, while another bore some of its most precious emblems on a
cushion. Two pages followed the Chancellor holding his gorgeous
robes. Six delegates had been selected to receive degrees at Cambridge, each from a different nation, and each representing a different branch of science. These were: Professor Rubens, physicist,
of Berlin; Professor Pavlov, pathologist, of St. Petersburg; Professor
Paterno di Sessa, chemist, of Italy; Professor E. Warming, botanist,
of Denmark; Professor C. E. Picard, mathematician, of France, and
myself. A printed diagram was handed to us showing just where
we were to stand on the prayer rug spread below the dais of the
Chancellor. I was the first to pass through the ordeal, and while I
tried to stand exactly as indicated on the diagram, I was evidently
three or four inches out of position, for the Chancellor sent down a
page to move me to the correct spot on the rug. Then the famous
university orator, Sir J. E. Sandeys, delivered a fluent oration in
Latin,[1] describing the line of work which I had done in science, and
the degree was solemnly conferred. The brilliant scarlet Cambridge
gown and black flat velvet cap were lent to me by the authorities
for the occasion, as they said it was quite unnecessary for me to
buy the silken robes. After all the degrees had been conferred and
the procession started down the main aisle to the Senate House,
there was quite a chance that some demonstration would be given

[1] Primum omnium respublica maxima trans oceanum Atlanticum nobis con-
iunctissima quasi nuntium quendam sidereum ad nos misit, qui lacus maximi in
litore astrophysica (ut aiunt) praeclare profitetur, lacus minimi in margine speculae
astronomicae celeberrimae praepositus. Ibi, astronomi praeclari, Societatis Re-
galis haud ita pridem Praesidis, vestigia secutus, stellas, quae inerrantes vocantur,
diligenter observavit, et spectri (ut dicitur) auxilio, earum motus aut recedentes
aut appropinquantes accurate computavit. Idem, cum collegis optimis conso-
ciatus, stellas duplices atque etiam multiplices plurimas detexit; siderum denique
illorum praesertim, quorum in aëre helium inesse comprobatum est, primus tarditatem quandam motus demonstravit. Astronomo autem nostro, viro impigro, viro
acerrimo, tarditatem mentis nemo exprobrabit. Etenim, talium virorum auxilio,
'caelum ipsum petimus,' non iam 'stultitia,' sed sapientia; atque, ut philosophi
cuiusdam Romani verbis utar, 'cogitatio nostra caeli munimenta perrumpit.'
Duco ad vos scientiae astrophysicae professorem illustrem, EDWIN BRANT FROST.

by the students gathered in the gallery. It took the form of a big toy poodle dog let down by a string as we passed. I caught it and passed it on to Professor Pavlov, who had made a great many experiments on dogs in the course of his medical researches.

After this ceremony was over, we were entertained at luncheon in one of the famous dining-halls in one of the colleges, and some excellent after-dinner speeches were made. There were no chances taken on losing the cap and gown lent to me, as two proctors soon stripped me of my finery, and I became an ordinary civilian again.

It was a source of great regret that Sir William Huggins, whom we properly regarded as the father of astrophysics in England, could not have lived to participate in the celebration of the Royal Society. He had been president of the Society when he was over eighty years of age, and had maintained his fine mental vigor until his death in 1910. We had the pleasure of spending an afternoon with Lady Huggins at their home in Brixton. The house was quite a museum, many of its doors and tapestries being of Oriental or Italian origin. At one time Sir William must have been a man of a good deal of means, for these collections were costly. We had tea with Lady Huggins, who afterward allowed our daughter Katharine to play on an original Stradivarius. We spent some time in looking over the wonderful garden which Lady Huggins had created. Artistic attention had been given to every detail. The iron hinges of the doors of the little summer house and all other fixtures had been specially designed by her. The garden had a great variety of the most interesting shrubs and flowers and plants. As she was planning to give up this home within a short time and go to live near the British Museum, she most generously offered to give me anything that I cared to take for my own garden in America. I could not then see how this could be done, as we were on our way to the Continent for a long vacation. I have often regretted that I did not make arrangements with some English dealer in plants and flowers to take over and hold for a year some of the most interesting specimens. Then, with good luck, we could have re-established on the grounds of the Yerkes Observatory a small part of this famous garden and have kept it as a memorial to Sir William and Lady Huggins. They both had many friends in America, although they had never been here, and Lady Huggins provided in her will that many of her treasures, scientific and artistic, should be given to Wellesley College. They are maintained there as a special exhibit and memorial.

We had enjoyed a day at Oxford with our whole party soon after our arrival in England, but Mrs. Frost and I were invited to spend the week-end with our friends Professor and Mrs. Turner. On Saturday morning we went with them to Henley, on the Thames, where the boat-races were to take place with special pomp and circumstance. A famous old royal barge which had not been used since an early part of Victoria's reign was brought from its museum retreat and put in condition for the King and Queen, who graced this occasion. It was manned by a crew of mighty oarsmen dressed in the quaint old scarlet costumes of an early period. They resembled the yeomen of the guard. Before the races began, the royal party was solemnly rowed up the river in this quaint old ark and could be seen by the great crowd, said to be of some fifty thousand, who were gathered for the festivities. When their Majesties wished to dine a few miles up the river a modern motor-boat took them to the home of their host on the river-bank. Every party of visitors who could do so rented a rowboat for the occasion. The day was bright and clear, and these thousands of boats filled with parties in their summer finery were a great spectacle. The private boats had to keep out of the course reserved for the racing shells, and this was well managed as usual. There was an intermission while the royal party had luncheon and the visitors picnicked on their boats or on shore. There were many handsomely decorated house-boats tied up at the best locations along the route, and not a few were said to have been rented by wealthy Americans. After all the events were over and the visitors attempted to return to the landing-places at Henley, the scene was one of great confusion. There were so many rowboats that it reminded me of a log jam in the Connecticut River. We might almost have gotten acquainted with another party as our boats hung together for some minutes, separating only momentarily, and meeting half an hour later, still trying to extricate ourselves from the confused mass of good-natured humanity. I think it took us more than an hour to move a mile. Among the throng we noticed Mr. and Mrs. Harry Selfridge of London who formerly were our neighbors at Lake Geneva, but we could merely wave to each other in that crowd. After landing, there was a grand scramble for tea. The afternoon was nearly over and the hour for refreshment by that beverage was almost past. Every table at the hotels had been taken by the throng. The urgency of the occasion, however, and the pressure of habit called for action. Professor Turner simply stopped at the first good-looking house and asked if we could be served with tea. This was done very simply and satisfactorily, and it seemed to be a matter of course for such householders to be prepared to supply the unquenchable thirst of visitors on such occasions.

After our return to London, we spent part of a day in trying to get interested in a cricket match which was played between Oxford and Cambridge at 'Lord's.' The game seemed more desultory than baseball and lacked the snap and business-like precision of our national game. There seemed to be no limit to the time which a player might have for his turn at bat and I understand that a skillful batsman may keep his turn indefinitely. When it was time for lunch, the game stopped to be resumed later, and the gaily dressed throng scattered in parties, making the event quite a social affair.

One day we made a visit to Eton under the guidance of Colonel Hills, an active member of the Royal Astronomical Society, who had been a guest in our home in 1910. His son was a pupil at Eton, and we were given the opportunity to see the tiny rooms occupied by the students. The rooms were just as they had been for years and the equipment was of the simplest character. I was impressed by the stairs which were worn into hollows by the feet of several generations. Colonel Hills took us in his automobile for the long drive to Winchester on our way to Bournemouth. The day was fine, and the trees, hedges, and fields were at their best as we drove through lovely Surrey. We lunched at one of those pleasant little English inns surrounded by charming gardens. Proceeding to Bournemouth by train, we found that the family had been well entertained by the various amusements of the place. We rested there for a few days, for the visit in London with all its functions had been pretty strenuous and had taxed our strength considerably. Again we packed our bulging grips and headed for Holland. *En route* we made a stop at the interesting old town of Canterbury and embarked in the evening from Folkestone for the Hook of Holland, where we arrived

Date 10/13 193 3

Name Prof Philip Fox

Address Adler Planetarium

Sold by _____ Amt. Recd. ch

1	An Astronomers Life		
2			3 50
3			
4			
5			
6			
7			
8			
9			
10			
11			
12			
13			
14			
15			

45

IN CASE OF ERROR PLEASE PRESENT THIS SLIP

much too early in the morning. We spent a sleepy day at Flushing and Middleburg and towards evening went to The Hague, where we stopped for a few days, making the usual excursions before proceeding to Amsterdam for another pause. We all tried our best to imitate the pronunciation of the Dutch name of The Hague ('s Graven Hage), but it is a difficult guttural sound which only a Dutchman can produce. Katharine and I took a dip in the surf on the celebrated beach at Scheveningen, its great sandy length covered as usual with bathing-machines and high covered chairs, and the waterfront gay with the bright colors and flying flags of the sailing vessels.

Holland gives one the impression of being a very peaceful, busy, and self-sufficient country. Its art treasures are certainly worthy of prolonged study and we enjoyed the cities with their clean thoroughfares and their beautiful government buildings. The trip to the islands of Maarken, Vollendam, and Edam were in sharp contrast to the busy streets of the cities. Many of the sights suggested Old World memories, but one got the impression that in that natural and truly picturesque meadowland, there was in the villages some posing for the benefit of the traveler.

After leaving Holland, we entered Germany and spent a few days at Bonn after stopping long enough in Cologne to see the cathedral quite thoroughly. At Bonn we found our friends Professor Küstner, Director of the Observatory, Professor Kayser, the eminent spectroscopist, and others. Both of these gentlemen had been guests in our home and were most kind to us in this interesting college town on the Rhine. Professor Küstner and his daughters took us for an *Ausflug* up to the Drachenfels, which was much enjoyed, especially by the boys.

We next spent a few days at famous old Heidelberg in the valley of the Neckar, so charming in summer. The whole town is full of interest, but the boys were shocked to see so many students who had felt that a scar on the face was an honorable necessity. Mrs. Frost and I visited the fine observatory on the Königstuhl, located in the pine trees high above the town and reached by a funicular. Here, over a cup of tea, we renewed old associations with our friends, Professor and Mrs. Max Wolf.

I was anxious to have my children see the old city of Strassburg where I had studied twenty years before, and we spent a day or two there. All of my academic friends had gone to other institutions, but we found much of interest in reviving my memories of the old town and its cathedral. There were still a few storks' nests on houses near the cathedral, and this amused the family.

One of the most beautiful parts of the trip was the ride through the Black Forest, past the Rhine Falls at Schaffhausen and on to Zurich. At this point and in several cities thereafter, we stopped at the *Christliches Hospiz*, corresponding to a high-grade Y.M.C.A. hotel. These were very clean and modern and served excellent meals. At Zurich we were entertained at dinner by my friend Professor Wolfer, of the observatory, our whole party making a trip with him up the Uitliberg, where we got our first view of the Alps.

At Lucerne we made a stop of about a week, making excursions into other parts of the country from this base. It was here that we were finally overtaken by my friend Professor Shin Hirayama, director of the observatory at Tokio, who had been following us from point to point in the endeavor to catch up with us. It was a pleasant reunion, for I had not seen him since our days together in Potsdam in 1891. We made the excursion up Mount Stansershorn with him and took him with us on many trips on the Lake of Lucerne. We all went to a performance of Schiller's *Wilhelm Tell* at Altdorf which was the very scene where the events of the play took place. It was a fine performance, but in a barnlike structure.

Very cheap monthly tickets were on sale at this time valid on both the railroads and steamers of Switzerland and one was allowed to travel as much as one wished during the lifetime of the ticket.

We located in the attractive city of Geneva early in September and made arrangements for the children to have French conversation and for the young girls to have regular lessons in French. *Le Journal de Genève* was the local paper which had quite a high position in Europe, and I read it thoroughly, as the autumn was rather a tense one with the Balkan War against Turkey in progress. In 1912 the city already had much of an international air, as there were many political refugees residing within its protection, and propaganda journals of various sorts were issued by Russians and others who were fighting the tyranny of the czaristic régime. It is indeed fortunate that there is a rugged republic in Europe where refuge may be found by those whose only offense has been a dissent from the lack of liberalism in the political administration of their own countries. No doubt this international quality has greatly increased since the League of Nations was established in Calvin's city. Geneva seems to me an ideal city to serve as the site for such an international body, except for its winter climate.

There was a continuous opportunity to hear lectures by famous speakers, and there were many excellent concerts during the winter. There was a distinguished orator who occupied the pulpit at Victoria Hall and his addresses were listened to by great numbers of young people at *pensions* and schools in Geneva. It offered a great opportunity to hear the best of French spoken with eloquence and clearness.

I did not get quite so strong an impression of the university as I should have, for the departments of astronomy and physics were not so outstanding as those in some of the other European universities. I probably should have introduced myself and become acquainted with the members of the faculty at the beginning and thus attended colloquia and other university functions, but I was too much occupied with the family to try to hear any of the regular lectures of the university. I presume that it excelled in the lines of history and economics and law. The Professor of Astronomy was very courteous and gave me every opportunity to use his office in the little observatory up on the hill near the cathedral, but I found that I had to open most of the astronomical periodicals myself in my desire to keep up with the current progress.

Just outside the limits of the city and on French soil are the two local mountains, La Grande Salève and La Petite Salève. This was a favorite trip for a nice afternoon for the boys, a street-car taking us to the foot of the mountain, and for those not wishing to walk, a cog-railway was available. The height, as I recall it, was only about four thousand feet above the sea, or three thousand feet above Lac Leman. A site here was being successfully used privately by one of the assistants in the observatory for some astronomical photography with a reflector which he had made himself. Geneva itself, from its location in the Rhone Valley, is very apt to be foggy and cloudy during the winter, but at the little elevation of the Salève, the percentage of sunshine was very much greater, and several hotels took advantage of this fact by locating in the higher elevation.

We had an experience, that often comes to families with small children, of picking up an infectious disease. While in many respects great attention is given to sanitary precautions in such cities, there does not seem to be a feeling of responsibility for avoiding the spread of contagion. So it happened that early in the autumn one of the boys developed whooping cough which was communicated to the others and really kept us much more secluded than we otherwise would have been. Our rooms were in the *dépendance* of a large *pension* in the Florissant District, and we felt quite a responsibility in keeping the disease from spreading to the other seventy-five or more children. Such precautions as we took were quite surprising to the other guests, but met with success. Of course we had what seemed to them a very reckless habit of sleeping with open windows. They still held to the ancient tradition that night air was dangerous and full of miasms. In our daughter's case, whooping cough was followed by a rather severe bronchitis which kept her in bed for nearly three months, where she continued with her French lessons with a splendid teacher who had been recommended to us by one of our colleagues at the University of Chicago. The doctor finally said that she would not recover until we got her into a better climate, and we left for Nice shortly before Christmas. There in the fine air and abundant sunshine she made an excellent recovery.

In Nice we lived at an old hotel owned by a Protestant Swiss family at the east end of the water front and built against the rugged slope of a high hill. To visit the garden located on the hill at the back of the hotel, we took the elevator to the fourth floor. The family of the proprietor included eleven children, so that among them there was a child to match each of ours and we were made quite at home, especially in the Christmas celebration, which brought the guests together quite successfully. There were a number of French and German families in the hotel as well as a large group of Russians. Our young people had to be restrained in their mirth in seeing the formality with which all the ladies in the Russian group had their hands kissed at breakfast every morning. We liked to look out of our windows the first thing each day and see the fishermen come in with their early catch. We particularly enjoyed the flower market from which we brought home large bunches of roses bought with surprisingly few centimes. The climate at Nice is not always certain, but during our stay the weather was remarkably fine. It was hard to realize that in this country of oranges and lemons and roses growing out-of-doors in midwinter we were really farther north than at our home in Wisconsin. We found it a good center for short excursions to quaint little villages up in the hills, part of the route being made by some kind of tramway and with the possibility of a long walk home toward evening through the old olive groves. The city itself was picturesque with some of the streets hardly wider than the spread of one's arms. Around the corner from the hotel was the Vieux Port which always had a few tramp steamers and pleasure craft in its safe anchorage. Near by was the Place Cassini and the street of the same name, one of the rare instances in which the achievements of a family of astronomers have been recognized by the assignment of a name. Four generations of Cassinis were directors at Paris, the last one closing his labors in about 1793. The trolley wound cir-cuitously over the hills around the shore at Villefranche, which had a most attractive harbor. Some of the French warships made a visit there during our stay at Nice and I took the boys over for in-spection when visitors were supposed to be allowed. We were just getting off the rowboat to climb the gangway to the flagship *La République* when something was said about Chicago, and it was intimated that foreigners were not permitted on board. Our boat-man felt sure that we would be received on one of the other vessels, and I cautioned the boys not to talk in English, but to use their best French. As we approached the *Suffren*, the older lad whispered in a loud tone, 'Daddy, may I sneeze?' We had an opportunity to look through this ship and to see beside it the *Gaulois* and the *Bouvet*. I mention these by name as within a couple of years at least two of them were sunk by mines in the Dardanelles.

Wishing to improve my very deficient pronunciation of French, I had registered at Geneva with the Berlitz School and had taken some lessons there, but the method was not suited to my needs. It enter-tained my French friends, however, when I would show my increas-ing acquisitions in their language by quoting such phrases as '*Les dames du téléphone sont insupportables.*' This phrase occurred in all the different languages of the Berlitz books and it seems to me that I have frequently heard it in English. I continued my studies again at Nice and had the same volume in a cover of another color for my Italian. The stately director of the school in his hot Prince Albert coat tried to give me a teacher who would talk to me about other things than the standard one-syllable words of the formal method. I did get some interesting points from a teacher of Italian who had once been secretary to Cardinal Merry del Val, Secretary of State to the Vatican. Finally I found just the person for my particular needs. She was a lady residing in Nice whose father was an Irishman who had married a French lady and lived in France. She herself had married one of the Sicilian barons from the sulphur district and she had written comments (not sulphuric) on France and Italy for the English papers and was a regular correspondent for the Sicilian papers. She had also written a large book on life in Sicily in that group to which her husband belonged and which had some elements of the frontier and the vendetta. Her sister had married a distinguished Greek surgeon at Athens and maintained a villa at Nice. When we sometimes went there on a Sunday afternoon for tea, it was as polyglot a gathering as one often sees. Madame D. spoke all the languages with great fluency. Her daughter was studying the violin with Ysaye and there was bright conversation and good music.

Out at the Pavilion on the *jetée* a fine orchestral concert could be heard for a few centimes, and so I took my Italian reading and my dictionaries and sat at a table where I could profitably enjoy all the interims of the excellent music. My instructress found in me a bug of a stripe with which she was not quite familiar, and I understand that she cited this unusual industry in her correspondence for the Italian paper.

One reason for our choice of Nice for a point of recuperation on the Riviera was the presence on the mountain back of the city, twelve hundred feet above the Mediterranean, of the Observatoire de Nice, the gift to the French Academy of Sciences of M. Bischoffsheim. It was a delightful climb up fine roads through orange groves, but one was in a warm glow on reaching the observatory, and it was dangerous to sit down in an unheated room to read the astronomical periodicals. The temperature would be perhaps from 50° to 60°, but it was safer to sit outside in the sun. The Director, M. Le Général Bassot, was very courteous to me and planned for us a formal dinner with the staff. I quite enjoyed the opportunity to establish connection with these gentlemen. The institution owned an automobile which was assigned to a staff member for a trip to the city one day a week, and we sometimes had the pleasure of riding up in their car, a much less tiring method than the hard, brisk climb. The splendid Route de la Corniche, which runs along the coast from Marseilles to Genoa, passes near the observatory. One day we went up on the diligence to join the astronomer and his family whom we knew best, and together we took the rather long walk to La Turbie where are the ruins of structures erected under Augustus Cæsar. The almost constant view of the blue Mediterranean and the noble mountains of Savoy to the north made a charming picture. From this village a cog-railway dropped directly down to Monaco, where we looked into the usual points of interest. We also had letters of introduction to the oceanographic museum maintained by the Prince of Monaco and thus had an opportunity of visiting this interesting institution before we took the train back to Nice.

The situation in Europe was a very dangerous one in the autumn of 1912, with various causes which might easily lead to war. Turkey had been carrying on an unsuccessful war with Italy over the treatment of Italians in Tripoli, and the leaders of the Balkan States buried their racial animosities for a time and built up an offensive alliance against Turkey, with Greece, Bulgaria, Serbia, and Montenegro as parties to the arrangement. They declared war on Turkey in October and were quite successful in their first attacks on their ancient Ottoman enemy. The European Powers were, of course, playing a hand in the situation, the French strategy and French equipment being influential in the success of the Bulgarian armies. Germany had furnished officers for the Young Turks, and Austria-Hungary was taking a firm position so that Serbia should not threaten her power on the Adriatic. Russia was generally sympathetic with the Slavs in their ambition to drive the Turks from Europe. A general conflagration on the continent was barely averted, and Turkey in 1913 gave up Thrace and Macedonia and practically all her possessions in Europe except Constantinople and regions immediately west thereof. During 1913 the perfection of the military organizations was given great attention in Germany, Austria, Russia, and France. The military machines were evidently being made ready for a test of their efficiency. It was, in fact, fortunate that the Great War could be postponed for another year, but some incident might occur at any time which would provoke a general conflict. During our stay the European newspapers were full of discussions of the various possibilities, and I followed the developments closely.

At the beginning of February we started our visit in Italy, proceeding first to Rome. We were fortunate in having the guidance there of our friend Dr. Giorgio Abetti, assistant in the observatory of the Collegio Romano. He had spent some months with us in study at the Yerkes Observatory a few years earlier. The Collegio Romano had had a distinguished astronomical history, and it was here that the renowned Father Secchi had worked many years before and had studied the spectra of the stars visually. The Collegio and its observatory were right in the heart of the city near the Piazza Venezia. The observatory itself was perched high up over the fifth floor of this rambling old building and was quite a climb, but they told us that the Queen of Italy would occasionally essay it when she wished to see something of astronomical interest. In the changes that have come in the educational institutions of Rome, the observatory has been given up in recent years. The other principal observatory of the city is located at the Vatican, and its director was Father J. G. Hagen. This fine old gentlemen was of German birth, but had taken the Jesuit orders and at one time was not able to live either in Germany or Italy and had been engaged in teaching for his order in the United States, where he became the director of the observatory of Georgetown University in Washington. I had known him in America for a number of years and he had been one of the guests at the inauguration of the Yerkes Observatory. When he was called back to Rome to become director of the Specola Vaticana, he enlarged the astronomical equipment which was erected on one of the ancient walls of the Vatican Gardens and was allowed to use for his office a building which Pope Leo XIII had maintained as his quarters during the hot summer months. Aside from the domes used for telescopes, there was one small dome under which an astronomical museum had been established and on the ceiling of which the stars in the constellation Leo were represented by electric lights in honor of Pope Leo XIII, who had during his pontificate placed expensive astronomical instruments in the Vatican Observatory and had provided accommodations and endowment for a staff of observers. We had contributed to the exhibit of photographs in this museum which we were told were of especial interest to many of the higher officials of the Vatican, including the successive popes. Having a card of admittance from Father Hagen, it was a ceremony of some interest to see the Swiss Guard line up and open the way for us so that we could enter and go through the gardens and come to the astronomical section. It might seem strange that the Papal See should maintain an astronomical observatory, but it has, of course, been the high duty of the Jesuit Order to care for the interests of science and knowledge in the Roman Church, and Father Hagen had made important contributions and evidently received the cordial support of the administration of the Vatican. We returned to the Vatican later for the customary 'audience' with Pope Pius X, and the fervor with which his entrance into the hall, containing one hundred or more persons, was greeted was full evidence of the high respect of those who attended the ceremony.

Soon after we reached Rome, I was asked by Dr. Abetti, secretary of the Italian Physical Society, if I would give a lecture before that body during my stay. I agreed to do so and sent at once to Geneva, where I had left my lantern slides. I had expected that I could speak in either English or German, but nearly at the last moment I was advised that I should have to speak either in French or Italian. Unfortunately for me, the slides were held at the border just long enough not to arrive on time, and I had to speak in rather halting French and without their great assistance. I had prints with me which could be passed about, but this did not give the opportunity for such a presentation as I would have preferred to make. The officers, particularly the president, Professor Blaserna (Senatore del Regno), was most kind in his introduction and comments, realizing that I was speaking in what was neither my own language nor theirs, and I was assisted occasionally by Dr. Abetti with a French or Italian word to fill a gap.

At Naples we found decided evidence of improvement in general conditions in the city since our first visit there fifteen years before. It happened to be rather a cold period in February, and the populace in some quarters were trying to keep their hands warm over outdoor braziers. There was even some snow while we were there, and an elderly American astronomer who had come down from Rome with us received rather a painful injury from a fall on the icy street. Many fine apartment buildings were being erected in the city, and there was every evidence of national prosperity in 1913. The observatory is on the high crest known as the Capodimonte, where I was hospitably received by the director and the staff.

Returning from Naples, we stayed again in our hotel in Rome for a few days, but on the morning that we started for Florence we had the unusual experience of finding a coating of almost two inches of snow over the whole city. We were up early, as one must be in traveling with a party of seven, but it was quite hopeless to get transportation to the railway station. The conditions were regarded as entirely unsafe for horses. There were no cabs to be had, and in order to catch the express for Florence I made haste to secure the services of a boy with a pushcart and, loading it with a dozen or more grips and parcels, I helped him push it a mile or more to the station while the family went ahead in the street-cars. The necessary delay made us lose the *direttissimo*, and we spent the whole day traveling in rather a wintry landscape up through the mountains into Florence.

In this interesting city, the site of many treasures of art, we had the pleasure of sessions with the director of the observatory at Arcetri, Professor Angelo Abetti, father of our friend in Rome. He had made his graduate studies in Germany and therefore there was no barrier of language, but he also took great pains in helping me with my Italian. It was a very pleasant walk out from Florence to the suburb of Arcetri up the hill through the olive trees. The new observatory is only about half a mile from where Galileo worked in his time, and is picturesquely located above the Piazza Michelangelo. We were entertained in true Italian style by the professor and his friends at a well-known restaurant in that Piazza and tried to learn for ourselves the proper way to eat spaghetti and tomato sauce without spreading the food upon ourselves or upon the floor. One of the guests was Count Ginori, who had an amateur's interest in astronomy. He suggested a picture of the antiquity of the Italian life when he quite casually remarked, as he pointed up the valley, 'About six centuries ago my mother's family came from that district a few miles up the river.'

Of course we inspected the Tribuna di Galileo under the auspices of its officials, and we saw at the physical laboratory many of the exceedingly ingenious and beautifully constructed globes, orreries, and astronomical models which had served for purposes of teaching and exhibition while the idea of the spherical earth was being gradually absorbed by the people. We also saw some of the very early and rare maps showing America as it was first thought to exist.

I recall with pleasure a visit that we made to the monastery of the Carthusian monks, known as the Certosa. Professor Abetti knew some of the members of the order and I was given opportunities to see some of the treasures not ordinarily displayed to visitors. My guide was a white-robed monk who had once been a dashing young officer of the Uhlans of the German Army until a severe accident had deprived him of any possibility of advancement as a soldier.

Venice can be rather a cold place for a visit in February, but the city never loses its charm. I had some introductions to scientific men which were of interest, and of course the family enjoyed all the usual sights. When one visits Venice in summer as is usually the case, the opera is over, but we were at this time fortunate in attending a performance of *Othello* which I can never forget. It was particularly appropriate to see this at the very spot where the scene was laid, and the artists were of high quality. A touch of realism was given to the picturesque unrealities of Venice when, standing on a bridge near the canal, we watched a group of prisoners, probably political agitators, being brought in a gondola and admitted to durance vile through the lower door of the prison.

We returned to our quarters in Geneva for a few weeks in the early spring, and now, with the family all in good health, we made excellent progress in our studies in French to which we assiduously devoted ourselves. The weather at this time was much better, with more clear skies, and the views of the Jura from our windows will never be forgotten.

I recall a demonstration which I saw of the real democracy which exists in the Swiss Republic. Some question was up for a decision by the people regarding the federal railways. The arguments had been presented at length in all the local newspapers, and on Easter Sunday morning an open-air referendum was held in one of the public parks in the upper part of the city. Speeches were made and the matter was finally settled by a *viva-voce* which had all the force of law and was actually an official referendum. The majority was so strongly on one side that it was not necessary to count the voters. Although special precautions were taken to see that each one was entitled to the suffrage, I believe that I could have assisted in the passage of that law without having my citizenship called into question. I cannot believe that such methods of expressing public opinion would be applicable in many other countries than Switzerland where there is such a fine sense of patriotism and loyalty to the Republic and maintenance of its laws and order.

Our next objective was Munich, which we reached by way of Zurich and Lake Constance. It is quite a lesson in geography to understand how many different political divisions border on that lake. I believe that we went through not less than three or four customs' inspections in a space of about ten miles. Munich, often called by the Bavarians the 'Athens of the Isar,' has long been a city of high intellectual standing, with its university, its technical high school, its many art galleries and schools of art, its textile schools, and particularly its museum for the 'Masterpieces of Science and Technology.' This museum differed from the many others in Germany in its plan and scope and has served as a prototype for others in different countries since its erection. Of course it resembled somewhat the South Kensington Museum and the Smithsonian at Washington, but its special aim was to concentrate on the real masterpieces rather than to multiply the quantity of different exhibits flowing from the primary one. The work of the museum had been planned most carefully and its leading officials had made a special trip to America in their desire to secure proper models and representations of some of the most important American inventions, such as the harvester and the Pullman car. Some members of the party visited our observatory, and they would have been glad to display a model of the Yerkes forty-inch telescope. The university, however, was not able to go to the considerable expense of such an exhibit, and the manufacturers (Messrs. Warner and Swasey) contributed large photographs instead. Our lads made quite a demonstration when they went into the room where these exhibits of our observatory were shown and tried to make the attendant understand the feeling of home that it brought to them to see the pictures. The museum was still in an old series of buildings, but the plans were being drawn for the splendid edifice which has since replaced them. There was a very realistic coal mine in which visitors could get a thoroughly comprehensive idea of the workings under ground. In general all exhibits were arranged so that they could be made to operate by pressing a button and could demonstrate to any visitor the principle of the invention. The new museum also contains a small planetarium, and thus astronomy is well represented. It is the plan of the new Rosenwald Industrial Museum in Jackson Park, Chicago, to follow some of the general principles which have been so successfully used in this Munich museum. With their families we found in Munich at this time our colleague Professor Andrew C. McLaughlin of the University of Chicago and Dr. Joel Stebbins, then astronomer at the University of Illinois, later at Madison.

Nuremburg has always seemed to me to present the best idea of mediæval Europe and the early Renaissance of any of the German cities. The Germanisches Museum, with its immense storehouse of treasures scattered through a group of connecting buildings, gives an idea of the handiwork of the woodcarvers and all the workers in industrial art that can hardly be surpassed elsewhere. I studied again the ancient features of the city, trying to get the viewpoint of the younger members of our party and found it to be still of unfailing interest.

The collections of art and science at Dresden are very notable, but the natural history exhibit in the Zwinger Museum, especially of the birds, was again rather overpowering. So many species are shown that one's acquaintance with those in a limited region is wholly dwarfed. It was as before difficult to find in it even a representation of American birds. One could not soon forget the fine performance of the *Flying Dutchman* to which we took our young girls in Dresden. Every detail of the opera had been carried out so carefully as to make it an almost perfect production, and the group of maidens at the spinning-wheels gave their chorus to perfection.

Of course we did not neglect the art treasures in Dresden and we found that our small boys never tired of the galleries if we called to their attention only those famous masterpieces which we hoped they might remember. They thus received a lasting impression of the highest accomplishments of the painter and the sculptor.

We found comfortably established in their home, 'Villa Vermont,' our friends for many years, Dr. and Mrs. William A. Spring. The Doctor told us some interesting tales of his dental practice in Europe and gave us a vivid picture of the happy domestic life of the Grand Duke Franz Ferdinand whom they had come to know quite intimately in the course of the Doctor's frequent visits to care for the dental work of the children in the family. It was the wicked murder of this couple at Serajevo, not many months later, that was the proximate cause of the Great War.

It seemed to me that the greatest external change noticeable in Berlin was due to the introduction of the automobile, and particularly the taxicab. This had seemed to speed up the activity of the capital. Unter den Linden has perhaps had a greater reputation than it deserves. It did not seem to me that the trees had grown very much since I had first gotten acquainted with them in 1891, twenty-two years before. There was a greater evidence of prosperity and even of extravagance in the windows of the stores, and some of the shops on the Leipzigerstrasse built great structures in what they called the modern style, which to me appeared far less attractive than the buildings of a quarter of a century before.

The location of the university buildings in the heart of the city had some advantages, but they did not make an impressive appearance. Many of the research institutions were at this time moving out to Charlottenburg in connection with the Reichsanstalt or Imperial Bureau of Standards, or to the suburbs near Dahlem. The growth of the city had quite hemmed in the fine old observatory at Enckeplatz, and the sale of this valuable land had made possible the erection of a new and entirely modern observatory in the suburbs in a part of the park of the old castle at Babelsberg. Professor Hermann Struve, the chief astronomer of the university, had planned this transfer with great foresight and skill and in the new site had established a highly modern institution for astronomical research. It was, in fact, not more than three miles away from the astrophysical observatory at Potsdam, but that was an independent institution without any teaching or any connection with the university. The small Urania Observatory, which had been in operation for some years in a suburb in the northwestern part of Berlin, was retained by the university for the teaching of practical astronomy to the students of the university. It was in that little observatory that the minor planet

Eros, until recently the nearest visitor to the earth of the planetary bodies except the moon, was discovered in 1898. Professor and Mrs. Struve were well known to us, having been our guests in 1910, and we spent a pleasant evening at their home in Berlin and a few days later were with them in their new home at Babelsberg.

We moved out to a *pension* in Potsdam after a fortnight in Berlin, as the spring was now well opened and the parks in that old city were at their best. I wished my family to get some of the impressions which I retained from my residence in the town in 1891-92. It seemed that there were more soldiers now than ever in the barracks in different parts of the city. We saw the cavalry in their maneuvers on their parade grounds. The municipal authorities had finally improved the street near which our *pension* was located, and had made a fine avenue of it, for this purpose removing the long row of small stables which had been built along its center one hundred years before to quarter Napoleon's cavalry. It seemed a little strange that these galling memories of the Napoleonic invasion should have been left so long, but German thrift was proverbial, and doubtless good use had been made of these small buildings until the time came for a general architectural improvement. Of course I sorely missed the presence at the Potsdam Observatory of my friends, the director of the observatory, Dr. Vogel, and his assistant, Dr. Scheiner, who had both passed on; but there were still active many good friends on the staff from my earlier years, and we had pleasant reunions, especially with Dr. J. Wilsing and Dr. Andreas Galle. The director at the time was the brilliant young Karl Schwarzschild who had been called there from Göttingen. He had one of the keenest mathematical minds of his generation and applied it very practically in many ways. The tension in Germany seemed to have relaxed since the Balkan War of the previous year, and the threat of war did not seem to be in the air in this fine spring weather.

We broke the trip to Paris by spending the night at Cologne, and thus had the full opportunity to see the country during the daytime. I often regretted that I did not study the contour of the railroad line more carefully as we passed through Belgium and on through Soissons into Paris. One could hardly believe that within a little more than a year the German forces would be ruthlessly invading France through that route in Belgium which was supposed to be protected by the treaties of neutrality. We saw a big military display in Paris on the occasion of a visit from King Alphonso of Spain. There seemed to be a spirit of fraternity and almost informality between the citizens and the cavalrymen while they were at rest, which I had not seen in Germany. On the whole, however, the discipline of the Germans seemed more rigid and all details of equipment more carefully maintained than in the case of the French troops. We had ten days in Paris before we sailed from Havre for home. Our time was spent in sight-seeing and some last shopping, with occasional visits with friends and frequent trips through the galleries. We stayed at a small hotel in the Latin Quarter and we were rather surprised to find how much interest our young children now showed in fine art treasures, such as those at the Louvre. Frederick and Ben, now eleven and seven, were quite accustomed to these visits to the art galleries, and used to purchase postcard copies of the pictures they liked best. The boys had been our best travelers, had assiduously collected and traded stamps, had been through the most important galleries in Italy, Germany, and France, and were particularly enamoured of Switzerland. They were well-behaved. Indeed, in a *pension* in Amsterdam, one woman remarked to Mrs. Frost, 'I never saw two such well-behaved boys.' Frederick, looking up in honest surprise, responded in a gentle voice, 'We aren't at home.'

We shall not forget one particular dinner party to which we were invited by an astronomer at the Paris Observatory. We were assured that it was to be a simple supper, quite informal, in fact strictly *en famille*, and that the children were expected. Arriving at the door, I inquired '*Quelle étage?*' The dignified butler, with some hauteur replied, '*C'est une maison particulière.*' The only young child of the family was twelve years old, had developed a temperature, and could not be present. Several guests arrived, and our simply dressed group were shocked and embarrassed when one grand lady swept into the room in a gorgeous evening gown and bedecked with jewels. Dinner was announced and courses passed in rapid succession. Mrs. Frost, opposite me, and to the right of her host, was earnestly practicing her recently acquired French, and her cousin was employing her easiest phrase, '*Je suis allée,*' and so forth. Our host was occasionally breaking into English to give my wife a breathing spell, and I heard him say, as he looked at my thick spectacles, 'I

see that your husband is very short-sighted.' Our efforts to tell some
of the humorous incidents of our travels were successful in producing
laughter, but it may be questioned whether this was due to the narra-
tives themselves or to the broken French in which they were told.
The table was a long one, and this prevented us from having a
strict supervision of our small boys. It was something of a shock to
see our youngest enjoying a glass of champagne shortly before midnight. On our way home we were a gay and relaxed party.

Versailles seemed to be a sleepy old town and its parks impressed
me again as being rather too formal. I visited the astrophysical observatory at Meudon under the guidance of one of the astronomers.
This is situated in the old royal park and was originally made from
the stables, but it has contributed in an important way to the advance of astrophysical research, particularly in the study of the sun.

CHAPTER XIX

AMERICA AGAIN

My good friend, Mr. A. C. Bartlett, of Chicago, had in addition to his estate on the lake shore a farm on the highway to Lake Geneva, Wisconsin. He used to urge me to join him in an enterprise to plant an apple orchard. I contented myself, however, by putting out a few trees on my own grounds while he, an optimist *par excellence*, planted a young orchard next to a schoolhouse! I once asked him, 'Does your farm pay?' 'In fun,' he replied. To Mrs. Frost's question, 'What have you sown?' he answered without hesitation, 'Greenbacks.'

And so it probably was with our inexperienced efforts with a miniature farm conducted largely on the edge of a hilltop and managed by one faithful man whose only assistants were Mrs. Frost and myself, whose primary interests were academic. David Harum said of a dog that 'fleas keep him from broodin' over bein' a dog.' So these urgent and perplexing problems of our little farm doubtless kept us from being too pressed academically.

Our eventual involvement was not premeditated, but was an unsuspected development which insinuated itself into our lives just because we happened to have a horse and a pony which required only the part-time services of a man. Coming morning and evening — why couldn't he just as well take care of a cow? So the faithful attendant accommodatingly purchased a fine bovine with the appropriate name of 'Star.' Her offspring and their offspring then had to be considered and planned for. When a pair of twin calves arrived, they were appropriately christened 'Castoria' and 'Pollux.' The line being led to pasture got longer and longer — the churn more and more full, the veal and baby beef increasingly difficult to dispose of. And what of the skimmed milk? — It must be meant for pigs, of course. A pigsty on a hillside and in all kinds of weather is not meant for one's best shoes, but is perhaps less muddy if dignified by the name 'Pennsylvania Avenue,' with the Presidential candidates 'Bryan and Taft' in their 'pigwams' at the end. Skimmed milk is naturally excellent for chickens also, and how a growing family consumes eggs, not to mention hens for Sunday dinner! Broilers are certainly much more choice and everyone knows that broilers are none other than young chickens. These are altogether too expensive to buy — so setting hens must be arranged for, a henhouse built, etc. The surprising percentage of fertility of those eggs made us feel like the woman who is presented with triplets. How it did increase our population! But production on a larger scale is the only paying basis. Why not have an incubator? There is plenty of room in our basement. No sooner thought of than one is installed, and before Easter Sunday we had box parties sitting before the mechanical mother and watching the whole process of the chicks pecking their way into the world. But what excitement we had one day when a sudden thunderstorm came up while dozens of tender little chickens were roaming through the woods on the hillside! Our friend Shirley Eaton arrived from New York with his bride just as we had gathered up a full bushel basket of apparently lifeless and certainly very ugly-looking little creatures and were at the moment reviving them in the oven of the kitchen stove.

After the war, when prices of labor and feed were so high, we gave up the farm work and were glad to be relieved of this strenuous activity. It had been fun and trouble. We had worked hard, but we liked it. The debit and credit side of the account was never balanced.

It may be suspected that my early habit of naming things has been continued by me in later life. My wife was surprised to find on the table in my office a notebook bearing the inscription in large letters, 'THE FLEA.' I explained that it was merely a 'scratch-book' which was used in our spectrographic program. 'The Lamb' and 'The Kid' were other books of this type, indicating their bindings. Our cars have had various names. I remember one that was named by my daughter. It was 'The Rabbit' because it hopped about so.

But we had no need in the early days of the observatory to give names to the small group of people who were in some way connected with it. It may seem strange that in such an institution the elements predominated in the names: Frost, Hale, Gale, Snow, Rainey, Thaw, Lowater, Moulton, Furness, Burnham, Burns, Firey, and Freeze. Another group was: Hawks, Crow, Fox, Wolf, Dobbin, Hart, and Roe. Then came the savory names: Cook, Pease, Bacon, Salt, and Baker. The rather lugubrious group was: Hurt, Parsons, Graves,

Hole, and Clay. We combined Foote, Hill, Street, and Carr; Brown and Gray; Poor and Ritchey; Slocum, Dodge, Heiden, and Stillhammer. In later years, when we had a larger number of graduate students or doctors coming to us from abroad, we found their names rather long for daily use. Therefore Dr. Paraskevopoulos of Athens himself adopted the abbreviation of 'Paras.' We called Mr. Bobrovnikof, Mr. Bob. Mr. Pogorelsky shortened his name to Mr. Pogo, and was so naturalized. Professor Van Biesbroeck readily consented to the shortening of his name for common usage to 'Mr. Van B.'

I recall that on the first morning after the arrival of Mr. Fox to become an assistant at the observatory, I took him into the building through the basement door and there met Mr. Wolf, our skillful cabinet-maker and janitor. I said, 'Herr Wolf: Herr Fuchs.' 'Woof!' said Mr. Fox. Mr. Wolf was a character, and in the early days was elected by the wets, more or less as a joke, as justice of the peace for this part of the township. He was almost immediately called upon to perform a marriage ceremony, and how he did laugh when he told of his first legal efforts! But the laugh grew louder a week or two later when it was found that his commission had not yet become effective at the time of the ceremony.

In connection with our feeble efforts at farming, I recall a local character, George Williams, whom I nicknamed 'The Crown Prince' of Williams Bay, being the grandson of the man for whom our little village was named. In spite of his 'arrested development,' he became in many ways a useful citizen, for he faithfully kept the town free from the miserable rags and papers which inevitably clutter the streets. There may possibly have been a mixed motive for this energy, for he unfortunately saved all that he gathered, storing it in the quaint old Williams homestead among the pines on the hill. It must have been a heartbreaking thing for him when the village authorities felt obliged to cart away and burn this germ-laden refuse. 'George,' as we familiarly called him even at seventy, also did the odd jobs around the village, tasks not meant for the fastidious, and among these unpleasant chores was the cleaning of our henhouse. But at noon, Mrs. Frost couldn't deny him a seat at our immaculate kitchen table, and heated his coffee for him. One day, however, George saw a crumb, and calling Mrs. Frost, said in his simple way,"Tisn't very clean!' After his luncheon, he always liked to rest awhile and read. He bought many books and always watched for the book sale in the Ladies' Aid Bazaar. One year, *Love Letters of an Old Maid* was not shown to him, but he spied it, saying, 'Sounds good, guess I'll take it.' He often gave his books to the library of which he was janitor for many years, charging twenty-five cents a week for his services, but loving to read there. He was also generous in his contributions to the church.

The question of help in the country is not without its difficulties and perplexities and occasionally there have been days and even weeks when we relied upon help by the day. When even that failed, in a spirit of desperation Mrs. Frost asked George, 'Have you ever scrubbed a kitchen floor?' 'No, Ma'am, but I can try,' replied the optimistic soul. He was assured that he would be given directions from time to time, but in so doing, Mrs. Frost noticed with increasing concern that the poor old fellow kept feeling of the small of his back as if it distressed him. Finally, in reply to her question, 'George, does your back hurt you that much?' he grinned rather shame-facedly and said, 'No, Ma'am, I was afraid my shirt-tail wasn't long enough.'

Poor George walked up from the village one day for the sole pur-pose of asking one of our neighbors, 'What is that *staff* that they keep in the observatory?' I was much touched when after his death there was found in his simple diary the oft-repeated entry, 'Saw Professor Frost pass by today.'

A whole book could be written on the succession of kindly helpers who worked early and late for our comfort. They were representa-tives of many nations. Yocie, our Japanese cook, could walk on his hands, and he made griddle cakes with faces in them to entertain the children. He finally 'thought best to leave wordlessly.' Mrs. Firey worked for Mrs. Frost one winter and was succeeded by Mrs. Freeze as the summer approached. One woman, not quite happy at home, used us as an outlet, and would finally exclaim after finding a sympa-thetic listener, 'Wasn't I a fool to marry that man?' But many of those faithful young women who so generously served us are now mothers of fine children who have received a good education in the excellent public schools of Walworth County.

CHAPTER XX

WAR

My RESIDENCE in such an armed camp as was Strassburg in 1890, with its garrison of twenty or more regiments, and later at the imperial country seat in Potsdam, where military uniforms were almost more abundant than civilian dress, naturally led me to think often of the effect of such armaments on world peace. The haughty attitude of the gay officers when they walked the streets of Berlin and Potsdam always seemed to me offensive to the spirit of liberty. There was a class consciousness among the army men that the destiny of the nation lay in their hands, and this was, of course, fostered by the authorities in power around the Emperor. I often tried to impress my German friends with the fact that I seldom saw a soldier in the United States and that the peaceful expansion of a country could take place without the use of the sword. An army was the plaything of a king, and the best entertainment that he could lay before a visiting sovereign was a review of his picked troops. Of course the Hohenzollern family had developed into an imperial dynasty from being petty margraves in Prussia chiefly by pure military aggression against less powerful neighbors. The whole system was provocative. I always heard stories from men who had been reserve officers to the effect that under the guidance of that great military genius, von Moltke, plans for instant mobilization had been prepared for every possible contingency, and that even the master of every large railway station had in his safe sealed time-tables that were to go into effect upon the receipt of a telegraphic message. Germany always seemed to entertain the fear that some military adventurer would get into power in France and make it necessary for the Teutonic forces to go over and teach him the lesson of defeat. This had been done in 1870. It was openly said that the route to Paris would be through Belgium despite the agreement of different countries for the neutralization of that country in the event of war. Even in the nineties the young Emperor was being much influenced by those who wished the Reich to become a first-class naval power. All of this, as I have said,

seemed decidedly provocative and gave the impression that the empire would rise to still greater heights by impressing its domination
upon some smaller powers with relatively weak armies and navies.
Of course in earlier times, might rather than right had been the chief
factor in the argument. The fleets of England undoubtedly had
sailed the seas in search of the most important stations or whole regions for England to acquire. With the arrival of the twentieth century, however, such policies as 'grab where you may' ought to be entirely out of date, although the Boxer Rebellion in China and the
war between Russia and Japan had still opened opportunities for
this process of confiscation from weaker countries such as China.

I came home from Germany thoroughly convinced of the futility
of the constant striving for supremacy in military equipment and that
it could only lead to trouble.

The Balkan War occurred in the autumn of 1912 while we were in
Europe, and the Bulgars with their allies severely threatened the
Turks with the loss of Constantinople. On each side military experts for the other Powers were giving advice in this deadly game of
chess, German officers having held influential positions in training
the Turkish Army. The danger of a general conflagration was
plain, and there were some statesmen in Germany who were evidently
watching for the time when the big test for all this military preparation should be made. The members of my family did not share my
concern about the matter, but I made arrangements to obtain cash
readily so that we might return to America in case the strain of keeping the peace proved too great for Russia and Germany. It was not
surprising then that a *casus belli* was found in July, 1914, in the out-
rageous murder of the Austrian Grand Duke and his wife at Serajevo. A greater effort to delay mobilization by the responsible
leaders in Austria, Russia, and Germany might have postponed the
outbreak of hostilities, but I do not believe that the delay would have
been long.

A state of war quickly develops public hysteria. Of course we in
America were affronted by the deliberate disregard of treaties on the
part of Germany in respect to the invasion of the rights of Belgium,
but the propaganda that was being circulated throughout the world
against Germany because of alleged inhuman treatment of the citizens of Belgium was decidedly unjust. I suppose that the German

officers had received more instruction than those of any other army as to how to treat the populace of a neutral or invaded country. We sympathizers with the cause of the Allies spoke complacently of the expected advent of the great Russian 'Steam Roller' on the eastern frontier, but had *they* invaded the enemy's territory the civilian population would doubtless have suffered much more heavily than was the case on the western front. The German military authorities somehow had no regard for the sensibilities of America and always seemed to be doing just the wrong thing to affect American public opinion. It was, of course, inevitable that if we entered the war we should oppose the Central Powers, but the false propaganda developed on all sides constitutes one of the many outrages of war.

The idealistic utterances of Wilson in some of his great state papers certainly gave our intervention the character of a crusade in behalf of justice and liberty, and I believe that this was genuinely felt by a great part of our population and particularly by the troops which were being trained for service overseas. The aggressive action of our troops when they reached France under the strong leadership of Pershing was clearly in behalf of the French people who had suffered so heavily in a war that they had in no wise provoked. We also felt a strong sympathy for the sad losses of England and her dominions, as they played the rôle of defenders of the rights of weaker nations. The terrible losses on all sides were shocking to me as an ardent supporter of peace and strongly in favor of the outlawing of war, but it was apparent that the situation could not be brought to a definite conclusion except by the successful prosecution of the American effort. There were many ways in which each of us could do something to help the morale of our troops and of our people. My own service was necessarily limited to speaking as a four-minute man and to assisting in the drives for Liberty bonds and other monetary campaigns. I did, however, write, for the use of the Y.M.C.A. overseas, an astronomical lecture called a 'Picture-Look,' for which the observatory supplied slides. Many copies of this lecture and sets of slides were distributed for the use of our soldiers and sailors. I also began the construction in our shop of a small portable instrument, analogous to the Zeiss 'Blink stereo-comparator.' This was intended to show the existence of concealed emplacements of artillery by the comparison of successive pictures taken by scouting airplanes. The progress of this construction seemed to be of interest to the army, as at least two officers came to inspect it. It was never used, however, as the armistice came before the device could be completed.

It certainly is a profound regret to all thinking Americans that our idealistic intentions were not realized after the Treaty of Versailles had been finally adopted. Incidentally, it always seemed to me that Wilson made a great mistake in participating personally at Versailles. He might have been justified in making one trip to study the situation at first hand, but I felt that he should have stayed in Washington and should have sent as his representatives our greatest statesmen and diplomats regardless of parties to decide on such terms of peace as would ultimately best heal the terrible wounds of war. I thoroughly sympathized with Wilson's efforts in behalf of the League of Nations despite our traditional avoidance of European entanglements, and I believe that the cause of peaceful rehabilitation was greatly delayed by the selfish action of a few jealous Senators, chiefly in the Republican Party. When broad-minded statesmen like Taft and Hughes and Root threw their influence in behalf of the World Court and the League of Nations, I see no reason why less influential Republican members of Congress should not have followed their lead.

Our generation has never had a thrill equal to that which stirred our souls when we heard on November 11, 1918, that the war was at an end and that the terms of the armistice had been signed. Our little village was doubtless characteristic of many others in its demonstrations of joy. Men and women wept without constraint, church bells rang, locomotives in the yards blew their loudest blasts. There was open rejoicing in the hearts of men; there would be no more fighting. When will civilization educate man to control the fighting instinct which seems to be born in him! It shows itself even in early childhood, and was expressed by a young friend of mine who retorted after a reprimand from his mother, 'I never seem to like a boy until after I have licked him.' War will never be abolished as long as men, 'but children of larger growth' as Dryden says, cannot settle their difficulties by reason and intelligence instead of reverting to the methods of uncivilized man.

Fourteen years have passed since the signing of the Versailles Treaty and there has been, meanwhile, much discussion at Geneva

by the League of Nations and at separate capitals by leading statesmen of ways and means by which the burden imposed by competi-
tive armaments can be lifted from the shoulders of a weary world.
The good faith of the United States in all of these attempts to re-
move the specter of war as far as possible from reality cannot be
doubted, and the Kellogg Pact is a genuine contribution toward international idealism, but there is much to be done to rid the world
of the idea that armed force gives the only assurance that a country
can develop peacefully. I am not at all one of those who believes that
war cannot be eliminated from international relations and that the
scourge must continue as a perpetual threat. On the contrary, I believe very heartily that public sentiment can be educated to the
point of abolishing wars quite as well as we have succeeded in most
countries in eliminating the settlement of personal differences by
the use of arms, leaving it to the courts to decide troubles between individuals. The practice of privateering on the sea has been given up
within the century past, and there have been genuine signs of progress. But after all, good will and brisk and friendly commercial relations are the best guarantees of a fraternal spirit among nations.
The erection of high tariff walls does not seem to me to be consistent
with the best development of international relations. What would be
gained if every country adopted legislation which practically cut off
import trade? There is no doubt that another great European war
would shake our civilization to its foundations. We can no longer
be protected from air raids, and immense populations concentrated in
large cities might easily be snuffed out by the devilish use of poison
gases. Many of the newspapers that might do much toward spreading
the doctrine of good will are controlled by persons full of the jingo
spirit of aggression and conquest. It is hard for the many organizations in behalf of peace to counteract the daily insinuations and sinis-
ter innuendoes against other nations by cartoons, distorted special
correspondence, and editorials in irresponsible journals, many of
which have large circulations. The best example of what may be
done by good will is illustrated in the peaceful, unprotected frontier
more than four thousand miles long between our country and our
neighbors in the Canadian Dominion.

In spite of my strong sentiment for the maintenance of peace and
my ingrained opposition to military aggression against other coun-

tries, I believe most firmly in the maintenance of an adequate defense of our continent against its insidious invasion by those fanatics who desire most of all to overthrow our form of government and destroy our liberties in an effort to introduce the fantastic doctrines which have been dominant in Russia for more than a decade. I see no possible application in our country of any phases of communism. But leaders of the movement at Moscow have skillful agents in every capitalistic country who are ready to turn any unfortunate economic condition into an argument in behalf of their doctrines. I frankly fear these influences and believe that we must always be ready to take the most determined steps to prevent any encroachment upon our form of government from outside the country or within it. The fundamental effect of communism as practiced in Russia would seem to be to destroy every item of individual liberty, to make the citizen and his family wholly subservient to the deluded policies of the men in power.

Their government, with some brilliant exceptions, seems to be still guided by ignorant partisans. And the whole system where a party controls a state is the total abnegation of the doctrine of liberty. That the members of the party and only members of that party should exercise the powers of government seems to be wholly restrictive of civil liberty whether the members of the party wear red shirts, gray shirts, black shirts, or no shirts at all. To protect ourselves from the dominance of these crazy notions is the duty of intelligent citizens in every community and in their voting for the administration of their state. Education and good will are the best antidotes within the people against the spread of these doctrines which are so strongly opposed to liberty, while the proper military defense should be maintained against invasion by any delirious forces of communism.

Capitalism doubtless has sins enough to atone for and to correct in the sacrifice of men to things, but there has been an immense change, mostly in the direction of betterment, during the five decades since I began to take an interest in public affairs and to be influenced by the sturdy democracy of the *Springfield Republican*, which I regularly read in my youth.

The fifteen years that have passed since the end of the war have not, in spite of some optimism, greatly diminished international suspicion or inspired fraternal confidence. Travel between the different countries has been greatly bothered with passports and other regulations which were formerly passing into abeyance. I took my family to Europe in 1912 without a passport and had no difficulty. There has been plenty of trouble between the inhabitants along frontiers that were changed by the Versailles Treaty and no doubt much injustice was done by it. It seems to be humanly impossible to atone for early acts of oppression by interchanging the oppressor and oppressed. There is no doubt that some nations like that of Czecho-Slovakia have greatly improved their condition under an enlightened and independent government, and the fringe of small republics formed from the so-called Baltic Provinces have undoubtedly felt the breach of liberty, but Poland and Hungary have fallen into the hands of dictators. Political liberty for the individual thus far seems to be too strong a drink for them.

General W. T. Sherman in his famous utterance declared 'War is hell,' but he little dreamed of the indescribable hellishness and the awful turmoil of modern warfare as was practiced in the World War and which would be experienced even beyond our conception should we ever be plunged into another such devilish conflict. We are a generation saddened and sullied, saddened by the most fearful tragedy of our times and sullied by the filth and terror of crime which had its birth on the battlefields. What is civilization if it cannot abolish war, if it fails to give us happiness, freedom, and justice, and hence 'peace on earth'? It seems to me very strange that none of our many able economists have as yet suggested a satisfactory solution for the plight in which our great country, favored by Nature more than any other, finds itself in this year of 1933. There should be some way to break the vicious circle of overproduction, unemployment, and hunger. After the depression is over, we shall doubtless look back and find that it had some benefits. There must be less extravagance, less profligate expenditure of taxes, and better standards of conduct in the new order of things, or our civilization will break down.

CHAPTER XXI

BLINDNESS

BY RIGHTS I did not have the proper inheritance in eyesight to become an astronomer. My mother was strongly myopic, and I evidently inherited the characteristics of my eyes from her. As a small boy I could never see the 'lone pine,' a fine relic of the early growth on the crest of one of the distant Vermont hills and visible to normal persons in the village. Oddly enough, my parents did not definitely seem to detect my nearsightedness until I was about nine years old, although I had been an industrious reader for some time before this. I began to wear glasses at about ten years of age and had all the vicissitudes with them as to loss, breakage, etc., which was to be expected of a lively boy. Myopia increased as my studies went on, but I had no particular trouble until about 1907, when I was over forty years of age, when a rotation of the line of astigmatism puzzled and disturbed my oculist. At that time I had to give up reading for three months or more, and I at once saw the great advantage of training the memory so that the spoken word could take the place of vision. It was of distinct value to be able to remember things accurately and thus avoid the continual necessity of consulting books. Reading was a very important thing for me because we had in our observatory library about eighty exchanges for the *Astrophysical Journal*, in various languages, and I tried each month to look them over and bring to the attention of members of the staff articles that might be of interest to them, especially when these articles were not in English. It was a great relief when I was able to resume my reading and the measurement of photographs of spectra under the microscope. Serious trouble with my eyes began one cold winter night, specifically on December 15, 1915, when I was working alone at the forty-inch telescope, photographing the spectrum of a rather faint star, by name 20 Persei. I had difficulty in seeing the divisions of the circle and in guiding after I had brought the star into proper position upon the slit of the spectroscope. I carried on the exposure until an assistant arrived and then found that vision in the right eye was greatly reduced. I had my own fear of what was the trouble, because my mother had suffered from a detached retina. My fears were unfortunately well founded. Although there were on record cases of the partial cure for this difficulty, the process was so difficult and the treatment so long that we decided it was too doubtful an experiment. Vision in this eye thereafter constantly diminished and was entirely gone in about a year. It again became necessary for me to greatly restrict my reading.

Coming up on the train from Chicago one day in the spring of 1917, and not being allowed to read, I amused myself by inditing a brief advertisement which I asked the editor of the *Lake Geneva News* to insert in his paper. It was inspired by the fact that a male Kentucky cardinal was found to be spending the winter in the village of Williams Bay. I called him the Widower. My advertisement read as follows:

> *Wife Wanted* — Widower, who has found this region pleasant for permanent residence, despite the long winter, seeks a congenial mate. No qualification as cook or seamstress necessary, and dowry is no object. Successful applicant must be a home-maker and desirous of raising a fair-sized family. She must be musical, and preferably a native of Kentucky, No objection to a widow. Address — C. Cardinalis, White Oak Lodge, Williams Bay, Wis.

Some person not known to me evidently cut it out and sent it to B. L. T. of the *Chicago Tribune* for his Line O'Type column. He added the caption, 'Add Signs of Spring,' under the impression that the widower was human. I afterwards wrote to him that if he knew his Audubon as well as his Horace, he would not have been fooled. His column being sent out through the country by syndicate gave my widower much publicity. In consequence many letters were received at Williams Bay and given to me by the postmaster upon my representation that I was the nearest friend of C. Cardinalis. These letters came from blondes and brunettes in different parts of the country, and each applicant claimed to fulfill all the requirements. A selection of their replies was later printed for the amusement of the readers of the local paper.

I was quite accustomed to receive over the telephone word that my widower had been seen here and there. He fortunately made the wisest choice of a permanent residence by going to the charming lake shore estate, 'Wychwood,' of Mr. and Mrs. Charles L. Hutchinson. His coming gave great delight to them and their guests as they saw this brilliant fellow on their bird table. It occurred to Mr. Hutchinson that, as a member of the Lincoln Park Board, he might be able to get a female cardinal from the Lincoln Park Aviary. When he found that one could be spared, he brought her to Lake Geneva in a cage and placed her in the screened porch of the foreman's cottage. The widower courted her for ten days and then it was thought safe to release the lady. The pair promptly began to build their nest, and thereafter the number of cardinals in this vicinity multiplied rapidly. As many as five broods have been known to be raised at Wychwood in a single season. When once established, these birds do not migrate, and their song is heard through a long season. It pays to advertise.

It was not long before I found that I could get on quite well with one eye and I was even allowed to measure under the microscope to a limited extent. A new difficulty, however, soon arose. That wonderful oculist, Dr. Wilmer of Washington, and his associate Dr. Burke, began to give attention to my left eye. After a year they told me that they could see a small cataract beginning to make its appearance, but they could not foresee whether it would develop rapidly or slowly. The latter condition was what occurred. Of course, various palliatives were employed, but the impairment of vision went on gradually. Then in 1921, 'adding insult to injury,' a hemorrhage occurred in this eye which made reading quite impossible and even made it difficult to see for ordinary purposes.

After a few months, this hemorrhage cleared up entirely and I was left with three or four per cent of vision which served me in good stead for several years. The question of an operation had to be deferred until the so-called ripening of the cataract, and it was not until about 1930 that this stage was regarded as reached. There was always the danger that an operation would be followed by a detachment of the retina, and the best advice seemed to be against taking the chance.

When a misfortune like this comes upon a person, it calls for will power and a spirit of adaptation to the circumstances. The restrictions and hardships during the several periods when I had been unable to read or to see much, had trained me to meet this emergency. Since I knew so well the location of every object in the observatory and the details of the separate instruments, I found it far less difficult than might have been expected to fulfill my duties as Director, and keep in touch with the various researches being carried on by the specialists of our staff. With a good memory and an adequate imagination, one can see much without the use of the eyes. The descriptions in printed articles can be interpreted, but there is the added difficulty that one must imagine the appearance of the photographs or of the diagrams from the verbal descriptions, All members of the staff and the graduate students have been exceedingly kind in reading to me and in describing the progress of their work.

It has not seemed quite fair play that I should be expected to pose as a blind man just because I lost my sight after middle age and found ways of carrying on despite the handicap. It so happened that I had given careful attention to the phenomena of Nature, had traveled considerably, and had stored away many imperishable memories. I often say that I should have no cause for complaint, as I have perhaps been privileged to see more than is allotted to the average individual. It is surprising how many people go about their business with imperfect vision; in fact, I am told that perfect eyes are the exception. When our family was in Naples we picked up from the blind beggars on the street the phrase 'povero caeco' (poor and blind). I did not realize that after the depression this double term would apply so well to me.

For those hours when I was not at the observatory, it was necessary to develop new forms of interest. I had been very proud of my rose garden and it was a real deprivation to give it up. I had been raising roses for about twenty years and took much of my exercise in the garden. I had experimented with more than two hundred varieties and had been quite successful in obtaining fine blooms from many of them. Every day Mrs. Frost had a display of about a hundred of my best specimens on a fine old mahogany table in the living-room, and this attracted many visitors, both friends and strangers. I made some study of the pedigree of the roses and once lectured on the subject before the Lake Geneva Garden Club with the title, 'The Blood of the Queen.' It seems rather a pity that some of the fine hybrid tea roses which can be grown in gardens have been sacrificed to fashion. Among these my favorites were the La France with its unequaled perfume, the Etoile de France, the Hoosier Beauty, and the Killarney. And one will never forget among the hybrid perpetuals the lovely white Frau Karl Druschki or the gorgeous red Ulrich Brunner. After it became too difficult for me to work on the delicate roses in the garden, I specialized more in hardy varieties. One of these is the Siberian rose (*Rosa spinosissima* var. Altaica), which is not often found in the market. Mr. C. L. Hutchinson gave me a few plants which he had raised from shoots presented to him by Mr. Egan of Highland Park, Illinois. These are not only hardy, but grow rapidly, have no insect enemies, and develop many shoots around the roots from which new plants may be started. One of my pleasures has been the distribution to my friends of over ninety of these shoots. They seem to transplant easily in almost any section of the country. The plant blooms profusely, the blossoms being single like a wild rose, and of a creamy-white color. This is our earliest blooming rose, our first date being May 19.

It was natural with my impairment of vision to devote myself more than ever to the general study of Nature. I wrote for local newspapers or other publications on various topics, such as the seventeen-year locusts who had visited us in 1905 and came again in great numbers in 1922.

I took a good deal of interest in the lotus which grew abundantly in Grass Lake, Illinois, about twenty-five miles east of Lake Geneva, and gave some thought to the possibility of starting them in our neighboring lakes. There are, of course, many places along the Mississippi River where this interesting water plant grows, and I obtained a record of at least seventeen places in Wisconsin. It is the American chinkapin (*Nelumbo lutea*). The waters of Lake Como and certain parts of Lake Delavan seemed shallow enough and suited for the growth of this interesting plant, so I gathered quantities of the seeds in the autumn and planted them in all sorts of ways in Lake Como, but without apparent success. Probably the fresh shoots from the germinating seeds were too attractive to the fish and the muskrats. The plant grows in the mud from large tubers, in appearance something like sweet potatoes. Friends who had heard of my interest kindly secured some of these roots which I planted in what seemed to be suitable places. Only once was I successful in getting a start from these tubers, but something prevented the continued growth of the plants. However, I was able during the winter to cause the seeds to germinate in a vase in my office and even got them to grow to a height of thirty inches. It was impossible, however, to transplant them. They always died. But I believe that with peristence it could be done.

The growth of the trees and shrubbery that were set out in the beds around the observatory according to the Olmsted plan in the years 1914 and '15 was a great source of satisfaction to me and I took much of my exercise in going about to inspect them. We have made a card catalogue of the trees and of the beds of shrubs. Thus we will have a permanent record of their history. Some of the elms planted in 1914 with a diameter of four inches had reached in sixteen years a diameter of sixteen inches.

One naturally gets to have his favorites among the trees. Aside from the original oaks, hickories, cherries, locusts, and poplars, there are about eighty varieties of trees and shrubs on the grounds. Among the evergreens, my prime favorite is the Colorado Concolor fir (*Abies concolor*). Excellent specimens of these from a reliable nursery were set out, but they were of small size. They are a little slow in getting started, but after a couple of years they begin to grow rapidly into shapely trees forming a dense mass of green with a distinct shading of grayish-blue. Their needles are very fragrant, and for a few weeks in spring they are soft and pliable. The European larches are also attractive. They are, of course, not evergreens, but deciduous. Their new growth is always bright and delicate, and the tracery of their branches is pleasing in winter. The Olmsted plan called for a large number of white pines of which only about twenty-five were set out. They have given us much trouble and have required constant spraying, but after they reach a height of ten to twenty feet they will probably outgrow this difficulty. It seems rather peculiar that they should be hard to raise here, as they probably originally covered much of this region and still abound in northern Wisconsin.

The oleasters (*Elæagnus angustifolia*), commonly known as the Russian olive, were planted around the two small domes, and have produced a pleasing effect with their gray-green leaves and their somewhat gnarled habit resembling the European olives. They have grown rapidly to a present height of nearly thirty feet, and produce quantities of small fruit, about as large as peas. Near them is a fine bed of the old Persian yellow roses, so gay in June. I planted this bed from shoots which I brought over from my own garden. The lindens, both of the American and European variety, are beautiful, especially when in blossom, and have a pungent odor. I have taken a special interest in two specimens of the yellowwood (*Cladrastis lutea*). Their bark is smooth and gray like that of the beech, and they are so covered with white blooms that Professor Liberty Bailey has called them the handsomest flowering tree in America. Our Norway maples have been successful and are in foliage about a month longer than the sugar maples, but their autumn coloring is yellow rather than red. I hope that my experiment with three or four beeches will be successful, as it has been thus far, as they are lovely both in summer and winter. The honeysuckles, hawthorns, and spireas make a fine show when they are in bloom. One of our striking exhibits at the end of June and the beginning of July is a large bed of the common prairie rose (*Rosa setigera*). They are entirely hardy and require little attention, and they probably have more than ten thousand blooms during the two or three weeks when they are in flower. We have a fine specimen of the tamarisk (*Tamarix odessana*), which I put in a protected place south of the meridian room where it has grown to be nearly twenty feet high. Its foliage is very delicate, and the lavender blooms come twice in the season, sometimes giving us almost eight weeks of flowering.

We had an interesting experience on a Sunday morning late in August. Dr. A. A. Michelson was spending the week-end with us and shared our surprise at the phenomenon new to us all. On looking out of our sleeping-room that morning we were greatly astonished to find that two thrifty oaks had apparently suffered a complete blight during the night. The verdant leaves of the previous day seemed to be a mass of brown more than a month before there was any reason to expect such a change. Later examination showed that a countless swarm of the large monarch butterflies had alighted upon those two trees in the course of their migration, spending a night and a part of the next day almost motionless, as if resting. We knew, of course, that this species and some others do regularly migrate. A zoölogist informs me that the monarchs do not travel far and seldom survive a winter.

During my period of exercise, I used to be joyfully accompanied by our faithful thoroughbred pointer dog, 'Pepper' by name. He was almost pure white except for his brown ears and a few characteristic light-brown spots on his body. He really belonged to our boy Ben to whom he had been given by Colonel Davidson of the Military Academy across the lake. Pepper lived with us for six years, a perfect gentleman, no bad habits, and devoted to us all as we were to him. During the time of his 'puppyhood,' we had a large screened tent in the yard, a tent large enough for five beds, many of which were occupied most of the time by our two boys and their friends, and, we later learned, by the dog. He did not always choose to sleep alone, we now understand, but his frequent scrubbings, of which he was always apprehensive and which he thoroughly detested, kept him fairly clean. Perhaps all dogs are intelligent, but we, of course, felt that Pepper was unusually endowed. For instance, on our village highway, Pepper, trotting along in quest of company or food, would watch, out of the corner of his eye, all passing automobiles. Ours never escaped him, and having changed our car nearly every two years, passing through the gamut from a Ford and a Reo to several Buicks, we could never understand what part of the outfit gave him the clue.

It was said of him that he doubtless resented being deprived of his hunting inheritance, and consoled himself by spying out the village garbage-cans, every one of which he evidently located. He was very friendly to everyone, but especially devoted to our friend and neighbor, Dr. Paul B. Jenkins. Pepper knew that Dr. Jenkins loved dogs, and that there was a comfortable and very elegant couch upon which a favored dog might slumber any evening when he scratched upon their door. On winter evenings we were sometimes worried by his long absence, and would ring their telephone 1274-J-3 (one of those grand long party-line numbers) to ask for our wandering dog. When that telephone rang, Pepper's head and ears would give an answering response, and as soon as he heard my whistle through the receiver would rush to the door and, with a questioning look and rapid wagging of the tail, ask to be allowed to depart.

It is a calamity in the home when the span of a dog's life is over, but it is a real tragedy when a shot from the gun of a despicable man takes the life of a dog in his prime, as happened to our

beloved Pepper on the Saturday before Easter in the year 1926.
It is surprising how many interests may develop along a short and
perfectly familiar pathway from the house to the observatory, a distance of only one hundred and fifty yards. It is perfectly evident, too,
that with the loss of sight the other senses, particularly those of hearing and smell, may be enhanced by deliberate intention. The
character of the adornments of this walk changes greatly in the different seasons. In lilac time, it is fragrant with the tall bushes that bend
over it, and after a rainy day they often bring an unexpected shower
to my face. Across the road in June is the fragrance of the bloom of
the high-bush cranberry, and farther on the *Euonymus alatus*, a tall
shrub of Japanese origin, whose every twig has an odd four-sided
section, each side slightly concave and roughly irregular. For about
three weeks in the autumn this bed is ablaze with flaming cerise-
colored leaves. Just beyond this bed the pungent odor of the
European linden and the medicinal perfume of the Russian olives are
tempered by the fragrance from a small bed of roses of the hybrid
Madam Charles Frederick Worth. This remarkable rose was produced at the experiment station of the State of Iowa. It has the
flavor of international romance. The hybridizer succeeded in crossing the fragrant and delicate General Jacqueminot of France with the
hardy, stalwart Madame Rugosa of Japan. It thus possesses the
fragrance of the General with the floriferous quality of the Rugosa.
I have sometimes counted over a hundred buds and blooms on these
four bushes at their first blooming in June, and they normally produce their scarlet and very double flowers in each month, sometimes
even late in October. So I stop at this point in the path and pick me
a bloom for my buttonhole, for it has been a habit of my life in the
country always to wear a favorite flower beginning with the first
Narcissus poeticus from my garden. There are six other kinds of roses
in the bed as we near the brownstone steps, and three kinds of dog-
wood, each of which blooms twice, but all at slightly different dates.
As we go up the steps we pass the tall honeysuckles which are full of
bloom in their season and give a fine place for the nest of the catbird.
The Japanese barberry is so dense and so well protected by thorns
that the brown thrashers find it an ideal place for their housekeeping,
and baby bunnies hop under it in safety from the dogs. The greatest
glory of the Japanese barberry is in the autumn when both leaves

and scarlet fruit are brilliant. If I am out for exercise, I may follow this path an equal distance beyond the steps to the door of the building of the Bruce telescope, where one can hear the wind soughing in the branches of the *Ponderosa* pines which were planted near that building.

And here, as elsewhere along my path, I am greeted by the call of the chickadee, its note which many mistake for that of the phœbe. When I repeat their high-pitched tones they usually answer and often come within a few feet to inquire who is using their call without permission of the copyright owner. These friendly little black-and-white titmice are with us the whole year, and like their friends the nuthatches are our most constant visitors at the birds' feeding-table. In spring and summer the orioles and rose-breasted grosbeaks are favorites who sing in the maples near the path and whose warbling songs can be imitated with some degree of success. In early spring I have the rare pleasure of hearing the exquisite morning rhapsody of the ruby-crowned kinglet. It was also on this path that my attention was once attracted by a fine imitation of the whip-poor-will given at the very end of the rollicking medley of the brown thrasher. He had learned his lesson well when he added this unusual call to his efforts in mimicry. This particular thrasher spent two different summers with us, not consecutive, but I have not heard of another case like it. It is from this path that on a May evening one sometimes hears high up in the air the rush of a million wings of the June-bugs which have emerged that day from the ground and are taking their first flight in a great cloud. It reminds me of the words in Haydn's *Creation*: 'Unnumbered as the sands, in swarms arose the host of insects.'

When my sweet little granddaughter Holly, 'half five and half six,' as she used to say of her age, spent six weeks with us in the spring of 1931, she always wished to lead her granddaddy along this path as he went to his office, and before we crossed the road, she invariably followed the precept which I had given her, 'Stop, look, and listen,' lest we might be overtaken by an automobile driving through the grounds. The little girl had great delight in watching some birds' nests with me, and each day we must stop and see the full-breasted mother robin sitting on her nest in the honeysuckles, 'that big, fat woman,' as she called her. We found in a Concolor fir the robin's nest which I knew must be there from the hasty flutter of the wings and anxious call of the birds as they flew away when we approached the tree. The nest was hardly two feet from the ground, and we watched them finish it, each day afterward making one visit to see if an egg was added. Only three were laid. After that we made our visits carefully, as the little ones were hatched, and we finally saw them large enough to leave the nest. To those who are less familiar with bird ways, one who knows the birds well may perhaps seem to have an extra sense in regard to them. When I pointed to an indigo-bird singing in the top of a tree, my friend from New York found it difficult to believe that I did not see the singer. Of course I knew that it was his regular habit to sing from the very top of the apple tree.

Shortly after midsummer, when the voices of the song-birds have become silent, there is much to hear of the music of the multitudinous insects of the evening chanting their rhythmic, persistently repeated tones. It may seem strange that the sense of hearing suggested to me the study of the little creatures which give the greatest volume of insect harmony in August and September. For years, I knew neither the name nor the habits of these insects. They proved to be the 'snowy tree cricket' (*Œcanthus niveus*), who live in bushes or low trees, are very small, have tiny transparent light-green wings, and have no resemblance whatever to the ordinary house cricket. I was surprised to find that the specimens which I located by their continuous chirps occupied the same bush for the whole season of their song. It was amusing to give them names of current cartoon celebrities, such as *Sam* and *Henry*, *Andy Gump*, etc. Half a dozen of these little creatures can make an acre ring as if there were a thousand cricket musicians expressing their satisfaction with Nature. The male cricket, strange as it may seem, is the one that does the talking, and it is interesting to watch him (if you can catch him) as he raises his gauzy wings at right angles to his body, shuffling the edges of the wings together to give his high-pitched chirps.

It began to be obvious that the speed of their chirping was closely related to the temperature of the air. After recording the number of chirps per minute on a warm, a medium, and a cold night, it was readily possible to draw the straight line which gave the law of this correlation. The formula is $y = ax + b$, where y is the temperature, x is the number of chirps per unit of time, and a is the coefficient to be determined, while *b* is the temperature at which the chirping stops, 42°. This is the point at which his sensitive mechanism is apparently too chilled for action. The formula shows that the number of chirps will be one per second at 55°, two per second at 68°, three per second at 82°, and four per second at 95°. I am greatly impressed by the effect of the environmental temperature upon the nervous systems of these small insects. They are irresistibly compelled to time their considerable body motion to the temperature of the surrounding air, and this with the greatest precision. Incidentally, I have often observed the effect of beats when one of the chirpers happens to be more protected than his fellow a few feet away. By counting the beats between the two frequencies, it would be possible to detect differences of temperature of a small fraction of a degree, probably as little as one-tenth.

Putting my formula into the simplest terms, the temperature may be found by counting the number of chirps in thirteen seconds and adding this to forty-two. It is surprising how closely these living thermometers record the true state of the air, for the result is usually within a degree of the reading of the thermometer. It was after considerable correspondence with our State Entomologist that we learned that the thermal sensitiveness of this snowy tree cricket had been noted some years ago by a physicist whose formula was only slightly different from mine. A meteorologist in Florida suggested that it was a great pity that he could not have had some of these crickets when his thermometers were carried away in the great hurricane of September 16–17, 1928. These crickets are often guideposts for me, as are the katydids, whose stationary habits are the same. I missed my path one evening, taking a spur to the right, but a katydid, none of which live along my regular route home, told me of my mistake.

There is no doubt that the subjection to the influence of the surrounding temperature is felt by many other insects. I have distinctly observed it in the case of the katydid, but since his story is repeated only at intervals, it cannot be studied with any such precision. Entomologists, however, might well study the acoustical responses of other varieties of insects whose rate of emitting sound may be so fast as to produce an actual musical note, that is to say, of the order of several hundred vibrations per second.

I was much intrigued one evening to hear in a tree near the tennis court the curious throat-scraping tones of some young owls. Imitating the cooing notes of the mother owl, a very simple call, I quickly received an answering response from the young brood. These were young screech owls, little fluffy, brownish creatures who light upon a branch as softly as a feather.

Early this last spring, another slight sound attracted my attention as I walked past the tower of the twenty-four-inch dome. The leaves on the ground seemed to be stirred as by a light patter of rain. The sky was clear, for we had just spoken of the brilliance of the star Arcturus. And then it came to me that the sound must be that of the night-crawlers so dear to the heart of the fisherman! They were certainly in a hurry to have their first taste of freedom, for with the aid of a flashlight, we counted twenty-four to the square foot. Not long afterward, I heard of a highway so covered by them on that same day that a fire-engine was called out to wash them off in order to make traffic safe.

One evening I was walking home accompanied by the famous Willetta Huggins and three other girls from the State School for the Blind in Janesville. Willetta was at that time not only blind, but deaf, and could converse only through the medium of sound-waves. She said that she could feel the scratching noise of my cane on the cement walk. She could also feel, as I do from air currents, the approach to a wall or building. The most remarkable thing about Willetta was her ability to recognize colors and even shades of color entirely by the sense of smell. I understand that Willetta has since recovered both her eyesight and hearing, and attributes her recovery to Christian Science.

We invited this group of girls to have dinner with us and they were amused and pleased with a clock system which I had adopted for my dinner plate. One of the difficulties which a blind person encounters is to locate the special items of food. Although each article of food had been cut for me and carefully arranged upon my plate, it was at first confusing to find the different varieties. So we adopted the clock system where I am told, 'Your meat is at twelve o'clock, your beans at six o'clock, etc.' It has been a great convenience.

That evening at dinner, I told the girls about an expression which my father used and of which I should like to find the origin. When we were permitted to have that universal and excellent product of corned beef and potatoes with its fragrant brown crust, my father was accustomed to say, with some assumed solemnity, 'In the name of the Prophet, Hash.' On one occasion, when dining at the home of our gifted friends, Mr. and Mrs. Kellogg Fairbank, I raised the question with my hostess as to whether her father, a New-Englander and a graduate of Dartmouth a few years earlier than my father, might not have used the same expression. It was her recollection that the selfsame invocation had been used by him. My friend and colleague, James Weber Linn, who is also often a guest in these delightful groups, could not throw light on this particular phrase, but enlivened the discussions with pungent and pertinent comment. And speaking of the prophets, I happen to recall that Mr. Linn and my wife, who had both been reared in ministerial families, remembered how their parents had been taught to memorize the books of the prophets. Mrs. Frost's mother said that as a little girl she was taught them by stringing together the first syllables of the names in order: Ho, Jo, Am — Ob, Jo, Mi, Na — Ha, Ze, Ha, Ze, Ma. Of course she never forgot them.

From my walk there is a steep and rather stony path down through the shade of the oak woods to the lake and the observatory pier, where, every day in summer at five o'clock, gathers a jolly company of our staff with their families and guests. A springboard attracts those who like to dive, but of late years, I slip cautiously down the ladder, and with my cane swim out a hundred feet or more with someone in the water or on the pier to guide me.

In winter, we skate either here or on the ice in the Bay which may be frozen earlier. In the winter of 1932, I skated for the fiftieth year on the same pair of skates, those which I purchased with my hard-earned savings when I was fifteen. Winter sports have always added an enlivening feature to the otherwise dull season of the year. In the early days we constructed a course for coasting down the steep hill from the observatory through the woods, and then we negotiated the entrance to the Y.M.C.A. grounds, crashing out onto the lake over a special bridge of pier planks, which had to be adjusted every day owing to the heaving of the ice. Sometimes the momentum would carry the sled with its passengers a quarter of a mile out onto the ice, and then there would be much exercise in getting back to the starting point.

One of the most delightful sports is ice-boating, so keenly anticipated, but so frequently spoiled by snow. Our boys owned both ice-boats and a sail-boat, either given to them, or earned by them in various ways. Ordinarily the west end of the lake is frozen for eleven weeks, beginning on the average at the end of the first week in January. In a long, cold season, the ice may reach a thickness of over twenty-four inches, but there are always places to be watched where the wind pressure may make an open gap of water, changing in size from day to day. The ice usually breaks up eleven weeks later, or about March 27. I used to have a wager with Professor Barnard, and subsequently with Professor Barrett, in regard to the date of the final breaking-up of the ice. It was a rose against an apple. I generally won.

The presence of wild geese on the lake for about half of the year has been a matter of much interest and has added a flavor of pioneer days. The geese normally arrive from the North about October 10–15, spending their days in the prairies or in the cornfields, and returning to the lake over their various flyways toward evening, honking as they go, their V-shaped phalanxes forming and re-forming. There are often two hundred or more in a flock. The greater numbers go farther south, but many stay with us through the cold weather, squatting on the ice or sitting along the seams that have opened. As the warmer days of spring come, the influx of geese from the South is very great. We have estimated with care that there were sometimes as many as ten thousand geese on the lake at one time, but by the end of the first week in May, the last wild goose has generally left us for the North.

Of course, various kinds of ducks are on the lake in great abundance and the whistle of their wings can often be heard as they pass over the house. We have also seen quite a variety of the larger migrant birds, such as swans, cormorants, and eagles.

Sometimes we see from the window of our house a dozen or more ice-boats gracefully flitting about and with skaters enjoying themselves in groups at points where the ice is best. In recent years the municipalities of Lake Geneva and Williams Bay have aided in keeping the ice cleared and in providing electric lights and hockey rinks for sport in the evening. In winters when the ice was considered sufficiently safe, there developed a regular course for automobiles and teams between the villages of Fontana and Williams Bay and the city of Lake Geneva, six miles down the lake. Picturesqueness was added to the scene by the several colonies of fishhouses, flimsy little cabins that were pushed out onto the ice and provided with a stove for the comfort of the fisherman while he watched his lines and caught what he could through his holes in the ice. The cisco was a favorite variety for winter fishing, and the fish make delicious food.

A mysterious change took place in the life and habits of the cisco, which is a variety of whitefish and found abundantly also in Lake Michigan. Until about the year 1897, there would be in June a tremendous 'run' of the cisco. They would appear at the surface in immense shoals, and as they would bite at anything, large quantities of them were caught from rowboats hauled by steamers plying around these great swarms. At about this time in the spring, there appeared along the shores and over the lake a sort of fly known here as the 'cisco fly,' more properly termed 'day-fly,' so-called from the shortness of their lives. These flies were so numerous that it was sometimes very disagreeable to walk along the shore of the lake. There appeared to be a real connection between the flies and the swarming of the ciscoes on the surface of the lake. It seems to be a fact that after 1900 ciscoes were no longer seen at the surface in spring or summer, but after an interval of a few years they began to be caught in rather large numbers through the ice. Perch are also abundant in Lake Geneva, as are pickerel, of which specimens as large as twenty pounds have sometimes been brought in. Brook trout are also found in the lake, particularly at the mouths of some of the small streams. There are many more rock bass than largemouth black bass. However, in the early summer of 1932, the Conservation Commission, using a seine seven hundred feet long, procured near the shore of Williams Bay one hundred and twenty of the latter for breeding purposes at the State hatchery. From the ton of fish in the haul, only this variety of bass was chosen and only those which weighed between four and six pounds. They were returned to the lake in the autumn.

CHAPTER XXII

IN THE DAY'S WORK

AN ASTRONOMER who is observing at night as I did for many years from dark to daylight is, so to speak, burning the candle at both ends. I was often too weary to sleep and scarcely ever managed to get more than four or five hours.

In winter with the temperature fifteen to twenty degrees below zero one might not consider it a pleasant prospect to spend the night in a dome where the temperature has to be as nearly as possible like that outside, so that there shall be no rising currents of warmer air to spoil the definition of the stellar images. The greatest difficulty with which an astronomer has to contend is the weather. Cloudy skies prevent at critical times the observations for which preparation may have been made for days and weeks in advance. Still worse are the nights in winter when a beautifully transparent sky is spoiled by a sudden change of weather and a consequently troubled atmosphere. Then the images of the stars in the telescope, which should be sharp points like diamonds, are spread out to look like the flickering light of a candle. Often a long exposure has been begun and carried on for some time, only to be interrupted by this condition of 'bad seeing' so that it cannot be completed. Then the astronomer might as well fold up his tent like the Arab and quietly steal away.

Those who have visited a large observatory on such a night say that they will never forget that cold eerie place, silent except for the persistent ghostly ticking of the driving clock and the wind howling around the slit in the dome. But there the astronomer sits in his Eskimo suit or fur coat and cap with his eye glued to the eye-piece of the telescope, watching closely to see that his star does not drift away from the crossed spider-threads which mark the center of his field while a plate is being exposed.

Those long hours afford ample opportunity to consider not only the various unsolved riddles of the universe, but also to ponder upon the daily problems of life. Alone with the faithful engineer who never misses a night, there are things discussed in an intimate exchange of what might seem at times rather quaint philosophy. We relieve each other at periods when one 'goes below' for warmth or for a cup of coffee. The telescope is never idle except when something unforeseen gets out of order or the wheels upon which the dome rests and turns are completely frozen and refuse to move. This, however, rarely happens. During the day solar observations are constantly in progress. It is evident that we could never belong to a labor union. Of late we have more humanely divided the nights and have adopted a schedule whereby a man works either the first or the last half. Certain hours are given for the spectroscopic work; other hours for the program of determining stellar parallax (finding the distances of the stars); others for photometric work (the determination of the brightness of the stars), or for visual observations of double stars and other interesting objects with the micrometer.

It is perhaps fortunate for the astronomer that the severity of winter is relieved by the shorter, more comfortable nights of summer, and that he can rid himself of the weight of his heavy clothing.

We seldom have visitors during observing hours, as each observer is jealous of a moment's loss of time. About 1900, Mr. Hale, who was then Director, planned that several lectures should be given in the big dome. This proved to be of great interest to the summer residents and their guests around Lake Geneva, but the preparation was a serious one, as the floor which is an elevator had to be strongly propped from below, a distance of about twenty feet. After the lecture an opportunity was given to look through the telescope, but with a group of even fifty it is a long wait for someone if even two minutes are allowed for each person. It is really an unsatisfactory proceeding.

Occasionally, when one observer has finished and before the next one is ready to begin, we have shown our guests or friends of the university something of interest. Saturn with its rings is the favorite, but the Ring Nebula in Lyra (sometimes jokingly called the 'celestial doughnut') makes a popular appeal, not only because of its beauty, but because of its size. It is now estimated that the space within the Ring is large enough to hold thirty thousand of our solar systems. The Great Cluster in Hercules is another attractive object. When the conditions are good and the air is steady, thousands of sparkling points are seen, but packed so close together at the center as to be irresolvable. There are more than a million stars in the cluster and its distance from us is thirty thousand to forty thousand light-years. Its diameter is two hundred light-years. On one occasion some distinguished visitors were given an opportunity to see this great object in the telescope. One of them was much impressed. He remarked to the astronomer: 'So you say that each of those points of light is a sun and each one is larger than ours. And you allege that this cluster is so far away that the light requires thirty thousand to forty thousand years to reach us? Well' — with a sigh — 'if this is so, I guess that it doesn't really matter whether Bryan or Taft is elected.'

I recall one evening long ago when the serious Mr. Burnham was asked by a light-hearted débutante, as she coyly approached him at the telescope, 'And what are you going to show us, Mr. Burnham?' He replied in a matter-of-fact tone, 'A double star.' Said the young woman, clasping her hands, 'Oh, I'm perfectly crazy about double stars!'

In order to insure the admission to the observatory of his students and academic friends, Professor Philip Fox, who had been a member of our staff for a number of years and then director of the Observatory of Northwestern University at Evanston, Illinois, gave them as a password the astronomical term 'syzygy.' This is a Greek word meaning 'a yoking together' or 'in line,' but it can be so uttered as to simulate the discharge of a soda-water fountain. This word has served as an introduction to many in the course of the years and has probably never failed to open the doors to these special visitors. We might return the compliment by the use of the same term to introduce our friends to the office of the Adler Planetarium in Chicago of which Dr. Fox is now director.

It is unfortunately the case that the administrative duties of the director of a large observatory occupy much time that he would be glad to devote to research. I sometimes wonder how with so little sleep I could measure my plates under the microscope after a whole night of observing and still carry on my other work. Many of these duties were strictly of a research character in planning investigations for and with the members of the staff and overseeing the construction of new types of apparatus. The graduate instruction for students specializing in astrophysics and observational astronomy has always been an important function of the Yerkes Observatory, and much time and effort must be expended in directing and supervising this work in which the members of the staff co-operate.

In many cases the graduate students have come to us from foreign countries, and their induction into American ways of life and study has been pleasant and interesting. We have had students from at least ten different countries. The advent of these young men was sometimes amusing. I remember that on one dark night, as we entered our garage rather late, we heard on our path modern Greek being spoken by a new arrival. The visitor fortunately had an interpreter with him, but later learned to speak English. On another day a Japanese came to make his first call, and his English vocabulary consisted of the single word 'yiss.' In some cases advanced students come after they have received their doctors' degrees and are then registered as 'Volunteer Research Assistants.' Besides participating in the regular observations they are given a problem to work out and to publish over their own name.

Doctorates of Philosophy have been awarded by the university to seventeen for graduate work done at the observatory, and such a group constitutes a body of loyal alumni. It so happens that during the years of my directorship there were developed among the members of our staff no less than ten men who have assumed the directorship of other observatories. Thus there has been formed a group of men brought up under the influence of the Yerkes Observatory just as has been the case with certain of the older institutions.

During my years at the Yerkes Observatory my own researches have been chiefly in the study of the motions of stars in the line of sight. The results have been published either in the *Astrophysical Journal* or in the quarto volumes issued as 'The Publications of the Yerkes Observatory.' Six volumes have appeared and two parts of the seventh volume are in print. It has been difficult to raise funds for these special publications. As managing editor of the *Astrophysical Journal* for the last thirty years, I have necessarily had to devote much time to the reading of manuscripts and to the details of the proofs and of the illustrations. In the earlier years, I translated at the request of the authors many papers which had appeared in the *Proceedings* of the Prussian Academy of Sciences and other learned societies in Germany and in France. I have also written numerous scientific reviews and some biographies of deceased astronomers for the *Journal* as well as for the biographical series of the National Academy of Sciences. In 1906 I edited for the Carnegie Institution a long series of unpublished observations by the late Professor C. H. F. Peters of Hamilton College, New York. Mr. Elihu Root, an influential member of the Carnegie Institution, was much interested in having these researches printed, as they represented the work of his old teacher.

My scientific publications, aside from those already referred to, number somewhat over one hundred titles, many of them written in collaboration with other members of our staff. These papers are listed in a section on the publications of the faculty in the annual reports of the president of the university. A part of this list was collected in a special volume of the university publications and covered the first twenty-five years of the achievements of that institution.

There has been, of course, considerable serving on committees of the national scientific societies and of the International Union. I was for a good many years a member of various committees of the National Academy of Sciences on grants from the Bache, the Watson, and the Draper Funds. And I was for some years the representative of astronomy on the editorial board of the *Proceedings* of the National Academy of Sciences.[1]

During the famine winter of 1922–23, I organized a committee at the observatory which would act as a clearing-house for funds to be used for the relief of Russian astronomers and their families,

[1] Personalia: A.B. Dartmouth, 1886, A.M., 1889, D.Sc., 1911; D.Sc. University of Cambridge, England, 1912; Fellow, American Association for the Advancement of Science, 1889. Member: American Astronomical Society, Astronomische Gesellschaft, 1891; National Academy of Sciences (Washington), 1908; American Philosophical Society (Philadelphia), 1909; American Academy of Arts and Sciences (Boston), 1913; Washington Academy of Sciences, 1915. Foreign Associate or Honorary Member: Royal Astronomical Society (London), 1908; Societa degli Spettroscopisti Italiani, 1909; Astronomical Society of Mexico; Royal Astronomical Society of Canada, 1909; Russian Astronomical Society. Assistant editor *Astrophysical Journal*, 1895–1901, Editor, 1902–. Clubs: Honorary member University Club of Chicago, Lake Geneva Country Club, Big Foot Country Club.

my associates being Mr. Van Biesbroeck and Mr. Struve. We were able to obtain a list of the men and their dependents, and the calls for help met immediate response. Through subscriptions collected from astronomers at American observatories, we were able to provide for the distribution of two hundred of the ten-dollar packages of balanced rations provided by the American Relief Administration (A.R.A.). We found that one such package had carried two persons through a month. The letters of appreciation which we received were too intimate and touching to be published, but all of the contributors had the opportunity to learn of the great benefit conferred by them on their Russian colleagues. At my suggestion the Russians named an asteroid 'ARA,' but in wishing to express their appreciation of my efforts in their behalf, they did not consult me when they named asteroid No. 854 'Frostia.' This was not in accordance with practice, as asteroids are not usually named for living people.

Soon after the war our little community began to show signs of municipal consciousness, and after due deliberation the village was incorporated. Thereafter we could cast our votes in our own community instead of driving nearly five miles to the voting headquarters of the township. When we drove thither in the spring of the year, when women were first allowed to vote on state public school matters, Mrs. Frost asked the venerable guardian of the sacred booths how many women had voted that day. She received the laconic reply, 'The hull o' two.' As she came out of the building, she met a neighbor, a farmer's wife, who in her friendly way exclaimed: 'Well, who won't you see when you ain't got a gun!' I served on the Village Board for three years, thus fulfilling my civic duties in that direction. It often takes patience and some philosophy to serve on such committees when it means giving up time from one's regular and exacting duties. We sat late on many evenings, hugging the iron stove in the village library, while we attempted to introduce such modern extravagances as electric lights for our streets without unduly increasing the taxes. For some years I have been a member of the Walworth County Park Commission, and for a long period a director of the County Y.M.C.A. It should be the duty and privilege of every citizen to assist, not only in its civic work, but also to aid in promoting its religious interests. No village can expect a normal development without the influence of the church. Mrs. Frost and I long ago transferred our memberships from venerable churches in the East to our little village Congregational Church in which I have for some time acted as trustee.

Not a little of my own personal pleasure has come from entertaining notable visitors, many of them friends from abroad, astronomers from nearly all the civilized countries. We look upon Einstein as our most distinguished guest. He spent a day with us when he was in this country in May, 1921. The tests which he proposed for the establishment of his theory were all of an astronomical nature, and it is natural that he should be interested in the work of astronomers, and conversely that they should recognize the importance of his theories, in the application to astronomy. His contributions to mathematical physics would be recognized as of the utmost importance quite aside from his theory of relativity which plays an important part in cosmic philosophy and has greatly broadened our intellectual conception of the universe.

Guests from Europe never fail to speak of their surprise in seeing our wooded areas which have been untouched by the hand of man. It is difficult for them, as indeed it is for us, to believe that less than three hundred years ago the first white man to set foot on the soil of Wisconsin was a French explorer who landed on the shores of Green Bay, thinking that he was entering China. It is still more difficult to believe that only one hundred and two years ago the first white person came to Lake Geneva, and that at that time three settlements of Pottawatomies, numbering about five hundred souls, were still located on its shores. They called the lake 'Kishwauketoe,' or 'Clear Water,' and their Chief 'Big Foot' once lived in Williams Bay. Arrowheads are still frequently unearthed during plowing, and several Indian graves have lately been found and opened.

The railroad reached Lake Geneva in 1856, but was not carried to Williams Bay until June 1, 1888. The present beautiful homes, lovely gardens, and extensive cultivation around its shores seem a far cry from wigwams and the hunting of wild deer with bows and arrows in these woods. 'From Wigwams to Mansions' might easily be the title of a book on Lake Geneva depicting the last hundred years of its history.

Public lecturing has not been a large factor in my educational duties, but it has brought a pleasant variety to my life and widened my acquaintance and, it is hoped, my influence toward higher education. It is interesting to go to different communities and meet some of their leading citizens and establish contacts which are often inspiring and lasting. I have generally given illustrated lectures when speaking to popular audiences, and the wonderful progress made in astronomical photography since I began to teach has made it possible to display the glories of the heavens far more effectively on the screen than could be done by any verbal descriptions. As I have grown older I have tried to present my subject in a less technical and in a simpler way than formerly. One may not assume too much knowledge in a given field of science on the part of a general audience. The presentation may well be restrained, for an audience should feel the power of the knowledge that is unexpressed by the speaker; he must know a thousand times as much about a given topic as he presents.

In the autumn of 1929 at the inauguration of my friend, Dr. John Timothy Stone, as president of the McCormick Theological Seminary, I spoke at his request on the topic of 'Science and Religion.' As a consequence of this address, I was invited to give a series of three lectures under the Norton Foundation before the Southern Baptist Seminary at Louisville, Kentucky. This was in March, 1931. Thence, on a lovely spring day, we motored to Galesburg, Illinois, where I gave a brief Vesper address in Beecher Hall at Knox College. I stood almost on the spot where Mrs. Frost's father and mother had been united in marriage by Dr. Edward Beecher many years earlier.

In the winter of 1927 I gave several lectures in the South. Five of these were in Florida, where we spent some time in St. Petersburg in order to be near Mrs. Frost's father and mother who were spending their winters there. Dr. Hazard had retired at seventy, after twenty-five years as editor of the publications of the Congregational Society under the imprint of the Pilgrim Press. Thereafter he not only wrote short articles occasionally, but compiled for Nelson and Sons a colossal concordance of the American revision of the Bible. Beginning as a lawyer after graduating from Knox College, he had a busy life. His literary ability brought him to Chicago as one of the editors of the *Advance* and from that time he continued in the field of writing for religious education. His was an eventful life and he gained from it a cheery philosophy. Dr. and Mrs. Hazard both passed away in 1928, having lived together for the unusual span of nearly sixty-seven years.

In our two visits to Florida we found it an attractive playground, and it was interesting to meet at nearly every turn a friend from some part of the country. We often found them basking in the sunshine on one of those cosmopolitan green benches along the streets of St. Petersburg. We greatly enjoyed, too, the daily open-air band concerts in the park of the 'Sunshine City.' Visitors to Florida also appreciate very highly the lyceum courses which bring musical artists of the highest rank to their platforms.

There are many amusing incidents bound to occur on the lecture platform. An introduction is often made with unconscious humor and sometimes must call for quick response. I was once introduced by a widely known financier and philanthropist in a neighboring city with the remark, 'And now Professor Frost will tell you what he knows about astronomy.' This could not be left unchallenged, and so I was obliged to assure the audience, 'I will not detain you that long.' My wife says that she never knew me to fail but once of an appropriate retort, nor ever saw me with so sour an expression as when I was once introduced as 'Mr. Frost, the famous astrologer.' I simply had to let that pass.

A speaker is quick to feel a responsive audience, and I have never known a lecture on astronomy which was a failure from this standpoint. It surprises me, too, that so many come to the platform after a lecture, asking keen and intelligent questions. During recent years there has been most certainly a marked increase in the interest in this now very popular subject. This may be due to the many articles and books written during the period, but perhaps the newspapers are more responsible, for the flaring headlines of crime are now occasionally replaced by the record of some scientific achievement.

I lectured once in Oak Park in the Congregational Church of which Dr. William E. Barton was pastor. This church was the center that season for a course in science given by some of the professors of the University of Chicago. I was explaining the mysteries of the spectroscope. As this is a difficult subject for a popular lecture, I paused at a certain point and called out in the dark, 'Have I made this quite clear, Dr. Barton? Do you understand it?' To his reply that he did, I answered, 'Then I am sure that everyone does.' He laughed with the rest.

I never told an audience, however, that when I speak I pick out the dullest person I see and try to be sure that I am making myself clear to him. A lecturer once made this announcement, but was shortly interrupted by a man in the rear of the room who called out in an angry voice, 'Say, quit looking at me!'

When I was speaking before the faculty of the Medical School of the University of Illinois in Chicago at one of their noonday assemblies, Dr. D. J. Davis in his introduction of me sought to establish the contacts between medicine and astronomy and referred to the tragic history of Æsculapius. This ancient Greek was so successful in his medical ministrations that he aroused the enmity of old man Pluto, for people delayed too long to suit him their journeys to the lower regions. There was a decided falling-off of business and of some of the concessions which were his racket — for example, in 'The Styx Navigation Company' Jupiter yielded to Pluto's request and let a thunderbolt smite Æsculapius with a fatal result. His protectress had been the goddess Minerva, who now complained to Zeus of this outrage against a human benefactor. All that Zeus could do was to promise Æsculapius a place among the stars in the heavens.

It at once occurred to me that this Olympian promise had not been fulfilled and further study confirmed my suspicions. But it seemed to me not too late to rectify this omission covering divers æons. A good many asteroids had been discovered by my colleague, Professor George Van Biesbroeck, with the twenty-four-inch reflector of the Yerkes Observatory, and while numbered they had remained unnamed. He readily agreed that one of these should receive the name 'Æsculapius,' and I so reported it to the Central Foundling Hospital for Asteroids at Berlin-Dahlem or the Astronomical Computing Bureau. It is customary to feminize the names of asteroids if possible and so the director of the Institute requested my assent to christen Asteroid No. 1027 'Æsculapia.' Thus the injustice of Walhalla was in a measure requited.

In 1905, the Northwestern Military and Naval Academy came

from Highland Park and camped at Kayes Park on the south shore of the lake. As the situation seemed so favorable, they soon located here permanently and erected a fine building on spacious grounds. Colonel Royal P. Davidson has always wished to have the cadets make a special visit to the observatory during the course of the year and it has usually been my pleasure to explain to them the aims and operations of the institution. For some years also, the Colonel has asked me to speak at one or two of their Sunday afternoon Vesper services and I have gladly complied. The type of address which I might present differs perhaps rather widely from that of the usual speaker of ministerial training. However, I have always believed in the frank use of the findings of science as contributory to religious and moral ideas. I remember that I spoke to the boys on one occasion using the fictitious text from the book of *Trigonometricus*, 'And Nahum said unto Habakkuk, Habakkuk, get your base-line right.' I was asked to repeat this address elsewhere, but declined, as it was meant for those cadets and for them alone.

Since the loss of my sight Mrs. Frost sits beside me during my lectures in order to watch the progress of the slides. I should hate to take the chance of having the operator get ahead of me — and perhaps have Halley's own picture on the screen while I might be describing the slide as 'This is an object with a tail so many miles long.' I sometimes use a slide about which I say to my audience, 'In the right-hand upper corner you will see — so and so.' Once, to be doubly sure of my description, I asked my assistant *sotto voce*, 'I am correct, am I not?' This happened at one of two lectures which I gave in Rochester, Minnesota, one evening. At this lecture given before the doctors, my host was sitting beside their leading oculist, and my question, which I asked after the lecture was half over, brought the quick remark from him, 'Why does he ask that? He can see it for himself, can't he?' We fool them sometimes.

I am often asked, 'What are the practical uses of Astronomy; what bearing has it upon our everyday life?' I usually take out my watch and ask, 'How important is time to you?' People do not stop to think that every appointment is in reality a rendezvous with the stars; that time is measured by the rotation of the earth as indicated by the passage of stars across the meridian. In no other way is time accurately determined, although it may be found approximately by observing the sun. No clock or watch can be trusted to keep perfect time, but must be checked every two or three days by an astronomer at the Naval Observatory and then universally distributed by radio and telegraph.

Then, too, the position of every acre of land or portion thereof in country or city is ultimately referred to a parallel of latitude and a meridian of longitude defined by the stars. This is true of the survey of our coasts and inland points. The accuracy of these findings is a very important matter to anyone who owns real estate, especially if it is worth a small fortune per linear foot. In the early determination of the boundary between Illinois and Wisconsin, which was by law to be along the parallel of 42° 30′, the first surveyors, depending largely upon a compass, laid out the line so that it was at least half a mile too far south at one end and a quarter of a mile too far north at the other.

Furthermore, a safe passage of all the merchant ships that sail the seas depends upon careful observations of the sun and stars to determine the ship's position. The fact that wireless signals can be received at any point on the sea does not relieve the navigator from the necessity of making his observations whenever the sky is clear. The magnetic needle is notoriously erratic, not pointing to the true pole, but toward the magnetic pole which is several hundred miles distant from it. Moreover, the needle changes its pointing from year to year in a long period for causes not yet understood. Therefore, before the compass can be used at any given place, its pointing must be checked by the sun or stars.

I recall a conversation with the late John J. Mitchell, a prince of gentlemen, as we were going to the city on the morning express. I was telling him the story of the gas helium which had then rather recently been found in crystals and waters of the earth, although discovered in the sun more than a quarter of a century earlier. He doubtless regarded this as far removed from any practical application to his activities as president of the Illlnois Trust and Savings Bank. But the use of helium in airships soon became feasible and eliminated the danger of fire so ever-present with hydrogen-filled balloons. However, it happened that on a summer's day, July 21, 1919, the blimp Wingfoot Express, filled with hydrogen and circling over Chicago, fell through the skylight of Mr. Mitchell's bank, bringing sudden death to thirteen of the one hundred and fifty employees who were working there. Had the findings of science been applied, this tragedy would have been averted.

These are some of the practical points of the application of astronomy to daily life, but the greatest service to mankind is the outlook which astronomy gives to his mind — the broadening of his horizon — and a philosophy regarding the place of his earth and his sun in the universe.

I have had some amusing and interesting experiences with reporters, many of them brilliant writers, and in general they are careful and considerate and make every effort to have their facts correctly stated. They make blunders — serious ones — but what are a few ciphers in their consciousness of the distance, for instance, of a nebula millions of millions of millions of miles away.

Coming up on the train one morning at the time of Halley's Comet, there seemed to be a baseball nine on board. They proved to be reporters, and that afternoon our observatory library was a classroom. When about midnight a friendly and interested neighbor, a well-known Chicago business man, telephoned that drinks would be served in his home — what do you think? — not a man left!

Reporters find it easy to telephone or telegraph, 'Won't you please give your opinion,' and so forth. I was particularly amused by one message which came over the wires, 'Send us three hundred words expressing your ideas of the habitability of Mars.' My reply was, 'Three hundred words unnecessary — three enough — no one knows.' This reminds me of a short and impromptu talk on Mars given by my son Frederick at the age of six. He invited a group of a dozen or so at the observatory (including his grandparents who were visiting us at the time) to hear his discourse. He had declined offers of assistance in regard to his facts. Barefooted and dressed in overalls, he spoke from a spiral staircase and really surprised me with a speech much better than I anticipated. But his conclusion, given in his then stuttering fashion, brought down the house, so to speak. It was, 'M-M-Mr. Percival L-Lowell of Flagstaff, Arizona, thinks that Mars is inhabited — b-b-but I disagree with him.' Now where — but then, as I said, he hadn't consulted me.

At one time there was a controversy raging in astronomical circles in France in regard to the so-called 'canals' on Mars, and most of the observations were being made with small telescopes. I was cabled, 'Please state whether the forty-inch telescope shows canals on Mars and with permission to print your reply.' I didn't quite like to become involved in an argument, not knowing just how my reply would be used. I sent therefore the rather cryptic answer, 'Forty-inch telescope too big to show canals.'

I have been called upon to speak informally in various institutions and on subjects other than astronomy. One month I spoke on bird life both at the State School for the Deaf and at the State School for the Blind. At the first, an interpreter kept up with me with his finger language. I rather questioned their interest in the talk, but one little girl remarked afterwards, 'I have always wanted to know what that bird is that goes head downward on the trunk of the tree. Now I shall always know a nuthatch.' At the School for the Blind, I gave them some bird calls and they were delighted to learn how to identify some of the birds in this way.

Most of my writing has been naturally along scientific lines — scarcely any in book form. I contributed a chapter in a book by Dr. Shailer Mathews entitled *Contributions of Science to Religion*, my chapter being called 'The Structure of the Cosmos.' Professor R. A. Millikan and Professor J. M. Coulter, and others collaborated. I also wrote a small pamphlet in 1924 for the American Institute of Sacred Literature. This was entitled 'The Heavens are Telling,' and apparently it has a wide circulation as have their other publications. I was pleased to find that it appealed to business men, for I understand that one banker ordered five hundred copies to distribute among his employees and friends. Incidentally, this little pamphlet identified my son Frederick when he was quite far from civilization on a field trip in northern California. When he went to a small town to have a check cashed, the banker took from his desk a copy of this little publication and asked him if he knew the author. The answer was, 'Why, that's my Dad,' and his check was cashed.

For many years it has been my custom to keep on my desk a small calendar upon which I enter all kinds of data, but especially those of the weather, of the blooming of flowers, and the dates of the arrival and departure of the birds. I found that these were of so much human interest as to warrant collecting them for a monthly report which the local papers requested. I have kept these dates of the migration of the birds for many years, and it is one of my pleasures in the spring to know that on or about a certain date my friend the bluebird will give me his charming greeting from my apple tree.

My 'bird calendar,' which may be of interest to bird-lovers in this latitude of 42.5°, reads for the common birds as follows:

Robin, March 6; bluebird, March 7; red-winged blackbird, March 18; song sparrow, March 19; meadowlark, March 20; phœbe, March 27; field sparrow, March 28; golden-winged woodpecker or flicker, March 29.

In April it reads:

Red-headed woodpecker, April 6; chewink, April 10; mourning dove, April 17; white-throated sparrow, April 20; brown thrush, April 27; whip-poor-will, April 30.

May is the time for the migrant birds:

Chimney swift, May 3; house wren, May 3; Baltimore oriole, May 5; ovenbird, May 5; yellow warbler, May 6; catbird, May 6; rose-breasted grosbeak, May 7; bobolink, May 7; kingbird, May 9; scarlet tanager, May 10; great crested flycatcher, May 11; ruby-throated hummingbird, May 16.

On several occasions, naturalists interested in bird migration have come to the observatory in the autumn or spring to watch through some of our smaller telescopes the flight of birds across the face of the rising moon. To some of these ornithologists it seemed a little uncanny that the astronomer could tell them the distances of the passing birds provided that one could identify the birds and say what fraction of the moon the stretched wings covered. It is, of course, simple arithmetic. We know that the moon's diameter is one one-hundred-tenth of a radian. This means that a disc one foot in diameter held at a distance of one hundred and ten feet would exactly cover the moon, or a coin one inch in diameter held at one hundred and ten inches would do the same. The normal extent of wing of each bird, correctly identified, is of course known. As an example, let me say that a waterfowl having a normal wing-spread of one foot is estimated to cover in its flight across the moon one tenth of the lunar diameter, and therefore must be at a distance of eleven hundred feet. Sometimes during the fall migration at the Hunter's Moon, birds have been seen to pass the surface as rapidly as over a hundred in an hour, practically one every half-minute. Of course quite accurate measures may be made which would determine the speed of flight and height above the ground as well as the distance from the observer.

Many organizations having sessions around Lake Geneva during the summer have requested the opportunity of visiting the observatory in a body outside of the hours when the building was open to the public. When I was too good-natured to refuse the privilege, I have usually accepted the burden of speaking to these groups, sometimes quite large, rather than to impose it upon my colleagues. There have been many interesting and stimulating people in these organizations.

Among the professors engaged in scientific research at the University of Chicago, Northwestern, Illinois, and Wisconsin, there has been a very informal organization called the Chaos Club which has met half a dozen times a year on Saturday at the luncheon hour at the University Club in Chicago, with autumn or spring migrations to some of the other institutions. The Chaos Club has the absolute minimum of formality and keeps few records. Professor T. C. Chamberlin was an enthusiastic member from the beginning. It has always been a pleasure to have this group visit the observatory, and they have usually spent a night at one of our local hotels where we met for an informal dinner to be followed by a talk and demonstration at the observatory. Membership includes all types of scientific research workers, from neurology to mathematics and botany. They have fortunately come to us in May or October when the country was especially attractive. The informal discussions of small groups as they have strolled about the grounds or waited their turn at a telescope have been both stimulating and delightful. On one of their recent meetings here on a lovely afternoon and evening in May, I spoke to them on 'The Drama of the Bursting Star,' referring to the origin of the Novæ by explosion.

One of my astronomical colleagues at a neighboring institution who was formerly on our staff had the habit of shaking hands with me when we met without any word to identify him, and I had always recognized the vigor of his hand-shake and made a quick identification. We received word that he would not be able to attend this particular meeting of the club, but at the last moment someone picked him up and brought him along. He told his friends that he would not say a word to identify himself, but he expected to be recognized. I was near the entrance, greeting the arrivals as they drove up to the steps, and when this new group of three or four shook hands with me, my friend gave me his usual silent greeting. They were amused to hear me reply at once, 'Why, I thought you said that you couldn't come.' This was Dr. Philip Fox.

We have naturally tried to give an opportunity to the students in astronomy in neighboring universities and colleges to see our instruments in operation, although it is very rare indeed that there was any chance to use the great telescope. It was for many years customary in the first instance that a general excursion from the University of Chicago should come about Decoration Day, spending the evening and sometimes the night. Similarly, smaller numbers sometimes came from the University of Wisconsin at Madison and from the Milwaukee colleges.

On one occasion I was requested to give a special opportunity to the State Conference of the Federation of Labor meeting in an adjoining city. I took the occasion to show how research in astrophysics, particularly in the study of the sun, might have a very direct bearing upon our understanding of our dependence upon the sun, of its inestimable importance to our lives, and how this is a free gift, unrestricted by the control of any privileged group. So I explained the recent view that the sun gives up its matter by transforming it into radiant energy, heat and light, and that this radiation is reconverted into matter in the grain and fruits which can be produced only with the beneficent action of the solar rays. So I said, 'In effect, we thus eat the sunshine.' I afterwards heard that at their banquet they spoke about this fact, saying that, 'He told us that we eat the sunshine, but fortunately he did not add that we drink the moonshine.'

Thus there have been groups of the editors of Wisconsin, the Wisconsin Club of Chicago, and many other varieties of social and educational units to whom it has been a pleasure to speak. The effort has been to interpret scientific research and its bearing on any philosophy of daily life. There has been no doubt a preponderance of religious groups who have been in session at the Y.M.C.A. Camp or others around the shore of our lake, and thus there has been the opportunity of trying to present to many thousands the harmony rather than the discord between the ideas of science and the ideas of religion, broadly considered. There have also been many hundreds of students from foreign countries participating in conventions who have had contact with our observatory. I have always tried to have these meetings offer no interference to our fundamental duty of scientific research and scientific instruction, but I believe that it is a real duty of the university to interpret to the public such of the results as can be easily grasped, whether to youthful or to adult visitors. Ordinarily, during the last twenty years there have been about twelve thousand visitors on Saturday afternoons through the summer. Different members of the staff take their turns as lecturers and demonstrators on these public afternoons, and no doubt many different viewpoints have been taken by the speakers. We have sometimes found that some people spending the summer on or near Lake Geneva have been accustomed to come to the observatory almost every Saturday afternoon during their stay. Usually the people are admitted in groups of from two hundred to four hundred, and the speaker must be audible and interesting enough to keep them quiet because it is not possible to provide seating facilities for over one hundred on the balcony inside the dome. With small groups we used to permit questioning, and this brought out some queer ideas. Ordinarily it is rather futile to permit questions from the balcony after a talk because they are apt to deal with some trifling subject as compared with the vast one which has just been presented.

In the early days some woman questioner was quite concerned to know why our power house was placed some seven hundred feet away from the great dome. She tried to make me admit that there was danger of an explosion that might threaten the safety of our hundred-thousand-dollar telescope. My reply was that I had a million-dollar baby within two hundred feet of the power house! Of course it is desirable to keep all smoke and vibration as far as possible from the telescope. As soon as it became feasible to buy electricity during the summer months and not consume any coal, we adopted the plan which has brought considerable economy in operation. In winter it is, of course, necessary to heat the large building with steam, and the use of smokeless coal in recent years has kept down any disturbance of the observational work from smoke.

One of my frequent callers at the observatory was my friend, Dr. George S. Isham, of Chicago and Lake Geneva. In addition to the Doctor's keen interest in the development of the medical sciences, he was anxious to keep in touch with all advances in practical physics and astronomy. Being skillful in operating his own lathe and milling machine, he was a frequent visitor in our shops and in my office, and often contributed helpfully in the design and construction of our astronomical apparatus. His brother-in-law, Henry H. Porter, has also contributed, not only financially but by the work of his own hands, in adding new auxiliary instruments. One of these I named the 'Astrogon.' This is a type of armillary sphere which serves for the conversion of one set of co-ordinates to any other on the celestial sphere. It thus may be used to derive the new co-ordinates mechanically and without laborious computation.

Dr. Isham had received a classical education and was also a good German scholar. We both appreciated the value of the classics, but did not neglect opportunities to assail each other's accuracy as to rules of Latin grammar even at midnight when we were spending a week-end with him as we often had the pleasure of doing in his beautiful home on North State Street. In the public press at this time there was considerable discussion of the value of the classics in modern life. Dr. Wylie, Chief Chemist of the United States Department of Agriculture, was a protagonist for the advantage of this kind of education to students of science, and sent out a questionnaire regarding the benefits one had derived from the study of Latin and Greek. Dr. Andrew West of Princeton requested the same opinions to be used for a magazine article which he was preparing. It is frequently argued that standard translations are so much better than anything that may be produced by the young student that his time is wasted and his English is not improved. I am far from accepting this view, as I have stated elsewhere in these pages.

After the sudden death of Dr. Isham's wife, the Doctor was a very lonesome man. Toward the end of the winter of 1921, he invited me to accompany him on a trip to California with the particular intention of being near our friends at the Mount Wilson

Observatory. He sent his automobile ahead by train to be available at Pasadena while we went *via* New Orleans and the Southern Pacific, stopping at Houston, Tucson, and Phœnix, and incidentally driving over the Apache trail to the then recently constructed Roosevelt Dam, a marvelous piece of engineering.

During our seven weeks in California, we spent a short time in Santa Barbara, and I paid a brief visit to Berkeley to act as a representative of the University of Chicago at the inauguration of President Barrows. Upon my return home, I was shocked to find that only two days after I had left home, my wife had been thrown from a sleigh and had sustained a badly broken arm, but had refused to let the news reach me, knowing that it would spoil my vacation. That autumn, Doctor Isham planned for a trip to Europe, but a hemorrhage in my eye and his rather poor health prevented us from carrying out what would have been a most delightful expedition motoring through Europe, and with the opportunity of attending the meetings of the International Astronomical Union at Rome in May, 1922.

My next trip to California was made in order to observe the total solar eclipse of September 10, 1923. At my solicitation, Mr. William Wrigley, Jr., had generously contributed five thousand dollars to cover the expense of rather an elaborate expedition to Catalina Island which he controlled and which I had selected as the best site for our observing station. I began planning some months in advance and made a complete model of the station. Then different members of our staff successively journeyed to the Coast and began the erection of the necessary wooden buildings under the skillful direction of Mr. Foote. We were shown every courtesy by the Catalina Company in the erection of these buildings thirteen hundred feet above the town of Avalon and commanding a splendid view over the sea. For nearly every one of the forty-two days which covered our occupation of the camp the sky was clear at noon which was to be the hour of the eclipse. On September 3, one week before the eclipse, the day was entirely cloudy with some rumbles of thunder, 'very unusual in California.' Many representatives of other observatories asked to join us with their equipment, and thus, on the eventful day, our company of persons having observational duties numbered forty-two. Among these was my friend Father Luis Rodés, S.J., of the Observatorio del Ebro of Tortosa, Spain. Upon his arrival I immediately appointed him chaplain of the camp, and admonished him that I should expect from him sufficient supplication to insure clear skies. For the first time in forty-seven years, according to the Weather Bureau, the whole southern coast of California and into Mexico was covered on that date with what is euphemistically called a 'high fog.' Our efforts had been in vain. I told Father Rodés that I feared he had not been fervent enough in his prayers to secure the weather desired. The conduct of this expedition had been somewhat of a tax upon me because at this time I was obliged to do my work with less than three per cent vision.

And now about letters. Oh, the letters! Some from friends far and near are treated as cherished possessions and are acknowledged with due appreciation. The waste-basket is overcrowded with others. I try to answer some of those which show a seriously troubled mind and in which the lack of mental balance is quite evident. Some of them are amusing. For instance, not long ago a woman (probably colored) wanted to know how old she was. Her mother had told her that she was born in August a few days after a total eclipse of the sun. There were two possibilities. She probably chose the one which made her five years younger than the other.

We had many letters at the time of Halley's Comet, inspired by the fear that the end of the world was approaching. One woman expressed herself thus: 'I haven't et for two weeks. Shall I keep on feedin' my baby? I am a nervus reck.' I assured her that she need not worry and that the baby should certainly be fed.

One letter sounded a bit like a threat at first reading. It came from a well-digger and said, 'I would like to put you in a well.'

During the years since I lost my sight, and when the newspapers were too freely commenting upon it, I had many suggestions — all kindly meant — for the restoration of my vision. The only one which I remember, however, was this advice: 'Beat the white of an egg and use it in your eyes twice a day. If two eyes, use two whites.'

I began to be interested in the reform of the calendar in the years preceding the war. The plan which was receiving most consideration was that proposed in Switzerland whereby the twelve months would be equalized as nearly as possible, with a sequence of thirty-one, thirty, and thirty days in each quarter, making ninety-one days, or thirteen weeks per quarter. New Year's Day would not be given a week-day name, and in leap year the extra day would be called 'Leap Day' and would be inserted after June 30 instead of in February. This plan would have genuine advantages, although its introduction would doubtless lead to some confusion for a considerable period.

However, the arguments in favor of the thirteen-month calendar were being pressed upon our attention. Upon looking at the matter carefully I became convinced that if any change were to be made, we ought to make the complete reform so that each month should consist of four weeks and the calendar should thus repeat itself for each month, beginning on a Sunday and ending on a Saturday. The advantage in the payment of monthly wages of four weeks is very great, and many large corporations have already found it necessary to adopt some form of adjustment like this in payment of their employees and in their own accounting within their organizations. The introduction of another month between June and July seems to many people a radical procedure, but I believe that we could adapt ourselves to it. The objection that the year could not be divided into even periods of months for semi-annual reports does not seem to be serious. The late George Eastman of Rochester, New York, became convinced of the advantage of the thirteen-month calendar, and besides giving it his earnest personal support, financed much of the propaganda in its favor. I was asked to join a committee of the United States Chamber of Commerce which should discuss and report on the subject. Two or three meetings were held in Washington and I attended one of them. It was an interesting session of men who were leaders in the commercial world. Dean Wigmore of Northwestern University represented law on the committee, and several of us actively supported the thirteen-month calendar. A referendum was carried out some months later by the United States Chamber of Commerce as a whole with a nearly equal support for and against the reform.

Secretary of State Kellogg was asked by a commission of the League of Nations to appoint a committee to ascertain the state of public opinion on this proposal in the United States. This committee represented the different departments of the Government besides members from many national organizations. Valuable reports were made, showing the effect of the adoption of the thirteen-month calendar upon public and private business, education, and scientific research. Professor C. F. Marvin, Chief of the Weather Bureau, made an excellent analysis of the situation from a scientific point of view, and he became chairman of this general committee. The reform could be introduced only in years which normally begin with a Sunday, which would be the case in 1933, 1939, and then not again until 1950. It was too much to hope that public opinion could be brought to favor the plan as soon as 1933, but I hope that in 1939 or in 1950 the world may see the advantage of making the change. It is really not so difficult a matter to change a calendar as might be surmised. It has been done several times since the days of Julius Cæsar, and only recently Russia and the countries under the Greek Church have adopted the Gregorian calendar, which was a radical change for them, as they dropped twelve days completely.

The discussion of the subject at Geneva, including the presentation of the report from the United States, came at a very unfortunate time in the autumn of 1931 when the League of Nations, and the world generally, was greatly upset by the aggressions of Japan against China in Manchuria and at Shanghai. The scheme for the thirteen-month calendar did not receive adequate support from the representatives of the various organizations involved. I believe, however, that the item of a fixed date for Easter may well go into effect, as the necessary legislation has already passed the English Parliament on this subject, and awaits an 'Order in Council' from the King and his advisers to be effective. There seems to be very little serious opposition from the clergy. Father Hagen, the astronomer of the Vatican, took quite a broad view of the subject which was practically equivalent to his support.

CHAPTER XXIII

ASTRONOMY

THE advance in observational astronomy is due in no small part to the introduction of photographic methods which were rapidly applied to all branches of the science and greatly increased the wealth of available data. Special types of lenses were devised for photographic telescopes, and new forms of measuring machines were designed which much improved the precision attainable. The direct photography of large areas of the sky, such as the Milky Way, brought out astonishing revelations of the immense number of stars and their aggregations in great star clouds. Prolonged exposures (giving an accumulation of the chemical action of light on the plate) bring out faint objects and details that can never be seen with the eye using a telescope with a lens of the same size as that employed for photography.

The application of the photographic method with large telescopes for determining the distances of the stars was initiated by Dr. Frank Schlesinger with the forty-inch Yerkes refractor. At the beginning of this period the distances of hardly thirty stars were known with any considerable precision; now after thirty years, the distance of more than two thousand stars has been determined by trigonometric methods. By the remarkable application of these results in connection with photographs of stellar spectra, the approximate distances of many thousands of additional stars have been determined. Thus the structure of our stellar universe has finally been studied on the basis of definite knowledge of its scale. The result has been that our conception of the size of the universe has been in forty years magnified many thousand fold, perhaps a million fold in the minds of most astronomers.

The revival of the use of reflecting telescopes with which Sir William Herschel had made his remarkable discoveries also came at this time and contributed much to the advance of knowledge. Reflectors have some advantages over refracting telescopes, as they may be made in much larger dimensions, and they have but one surface to be figured instead of four. Their silver coating, too, may easily be replaced when it becomes tarnished. All of the rays are united in the same focal plane of the reflector (which is not the case in telescopes having lenses), and therefore they are especially valuable for photography. The twenty-four-inch reflector at the Yerkes Observatory, figured by G. W. Ritchey, was the first and most accurate of the new instruments of this sort, and it was soon followed by the sixty-inch of the Mount Wilson Observatory, originally begun at Yerkes. The success of the sixty-inch was so great that in 1906 Mr. Hooker of Los Angeles agreed to give funds to Mount Wilson for the hundred-inch reflector. The great reflectors have revealed vast numbers of what are called spiral nebulæ, which are in effect galaxies like our Milky Way, and their distances have been found to be of the order of millions of light-years.

A magazine article by my friend George Hale, dealing with some of the discoveries which might be expected from the construction of a reflecting telescope of even such immense size as two hundred inches in diameter, aroused an interest in one of the great educational foundations in New York. For several years past, experiments have been in progress, first with quartz and later with pyrex glass, in the hope that such an instrument may actually be realized. This project is being carried out under the auspices of the California Institute of Technology, but in friendly co-operation with the staff of the Mount Wilson Observatory.

Forty years of science! And what golden years for astronomy! The field of practical and theoretical astronomy had been well developed during the preceding half-century and the greatest opportunity for advance seemed to me in 1890, as it would to any young man, to lie along the lines of astrophysics, the study of the physical and chemical constitution of the celestial bodies. Most valuable pioneer work had been done by Zöllner at Leipzig, by Huggins and Lockyer in England, by Janssen and others in France, by Ångström at Upsala, and others. Hundreds of lines in the spectrum of the sun had been mapped and the physics and chemistry of the celestial bodies offered the most attractive opportunity for research. The feeling was abroad that some large generalization must soon come which would explain in a simple way the origin of the spectral lines whose positions, for the most part, seemed to be without law and order.

In the laboratory the spectroscope, which in reality is a very simple instrument, reveals a different sequence of bright vertical lines of many colors characteristic of each of the chemical elements. When in the gaseous form, some elements have their light concentrated in very few lines, as, for instance, hydrogen in the visible region with less than half a dozen. Sodium is characterized by a close pair of lines in the yellow, and iron is represented by several thousand bright lines. It was the work of more than half a century to identify and measure the positions of the lines of the different elements in the spectrum. A scale giving the length of the vibrating waves is determined and these wave-lengths are now measured to the precision of a thousandth of a millionth of a millimeter.[1] When the light of the sun is thrown into the spectroscope the picture is quite different, for here we have a band showing all of the colors from violet to red, crossed by great numbers of dark lines, some wide, some very narrow, some strong, and some faint. Some of the lines had been mapped by Fraunhofer early in the nineteenth century, but their explanation had not been given until the work of Bunsen and Kirchhoff in Germany and Stokes in England in 1855. They showed that the bright yellow lines seen in the spectroscope, when it was pointed to the flame in which sodium had been inserted, corresponded exactly in position to the pair of dark lines seen in the solar spectrum. It was a great triumph that we could reach across the void of nearly a hundred million miles and determine in our sun elements that were familiar to us on the earth. The identification of hydrogen and calcium and of the metals like iron, nickel, and many others was quickly made. Thus it was established that the chemical constitution of the sun and of the stars was the same as that of the earth's crust. H. A. Rowland made concave diffraction gratings on which were ruled with great precision as many as fourteen thousand lines to the inch, and with this apparatus he made his great photographic map of the spectrum in 1888. He also determined the wavelengths of thousands of the dark (Fraunhofer) lines in the solar spectrum. This formed the basis for most of the spectroscopic measurements for several decades.

In 1880, S. P. Langley developed his bolometer for measuring the heat received from the sun. This delicate instrument could distin-

[1] A millimeter is a twenty-fifth of an inch.

THE GREAT SPIRAL IN ANDROMEDA

Estimated to contain nearly two million stars. Its distance from us is nearly
900,000 light-years, and its longest diameter is about 45,000 light-years.

guish differences of a millionth of a degree, and he applied it to the invisible parts of the spectrum beyond the red, greatly extending the knowledge of the longer waves of light which do not affect the eye.

Total eclipses of the sun were assiduously observed by the spectroscopists in the seventies, and Professor Charles A. Young discovered what he called the reversing layer — a thin sheet of gases enveloping the sun. When the moon covered everything but this thin stratum, hundreds of lines, normally dark in the spectrum of the surface of the sun, flashed out as bright. Thus it was shown that the dark lines are only relatively dark against the brilliant background of the surface of the sun. By themselves the dark lines are dazzlingly brilliant.

Until the late eighties the only way possible to determine the rotation of the sun was by measuring the position of sun-spots and determining the time it required for them to pass across the face of the sun. Since they seldom occur farther north or south of the sun's equator than thirty degrees, this left a great part of the sun beyond the possibility of measurement. When the spectroscope was set on the eastern edge of the sun and then upon the western edge, the difference in the position of the lines due to the motion in the line of sight gave twice the speed of rotation, and this method could be used from the equator into high latitudes on the sun. It brought out the fact that at sixty degrees of latitude the rotation was accomplished in forty-five days, whereas at the equator its period averaged twenty-six days. In other words, it does not rotate like a solid body, and this gave a new problem for study and some new light on the constitution of the sun. Although co-operative observations on the rotation of the sun were made at several observatories over a period of years and the values determined with accuracy, the problem of the different speed at different latitudes has not yet been solved.

The realization that our sun was the only star which was near enough to show a measurable disc and reveal surface details led to more thorough investigations concerning the sun, its great eruptions, its flocculi, and the vortices around its spots. The invention of methods for photographically recording the fine details of the solar prominences and of the surface markings in monochromatic light was begun almost simultaneously by George E. Hale at Chicago, and later at Yerkes, and by M. Deslandres at Paris. It had been difficult enough to make drawings of these features, but now photography was applied to give a definite and permanent record of these conditions at any moment.

In investigating the spectra of the stars Professor E. C. Pickering at Harvard followed the simple method used by Fraunhofer and later by Secchi of placing a prism over the object glass. Thus each stellar image became drawn out into a narrow line of spectrum. With the use of the plates instead of the eye a great number of spectra could be photographed at one time, even with comparatively small telescopes, and the classification of the stellar spectra was thus undertaken on a large scale at Harvard under Professor Pickering's direction by Mrs. Fleming and Miss Maury and by Miss Annie Cannon. Miss Cannon has shown great skill in her analysis of the faint spectra and has classified the spectra of several hundred thousand stars.

It was found that the white stars, by far the most numerous, had their spectra distinguished by a few strong lines of hydrogen, magnesium, and some of the metals of the iron group. The yellow stars had spectra almost identical with that of the sun, with the hydrogen lines less strong, the lines of iron and other metals much more numerous, and with two very broad dark lines of calcium vapor at the extreme violet end of the spectrum. It was found that the red stars showed peculiar bands in addition to lines in their spectra. Bands, sharp on one side and shading off on the other, were characteristic of compounds, or molecular combinations, and it was soon established that the atmospheres of the deep red stars contained much of the vapor of the hydrocarbons. It was not until a number of years later that the oppositely shaded bands in the orange stars were found to be due to another molecular combination, the oxide of titanium. These stars were evidently cool enough to permit the existence in their atmospheres of molecules as well as atoms.

The other fruitful manner of investigating the spectra of the stars has been by attaching a powerful spectroscope somewhat similar to that used in the laboratory to the eye end of a large telescope. This arrangement permits only one star to be investigated at a time, but it makes it possible to place immediately above and below the stellar spectrum a comparison spectrum of a terrestrial substance produced by passing before the slit, at the beginning and end of the exposure, an electric spark jumping across terminals of iron or other metals. The wave-length of each of these comparison lines being accurately known, the positions of the stellar lines lying between them could be fixed with the greatest precision. This added much to the information which could be learned from the spectrum.

One of the remarkable services which the spectrograph (a spectroscope adapted to photography) performs is to enable us to determine the speed in the line of sight of stars, planets, and nebulæ. The principle is known as that of Doppler, the name of its discoverer. If the source of light, planet, star, or nebula is moving rapidly toward or from us, the positions of the lines of their spectra will be slightly shifted because an approaching star gives us more waves per second than one at rest. If the star is receding from us in the line of sight, we get fewer waves per second and a displacement in the direction of longer waves, that is, toward the red end of the spectrum. If the observer himself is moving toward or from the star at a high speed, a similar effect is produced and must be allowed for. Thus the earth in its annual orbit around the sun moves with an average speed of thirty kilometers, or eighteen and a half miles, per second. Therefore, for a star on the ecliptic, the earth's speed would change within less than six months from a recession of eighteen miles per second to an equal speed of approach, or a range of thirty-seven miles per second. This can easily be computed for any star at any date in the year and thus allowed for. Referring now solely to the speed of the star itself, this averages for the yellow stars twenty kilometers, or about twelve miles per second; any velocity of one hundred miles per second or over is very high for a star unless two stars of a pair are spinning about each other. On a powerful instrument like the Bruce spectrograph which I designed for attachment to the forty-inch Yerkes telescope, a speed of twelve miles per second would produce a displacement of about one nine-hundredths of an inch in the violet region.

Up to 1895, there were scarcely fifty stars whose velocities in the line of sight could be given, but by 1932 this speed, also known as the radial velocity, had been measured at various observatories, chiefly American, for over six thousand stars.

Measurements of photographs of the same field of stars repeated after the lapse of a number of years and made with great accuracy gave information as to the so-called proper motions, and relative movements across the sky of thousands of stars. These results combined with those obtained with the spectroscope give the real motion in space for stars whose distances are known. Thus was secured a vastly better foundation for further studies in the structure of that part of the universe which is within our galaxy.

A new and interesting type of double stars was discovered in 1888–89 when the spectral lines of some stars were found on the Harvard plates to become periodically double. The periods were in some cases astonishingly short. Interpretation was given by Dr. E. C. Pickering. If a star which appeared single through the telescope really consisted of two components whirling about each other, then at times one body would be approaching and one receding, producing displacement toward the violet or toward the red end of the spectrum which made the lines appear double. A quarter of the period later, the motion of each component would be at right angles to the line of sight and the lines would be single. The first two stars of this sort to be discovered were Mizar with a period of twenty days, and Beta Aurigæ, with a period of four days. At almost the same date, with the spectrograph, Vogel and Scheiner at Potsdam studied the motion in the line of sight of the well-known variable star Algol which for many years had been known to be eclipsed every two days and twenty hours. If this eclipsing theory was correct, then the brighter star must be going from us at a quarter of the period before the eclipse and coming toward us a quarter of the period after the eclipse. The measurements of the speed on the spectrogram confirmed this satisfactorily. Thus our ideas that double stars made their circuit only very slowly in periods of many years or centuries had to be adapted to these new discoveries in the following forty years.

Up to 1933 there have been over twelve hundred spectroscopic binaries recorded and the orbits of a large number have been determined. The shortest period thus far found is two hours and thirty-six minutes, that of Gamma Ursæ Minoris. There is doubt, however, that these very short periods of less than a day represent the orbital revolution of two separate stars. With the extension of the observations over a number of years, the motion in the line of sight of Sirius, for example, has been found to agree with the visually observed orbital revolution in a period of fifty years.

It is over one hundred years since Wilhelm Struve, first director of the observatory at Pulkova, Russia, discovered the actual change in position of a pair of double stars. Thereafter, on a careful observation with the micrometer, many were found in which there was evident motion around a center of gravity of the pair. This stimulated much interest in the observation of doubles in the last century, and Professor S. W. Burnham discovered some twelve hundred which had thus far escaped detection. Professors Hussey and Aitken began at the Lick Observatory a systematic observation of all stars to detect possible doubles. As a result of this survey, Hussey added 1650 to the list of double stars, and Aitken, who has consistently followed his program for about thirty years, found 3103. Careful observations after a number of years often reveal the motion which shows a physical connection of stars as a binary system. The shortest known period for visual binary stars is 5.7 years, but there are hardly more than fifty thus far known with periods of under fifty years. For many such systems it is evident that thousands of years are required for a revolution.

When the orbit of a binary star is well known, it gives us the very important datum as to the mass of the system in terms of the mass of the sun, and it has been found in general that the mass is ordinarily within the range of one tenth to ten times that of the sun. In many cases the relative mass of the two components can also be determined, and finally this leads to determining the distance of such binaries by the method known as that of dynamical parallax. From stars thus far investigated, it would appear that about one in nine, for stars brighter than the sixth magnitude, is a visual binary. Among spectroscopic binaries, mentioned elsewhere, the proportion is very much greater among stars characterized principally by helium, in addition to hydrogen, in their spectra. We have found that more than two thirds of these stars are binaries or are multiple. With certain limitations the masses of spectroscopic binaries can also be obtained.

The more minutely the spectroscopic motions of the stars are studied, the more complex they are generally found to be. Stars which had been supposed to be single are thus frequently revealed as having several components. It may not be too extravagant an idea to believe that there may be some parallel in celestial evolution to that tendency found everywhere in the organic world to multiply by cellular division. It gives us the suggestion that what we see does not represent a stage of permanence, but rather a flux, the organic and the celestial worlds being in a state of progression, not in a static condition.

The analysis of the motions of the stars in space revealed the existence of groups of stars having their movements directed toward the same point — in other words, these stars are moving parallel to each other. One of the first of these to be recognized was in Ursa Major and the group has been called the 'Bear Family.' Five out of the seven stars in the Great Dipper belong to this group, and this also includes other stars in widely different parts of the heavens, among which we may mention Sirius, the Dog Star. Upon investigating the motions of the Hyades group in the constellation Taurus, Lewis Boss found parallelism in the motion of more than forty stars and this is known as the 'Taurus stream.' When the motion of a few of these in the line of sight was determined, it became possible to find the distance of this stream, which is one hundred and thirty-five light-years. J. C. Kapteyn of Holland then took up the task of investigating the motions of great regions of stars and wrote important papers under the title of 'Star Streaming.' He advanced the view that in our galaxy we are seeing the result of the mixture of two great streams of stars coming from nearly opposite directions. The problem was so great that centuries would be required for its complete study, and Kapteyn therefore secured international co-operation in a plan for observing two hundred and six small selected areas scattered over the sky. Every possible characteristic of the stars in these areas was to be determined, and thus, by sampling, it might be possible in a few decades to secure a general idea of the constitution of the whole galaxy — of its structure and arrangement. This co-operative work is still in progress, as it is no small task to determine for all the stars in these areas the motions, brightness, distance, and spectral characteristics.

The accurate knowledge of the magnitudes of the stars is a very important item for the astronomer. It is unfortunate that the term magnitude was introduced centuries ago to indicate the brightness of a star, because *a priori* no measurement of the size of the star is implied in its brightness; it may be bright because it is relatively near to us or because it is actually highly luminous. An accurate knowledge of a star's distance must be had before we can speak of its actual luminosity. Estimates were formerly made by looking first at one star and then at another, and great skill was developed by some observers in assigning the brightness in a scale of six magnitudes allotted to the stars visible to the naked eye. Instruments have been devised comparing the brightness of the different stars with an artificial star brought into the field of view and illuminated by a constant kind of lamp. Little progress had been made in a systematic study of the brightness of the stars until Professor E. C. Pickering took up the subject at Harvard and devised his meridian photometer. He took the Pole Star as a standard for comparison, reflecting an image of it into his telescope with which he observed stars as they passed the meridian. By a combination of polarizing prisms, he equalized the light of each star with the light of the Pole Star. By this visual method Pickering determined the brightness of many thousands of stars and personally made over a million settings with his photometer. The results appeared in successive volumes of the *Harvard Annals* and were extended to the southern hemisphere at what was then the Harvard Observatory station in Arequipa, Peru. Thus the Harvard system of magnitudes was based on visual observations. A precise investigation of the magnitudes of all northern stars brighter than 6.5 was carried out by the Potsdam astronomers, Professors Müller and Kempf, during the two decades following 1886. This is known as the Potsdam system of stellar magnitudes.

But when the photographs of the heavens were taken in large numbers, methods were devised for measuring with fair precision and great rapidity the magnitudes of thousands of stars. Many researches have been made to compare the photographic and visual magnitudes which differ because of the varying sensitiveness of photographic plates to stars of different color. During the first quarter of the new century this work was carried out with meticulous care at our observatory by Professor J. A. Parkhurst. In 1930, we had available catalogues of the brightness, both photographic and visual, of several hundred thousand stars.

In the last decade a great increase in the precision of measurements of the brightness of stars has been made by the employment of a photo-electric cell. Such a cell converts the luminous energy falling upon it into electrical energy which may be measured as a current by a galvanometer, or as a difference of potential with an electrometer. This eliminates the use of the eye in estimating the equality or difference of luminous effect. Professor Joel Stebbins, our neighbor at the University of Wisconsin (now only two hours dis-tant on our excellent highways), had been foremost in the applica-tion of this method in America and he had achieved results of the highest accuracy. After I received a grant from the Rosenwald Fund for improving and increasing the equipment of the observatory, I invited Dr. Stebbins to apply his experience in designing for us a photo-electric photometer to be used for precise work with the forty-inch and twelve-inch telescopes. The instrument was built at the shops of the University at Madison under the direct supervision of Dr. Stebbins. As visiting professor at our observatory for two quarters, he brought this excessively sensitive and therefore very tricky and temperamental instrument into good working order and carried out a series of observations with Dr. C. T. Elvey of our staff who later took over the operation of the instrument as a part of our regular program with the forty-inch telescope.

One of the important by-products of photometric measurements was the discovery of thousands of variable stars, those whose light is not constant, but fluctuates in longer or shorter periods, in many cases with great regularity. There are several varieties of variable stars, of which I may mention the class of red stars which have a period in many instances of about eleven months. Another class is that of the eclipsing stars where one component of a binary system passes between us and the other component. The combination of the spectroscopic and photometric investigation of these eclipsing bi-naries, carried out by Dr. Henry N. Russell, Dr. Harlow Shapley, and others, has yielded much information about various characteristics of these systems. There are about five other principal classes of varia-tion to which stars are subject, and the photographs show that abso-lute constancy of light may not be assumed for any star without thorough investigation. It was found rather recently that the Pole Star itself varies by about a tenth of a magnitude in a period of four days, and this, of course, slightly affects all of Pickering's results with the meridian photometer, which assumed that the Pole Star was con-stant. The total number of stars whose variation has been estab-lished was about six thousand up to 1931, and there is no apparent limit to the number that may be added to our lists.

The wonderful globular star clusters were studied with great success, particularly by Solon Bailey of the Harvard Observatory, and hundreds of variable stars within these clusters with special peculiarities were discovered by him and Miss Leavitt and by other members of the staff. They found an important correlation between the length of the period of variation and the actual brightness of the stars. This was later developed by Dr. Shapley as a method of inferring the distances of these objects. His work concerning these globular clusters was based on photographs taken with the sixty-inch and hundred-inch reflectors at Mount Wilson, and his results were published in a series of about twenty papers of great value. In the period from 1890 to 1910 few astronomers would have placed the clusters at distances of more than a few hundred or a thousand light-years. But Dr. Shapley proved that the distance of such an object as the Great Cluster in Hercules could not be less than some thirty thousand light-years. Such clusters were therefore found to be great systems composed of some millions of highly luminous stars separated from each other by vast distances. Thus again astronomers had to increase their scale of the size and their idea of the immense numbers of separate objects in the different types of cosmic systems.

It was by using objects like clusters as stepping-stones in passing outward, and the employment of the Cepheid variables and novæ discovered in such a galaxy as the great Nebula of Andromeda, that Dr. Edwin Hubble found the distance of the latter to be of the order of nine hundred thousand light-years, and its diameter some forty-five thousand light-years (a light-year being slightly less than six million million miles), fully as great as had been previously attributed to our own galaxy, or Milky Way system.

By the application of the spectrograph requiring a single exposure extending over several nights, it was found possible, by V. M. Slipher at the Lowell Observatory, to determine the speed in the line of sight of some of these spiral nebulæ. These were found to be very great, nearly two hundred miles per second for the spiral of Andromeda. Dr. Slipher was able even to determine the speed of rotation spectroscopically of some of the larger spirals. And recently, in extending his work with the great reflectors at Mount Wilson, Dr. Hubble and his associates found spirals with speeds of several thousand miles per second. He also discovered that the distance of a spiral could be inferred when its speed is known. By the application of this correlation, distances as great as one hundred and thirty million light-years have been assigned to some spirals. In four decades our knowledge of the scale and structure of the universe has thus been wholly transformed and almost incredibly expanded.

The demonstration that our own galaxy, or Milky Way system, is in rotation is by no means easy. We ourselves must partake, with our sun, in this mighty spinning about a center perhaps forty thousand light-years distant from our present position. If we could infer the distances of the stars from their brightness, then we could know which ones are beyond us and which are nearer the center of rotation. The case is as if we were trying to locate ourselves while swimming in a violent eddy of water. We are turning faster than some parts of the eddy and slower than others, but we can only vaguely estimate our distance from the center. However, from a minute investigation of the motions of the stars across the line of sight (or the study of what we call proper-motion stars), Dr. J. H. Oort of Leiden has established strong evidence of the reality of the rotation. When Dr. J. S. Plaskett combines these data with his material on the velocities of faint stars in the line of sight gained from his extensive observations with the seventy-two-inch reflector at the Dominion Observatory in Victoria, British Columbia, the evidence becomes practically convincing. It will be the task of coming years to perfect the accuracy of our knowledge of this rotation and to find the part which is due to our own share in the turning, and which must therefore be subtracted from the apparent velocities in other parts of the galaxy. With increasing knowledge it seems to me that we shall thus find fuller evidence of order in the motions of the stars and that we shall thus be less inclined to think of their motions as random, or a matter of chance. I therefore fully expect that future observations will more and more confirm the view that all the operations of Nature are orderly and the result of natural causes.

The complexities of the lines forming the spectrum of the different elements have been puzzling to physicists and astronomers for a century. An accurate mapping of the separate lines was a necessary preliminary to any general understanding of the matter, and this has gone on for many years. There was a feeling that the different vibrations of a given chemical element such as hydrogen must bear some harmonic relation to each other. In 1885, Balmer detected relationships in the different lines of the spectrum of hydrogen other than merely numerical coincidences. A series of lines rhythmically related to those of hydrogen was found in the spectrum of a southern star by E. C. Pickering. The electronic theory of the constitution of atoms, closely following the discovery of radioactivity, was being pursued in many of the important laboratories. The interior of an atom was imagined to be somewhat analogous to the system of the sun and its planets or of a planet and its satellites. No simple picture of a minute and universal electron like an exceedingly minute hard body traveling around a more massive nucleus, which also is of exceedingly small size, could represent the discoveries being rapidly made in the laboratories. Of course the electron represented the smallest unit of negative electricity, and the proton a complex nucleus with a positive charge. Rutherford's model served as a basis, and the researches of Nils Bohr of Copenhagen carried the picture much farther for the case of hydrogen. The astronomical analogy became more close in this case with elliptical orbits and perturbations of the outer electrons. Meanwhile, the quantum theory, which was being developed by Max Planck of Berlin, was found to fit into the structure. The electric charge of the electron was experimentally measured by Millikan. Atoms were found to be capable of very different states, neutral, ionized, and excited in manifold ways. Predictions were made by theory which were very frequently confirmed by experiment with the lines of the spectrum. Relations were found with the spectra of the X-rays so that new lines could be sought for from the exceedingly short X-rays all through the gamut to those visible to the human eye and even to the longer waves beyond the red. Complex groups of lines, known as 'multiplets,' were discovered in different kinds of spectra, and there has been a brisk race between theory and observation during the last decade. In general, the method of classification of lines is rather complicated, and the whole theory appears to be waiting for some great generalization. Despite the gaps in our knowledge, however, immense progress has been made so that astrophysics has become the forefront of physical research.

Certain combinations of lines have been called 'forbidden,' meaning that the theory did not provide for them, but conditions prevail in celestial bodies which permit them to exist. Thus was solved the old problem of the origin of the principal gas in the nebulæ aside from hydrogen and helium. The strongest lines had been known for many years and could not be identified with any known gas, and many other lines were found as larger telescopes were applied to faint nebulæ. C. I. Bowen first decided theoretically that the lines might be unusual or unexpected ones of oxygen and nitrogen, and then he was able to produce the spectra in the laboratory. Theory has made it possible to determine the abundance of different elements in the solar atmosphere, and many difficult problems regarding the structure of the sun are being gradually solved by the combined attack of the mathematical physicist, the spectroscopist in the laboratory, and his brother in the observatory.

By 1900, we had been able to arrange the different varieties of stellar spectra in a series which definitely showed a progression or evolution. This did not indicate which way the progression moved, nor was the time in human experience long enough to give visible evidence of change. The child at a very early age, seeing about him children older than himself, young, middle-aged, and old people, reaches the conception of growth and the effects of time. So the astronomer can never expect in the age of a race to observe the change in this extremely slow process of evolution. We nevertheless are just as definite in the idea that it must take place as if we had witnessed the progression.

Twenty-five years ago we laid the stress on the mode and sequence of evolution, but in the last decade newer ideas and correlations between the masses, sizes, and brilliance of the stars have taught us a great deal about their resemblances and their differences. It is believed that evolution goes through a circuit, starting with a giant red star of immense size and slight density, that it gets yellower, then whiter, then bluer, reaching its acme of temperature, the height of its brilliance, in the blue stage, and then goes back again through the inverse sequence, ending as a dwarf red star highly condensed. I have come to believe from general reasoning that a star has neither birth nor death, but is indefinite in its duration, or perhaps perpetual, going through many phases, even that of possible extinction as a source of light. I believe, for example, fully in the ancient precept of Marcus Aurelius (following Lucretius from Epicurus), '*ex nihilo, nihil fit*' — 'out of nothing, nothing is made.' It is much more logical to assume that there is something to start with.

It seems to me that we can also derive from the motions of the fixed stars confirmation of the principle of a universe of indefinite duration. We find that the stars themselves are all in motion, and such motions seem to be one of their fundamental characteristics. We have no right to assume that the motions of the stars, for example, started from rest, increasing from zero to any observed velocity. It is as logical to assume that the stars are slowing down from a still greater initial velocity, but obviously no one can claim that the motion we see is a relic of a greater motion of the past. Therefore we are bound to believe that this motion is of necessity neither increasing nor decreasing, but must be perpetual.

The smallest unit of matter may be in as rapid motion as the greatest. Matter is made from the motion of certain small units of negative electricity (electrons) in rapid circulation around a unit of positive electricity (protons) under each other's mutual spell. Stop their motion in an atom and the matter ceases to exist. This again leads to the conception that where motion is a universal characteristic of matter, it must endure.

One of the most remarkable developments in astronomy and mathematical physics in the last two decades has been the introduction of the theory of relativity by Einstein and those who have extended its application in various directions. Fundamentally it depended upon the celebrated experiment of Michelson and Morley on the possible drift of light with the ether. This had been carried out at Cleveland in 1887. There had also been much discussion as to whether there is any way of determining absolute motion. Fitzgerald and Lorentz had dealt with these problems. Einstein contributed some papers to the *Annalen der Physik* in 1905. He gave to his first investigations the title of 'The Special Theory of Relativity.' I have the impression that astronomers generally, as well as some mathematical physicists, regarded this at first as rather speculative. It did not seem to be taken very seriously for the first ten years after it appeared. However, Einstein proposed three definite tests for his theory which were all astronomical, and it was therefore certainly fitting that the astronomers should make these crucial experiments. One of these was based on the advance of the perihelion of the orbit of the planet Mercury. This had been studied some years before by our leading investigator in this field, Simon Newcomb of Washington, who had adopted a value which Einstein found quite well confirmed the amount expected by his theory. Newcomb himself had regarded the adopted quantity as highly uncertain and therefore it seemed that this test could not be regarded as critical.

In a brief paper published in 1905, Einstein had shown mathematically that light must have inertia, that its energy could be expressed in mass of matter. Light then must have weight and partake of some of the characteristics of matter. Therefore, if a beam of light from a star should graze in its passage toward the earth the edge of some massive celestial body like the sun, the gravitational pull upon the light by the sun should change its direction slightly, or in other words, deflect the star's light and make it appear to come from a slightly different direction than if there were no attracting body to disturb its straight course. The only time when this test could be made would be at a total eclipse of the sun when for the few minutes of totality photographs could be taken of the stars in the sky around the obscured sun. If the same background of stars were photographed a few months later with the same apparatus, after the motion of the earth in its orbit had removed the sun from that part of the sky, then the distances between the stars around the sun at the eclipse would be found slightly changed. It was several years before this test was first applied. I was asked to allow a camera to be attached to the side of the Denver equatorial telescope at the eclipse of June 18, 1918, and I agreed that it might be done, probably without disturbing our spectroscopic program. Cloudy weather prevented any photographs from being taken. A notable eclipse occurred on May 29, 1919, its track leading from the Andes across the Atlantic to the shores of Liberia in Africa. In spite of the disturbance of the war, preparations were made for observing this by a party from the Greenwich Observatory. Although the conditions were not ideal, the plates that were subsequently measured did show a slight shift of the order predicted by Einstein. This was regarded as quite a triumph for the theory. At the next few eclipses elaborate preparations were made for this test, the most complete being those carried out by a party from the Lick Observatory in Australia in 1922. When the great mass of observational material could be discussed a year or two later, the result was confirmatory of the deflection expected by Einstein. These tests have been continued at every favorable opportunity offered by total solar eclipses. Members of a German eclipse expedition have lately questioned the closeness of agreement. It seems to me, however, that we must regard this as a practical demonstration of the correctness of Einstein's view.

His third test was a spectroscopic one. Light emanating from a massive body must have its vibrations slowed down by the gravitation. Rays from the sun's atmosphere should therefore appear slightly longer, or, as we say, 'shifted toward the red.' The amount is exceedingly small, only about 0.014 of a ten-millionth of a millimeter. Observations were made at many laboratories with contradictory results. Finally, after several years of work, Dr. St. John at Mount Wilson Observatory reached the conclusion that the shift did occur in the right sense and in about the right amount. The case was tested by Dr. Walter S. Adams, director of the Mount Wilson Observatory, for the white dwarf star which is the companion of Sirius, the Dog Star, making its circuit in fifty years. Professor Eddington had shown strong evidence that we must give to this dwarf a density of about fifty thousand times that of water, or seven thousand times that of iron. This would mean a tremendous gravitational field for this exceedingly dense star. Its lines, therefore, ought to be shifted much more than those of the sun. The difficulty in the experiment came from the great brilliancy of Sirius which is over a thousand times brighter than its companion and masked its light. However, Adams succeeded in getting photographs of the spectrum of the companion and they showed a large displacement in the way predicted. This therefore gave an important additional confirmation to the third Einstein test.

Einstein's theory introduced time as the fourth co-ordinate in fixing the position of moving bodies in space. Space and time became interdependent, and the philosophical consequences were many and far-reaching. Einstein has made other notable contributions to the mathematical theory of physics, particularly in respect to the emission of electrons from metallic surfaces exposed to ultraviolet light.

In the field of mathematical physics there has recently been introduced a theory which is called the 'doctrine of uncertainty.' There is no doubt much attractiveness to the mathematician in such a speculation, for he is not bound by the limitations of observed facts. It is also undoubtedly true that the modern physicist cannot predict the action of electrons under every condition, so that uncertainty at that point must be admitted. However, to me this merely means that our observational data are inadequate; the actions within the electrons and protons may be far too fine-grained for detection with our present methods of research.

There is a radical tendency among some able young physicists to abandon what have long been regarded as the fundamental principles of physics. Today one even hears in some quarters the statement that we must throw overboard the principle of the conservation of energy. My persistent belief in the regularity of the workings of Nature is heartened by a recent statement of Dr. Max Planck, for the last forty years the distinguished lecturer on Mathematical Physics at the University of Berlin, and founder of the quantum theory. I give my own translation from his article in *Nature* of April 18, 1931:

> Theoretical physics has been brought by the quantum theory into a condition of some confusion. It is certain that of the fundamental principles hitherto generally accepted, at least some must be sacrificed in order to maintain the others. It is one of the most important future tasks of research to make this perfectly clear. As far as I can see, we must include among those principles which we must preserve under all conditions the assumption of a perfect accordance with law (*Gesetzmässigkeit*) of all physical processes; on the contrary, among those principles which must be dropped is the assumption that the orderly course of a process can be represented by a separation of its elements of time from those of space. Therefore, it is the notion of entirety which must be introduced into physics as it has been introduced into biology, in order that we may understand and formulate the laws of Nature.

I must mention at this point some of the later investigations and developments at the Yerkes Observatory during the final years of my administration as Director.

The notable ability of Dr. George E. Hale in devising new types of instruments was shown in his recent invention of the spectrohelioscope. This he used with much success at his branch of the Mount Wilson Observatory in South Pasadena. An appropriation from the Rosenwald Fund enabled me to purchase one of these instruments which we set up in a vacant space under the twenty-four-inch reflector. I employed in the cœlostat two mirrors made of the new fused quartz by the General Electric Company. Surfaces of this material are not affected by the exposure to the sun. The instrument operates on the principle of the retinal retention of the visual impression from a vibrating image. It enables the observer to quickly make a drawing of the eruptions at the edge of the sun or upon its surface. It has now been in use for a few years and has been a valuable addition to our equipment for solar research.

An important piece of apparatus lately added to the equipment of the observatory is a recording microphotometer. Owing to the heavy cost of importing such instruments from Europe, we found it necessary to build the instrument in our own shop, and this was done with the special assistance of Dr. Elvey. An instrument of this sort makes a precise and magnified record of the intensity at all points across the width of the lines of stellar spectra and it has been extensively used in physical laboratories for a similar purpose. In the hands of Dr. Elvey this instrument has yielded important results in analyzing our spectrograms for the determination of the rotation of the stars upon their axes. The character of the dark lines is markedly affected by the shape of the contours which are traced by the apparatus, and some stars have been found to rotate with a speed exceeding one hundred miles per second, while others show slower rotations. Still others, whose axes are probably pointing in the direction of the earth (or which present their poles of rotation toward us), show practically no rotation. Many important conclusions are being drawn from observations of this sort and contribute materially to our knowledge of the atmospheres of these stars.

In recent years we also added to the routine of our program with spectrograms and plates to be used for photometric purposes the impression on the edge of each plate before exposure of a series of standard squares. This greatly assists in the photometric evaluation of the density of the luminous impression in spectral lines or stellar images.

It had been for some years my special desire to arrange for the safe storage, for an indefinite term of years, of the great number of negatives on glass of astronomical objects taken with our different instruments. By 1930 they numbered sixty thousand. It was also important that the plates should be placed in envelopes, which should be of indefinite permanence and should not expose the sensitive film to any cumulative effects of chemicals which might have been used in the manufacture of the paper. Photographic dry plates have not been in use for much more than fifty years, and when we attempt to preserve them for one hundred or one thousand years, when, in some instances, their value will be greatly increased for the astronomers of that era, we are obliged to act without the benefit of long experience. With the help of Mr. Barrett and later of his successor, Mr. Crump, we investigated the matter as thoroughly as possible, and I wrote to all institutions and individuals who could give us advice. Finally, in 1932, we found an unbleached paper of pure cellulose which promised to be permanent. A large room in the observatory attic having brick walls had been prepared for cabinets a year or so earlier, and in the last months of my administration I was able to see the cabinets completed for the storage of about one hundred thousand of our valuable negatives. It is thought that there can be no damage from fire or water, and perhaps tornadoes or earthquakes are the only elements which may endanger these important records.

Some years ago a wealthy citizen of Texas left a sum of nearly a million dollars for the erection of a research observatory in that State to be associated with the State University. Relatives contested Mr. McDonald's will on the ground that it was not an evidence of sanity that he should bequeath his money for what seemed to them so impractical a purpose. At the request of the lawyer interested in the case on behalf of the university, I wrote a brief of several thousand words citing the cases of many able men of affairs in business and statesmanship who had left large sums for the erection of such observatories which had proved to be lasting and notable memorials. Such, for instance, is the case of the donors of the Lick, Yerkes, and McCormick Observatories as well as of several others. The litigation was finally settled with the allotment of the greater part of the McDonald estate to the purpose for which he intended it. Upon the initiative of my successor, Dr. Struve, a co-operative arrangement has been planned between the University of Chicago and the University of Texas whereby a large reflecting telescope will be constructed for the McDonald Observatory. This is to be erected at a point in Texas where the atmospheric conditions are most suitable. The scientific operation of the institution is to be conducted for a term of years by experts from the Yerkes Observatory with funds provided by the University of Chicago. Thus the problem which I had tried to put into effect for some years, of adding to our equipment a sixty-inch reflector, an effort which could not be accomplished during the business depression, promises to be realized during the next few years. It is expected that atmospheric conditions more suitable than those in Wisconsin will be found in the milder climate of Texas.

CHAPTER XXIV

YEARS OF 1931–1932

I SPEAK in great humility of spirit about the events associated with my sixty-fifth birthday. My wife and daughter had entered into a conspiracy to have a little celebration for me knowing how much I would appreciate a word of greeting on this occasion from my friends both here and abroad. Little did any of us realize what would actually happen or that any publicity would be given to the event. When the *Chicago Tribune* telephoned that they were sending a man to cover the affair, I assured them that it was entirely uncalled for. The following day, however, Mr. Philip Kinsley arrived. He dealt with me most kindly, and I greatly treasure the article which was written by such an expert. I felt that there would be nothing left for my obituary notices.

Mr. Kinsley quoted two poems, one of them written by my son Frederick who had been at one time rather a regular contributor to the 'Line O'Type' column in the *Tribune*, under the pseudonym 'The Phantom Lover.' Frederick's poem was dedicated to me and was written not long before his marriage, and while he was still a student in the Department of Geology in the University of Chicago. The second poem was in turn written by me and dedicated to him soon after his marriage to Miss Helen L. Chapman on June 28, 1924.

THE BLIND ASTRONOMER

I see him day by day,
His clean, fine face —
His almost silver hair —
Smiling as he feels his way
Through awakening springtime days
He cannot hope to see.

His eager brain,
His search for Truth,
His finest hopes
Are caged and blinded
By the darkness of his eyes.

And yet I see him
Day by day
Smiling with the spring.

                                    THE PHANTOM LOVER

PATER FILIO: AD AMANTEM PHANTASMATEM

Go, Son, in quest of Nature's Truth
Wherever found — in star
Or crumpled rock, or in a leaf
Age-long imprisoned
In the hardened sand.
But let Imagination lead the way
To seek the path, or haply find
A vein of purest ore.
Keep well strung thy youthful lyre
To smite in leisure hour;
For Science is not all;
Beauty may walk with Truth
In harmony.
And in your cozy nest with her
Let Fancy also have its play
To brighten narrow places,
Though Phantoms now are banished far
In love's sweet certainty.

                                              E. B. F.

In acknowledgment of the simple announcement and invitation to my birthday party, I am the proud possessor of two volumes of letters and one of telegrams which brought to me immense satisfaction with their expressions of affection and loyalty.

The morning of July 14 was a busy one in our household. Newspaper men, photographers, and some friends arrived early while the approach to the house was being outlined with a trail of flags. Our neighbors and friends around Lake Geneva offered us all kinds of assistance, and the generosity of many of my friends, both singly and in groups, in their gifts to me is too intimate an experience to mention in detail here. I have never been so touched by any demonstration, although our friends have many times been generously considerate of our welfare. Into our living-room in the afternoon came one after another of our friends, each one dear to us. The line grew longer and longer until we had greeted over three hundred and fifty. Then we gathered in groups on the lawn passing the afternoon in joyous intercourse.

About twenty-five guests who were staying over into the evening for a glimpse of something through the forty-inch telescope joined us in the sun-parlor for a picnic supper. So ended a day with unforgettable memories.

That summer of 1931 was a busy one for all of us, both before and after the party. Mrs. Frost, who for some years has been president of the Lake Geneva Garden Club, was soon involved in the preparations for the 'Midsummer Flower and Vegetable Show' which occurs in August of each year. It is a remarkable exhibit made possible by the indefatigable and combined work of the members of the Garden Club and the Gardeners' and Foremen's Association and also due to the fact that Horticultural Hall is an ideal setting for such an affair. Lake Geneva is justly proud of this building and very much indebted to the late Charles L. Hutchinson who was largely responsible for it.

When President Hutchins's new system of education went into effect at the opening of the autumn quarter, in October, 1931, I had the honor of giving the first lecture in the division of physical sciences. This new scheme of education recently adopted by the University of Chicago has received much attention. The university now consists of the professional schools and five divisions of arts. The first two years are devoted to lecture courses in the humanities and the social, physical, and biological sciences. The student may or may not attend these lectures, but may choose his own pace for advancement. The first two years are intended to give a general education to those who wish nothing more, but to provide a specific orientation to those planning to enter the divisional fields without ruining their general education by premature specialization. No degree will be given to those who leave at the end of the second year. It may take some time to demonstrate how successful the plan will be, but it has begun auspiciously. If the sentiment could become general among college students that they have a great opportunity before them which they may embrace to the full limits of their powers instead of being under compulsion, then education as a privilege might produce results far better than previous systems.

Later, in October of 1931, I was far from well, and after twenty-four hours of severe pain, our local physician, Dr. W. H. Macdonald, felt that it was necessary for me to enter a hospital, which meant for us the Albert Billings Memorial Hospital on the Midway in Chicago and connected with our university. This was my first experience in such an institution, and although I was desperately ill and annoyed by many distressing conditions, the pleasanter recollections predominate, as every possible kindness was shown to us by a group of skillful and friendly doctors and nurses and by the members of the staff. It didn't take me long to distinguish them by voice or by some special touch of the hand or even by a gift of silence. In the latter class was one whom I nicknamed 'The Noisy One,' but in some way I usually knew when he was present.

After a week or so I began to improve, and was able to undergo a modern procedure of being X-rayed. These exposures of a few seconds were quite different from those which I had myself made thirty-five years before, when instead of a few seconds something like an hour was required to X-ray the bones of the thigh. The present technique is admirably carried out by the operators, some of them young women, and the drinking of quantities of barium compounds exposes 'the department of the interior' to the scrutinizing eye of the specialist. It was considered unsafe to operate at the time, and my problem thereafter was to get well and strong. We were in the hospital for six weeks, where my wife occupied an adjoining room, reading to me, giving me moral support, and attending to the heavy correspondence and the telephone calls. I was much touched by the beautiful flowers and the many kindnesses received from a great circle of devoted friends. As soon as it was permissible, there were many callers and I fear that we may have overreached the hospital rules, especially when we celebrated our thirty-fifth wedding anniversary on November 19. The white satin wedding dress was in evidence, stuffed to represent the slender form of its original occupant. Tea and cakes were served to our doctors and nurses and to a few friends who had gathered to greet us.

Among my visitors I had almost daily discussions of astronomical problems with my friend Dr. W. D. MacMillan with whom I particularly enjoyed talking over the apparent expansion of the universe as evidenced by the high velocity of the spiral nebulæ in the line of sight away from us, a recession which reaches values of more than ten thousand miles a second.

Frequent visitors were our good friends Dr. and Mrs. Edgar J. Goodspeed, who enlivened my convalescence with their stimulating presence. Different friends bring different stimuli to a person. Dr. Goodspeed tends to revive with me memories of the classics, as did my friend Dr. Isham. As I have said, I make no pretense of being a classical scholar, but there are little fragments of this and that from the Greek and Latin authors which still register an impression after fifty years. Something during my illness recalled an old memory of Herodotus in respect to the *Podanipter*, a golden vessel of general utility at the court of Cyrus. Its name implied its use for the washing of feet. My wife was surprised at the emergence of such an odd recollection from the haze of ideas that had accompanied a state of serious illness, and she sought from Dr. Goodspeed the confirmation I desired. The good man kindly checked the reference (Herodotus 2:172).

Of my colleagues at the university, the most intimate has been Dr. James Henry Breasted, mentioned before in these pages as my comrade in our early days in Berlin. When we are together, we always break into German, but we do not enter the field of classics. Rather do we try to cast reproaches upon the accuracy of each other's findings in our respective fields and we save for each other our best stories, Victorian and modern. It has been our custom for many years to walk together in the university processions when I have occasionally participated. At the inauguration of President Robert Maynard Hutchins, November 19, 1929, Dr. Breasted and I, as two of the older members of the faculty, marched together toward the end of the procession and in somewhat flamboyant colors, he wearing the gay crimson gown of Oxford and I the scarlet one of Cambridge. The two shades do not normally blend, but they have had to meet in a similar way in England for many generations and the dissonance in color seems to make no serious breach in harmony between two old friends. As we walked along together that day toward the chapel, I heard from the side-lines the call of the white-throated sparrow and knew that a wave of my hand would tell my daughter that I had heard our adopted call.

But to return to the hospital where so many contacts were re-established by my friends and by many students of a generation ago. I was particularly pleased to receive a greeting from those men of the class of 1898 who were assembled at a dinner in Boston at the time of the Dartmouth and Harvard football game. Twenty-three were present and each man signed the note. When I expressed surprise that they should remember me so long, my wife countered with the query, 'Don't you remember *them?*' I could certainly give a strong affirmative, 'Every one of them.'

Before I left the hospital, I enjoyed a visit to the adjoining Bobs Roberts Memorial Hospital and to the wards of the Orthopedic Hospital for Crippled Children. To both of these groups I gave a brief talk about Nature and birds, and as usual with children showed them my Swiss watch that strikes the hours, quarters, and minutes. This watch is a great comfort to me and I am justly proud of it, as it was given to me by my friends and colleagues at the observatory on my sixty-fifth birthday.

After my discharge from the hospital, I went home in a pretty fair state of health, returning occasionally to the clinic during the following months for observation and consultation.

I was very glad to learn in the late spring that Dr. Otto Struve, a brilliant young man who had been a member of the observatory staff for some years, had been, in accordance with my wishes, chosen to succeed me as Director of the Yerkes Observatory. Ten years ago, when I learned that he was stranded in Constantinople after the war, I tried to get in touch with him. I had known of his illustrious line — three generations of famous astronomers in Russia — and felt safe in offering him a position. It was by a mere chance that my letter reached him, as it had first been opened by a fellow officer who did not know where to locate Mr. Struve and who furthermore hoped that the letter might contain American money. This officer happened to pass Mr. Struve who for the moment, discouraged and almost penniless, was resting on a bench on one of the streets of Constantinople. Mr. Struve spent half of the small pittance he had in his pocket (the equivalent of fifty cents) to purchase a small dictionary to assist him in translating my letter, but finally sought further help in the Y.M.C.A. which in that city is written as one word and pronounced 'IMCA.' He asked the secretary in charge whether he could tell him anything about the Yerkes

Observatory. Through the interpreter, Mr. Struve received the astonishing reply, 'Well, I ought to know it. I was brought up within seven miles of it in Elkhorn, Wisconsin, and I have often met Mr. Frost there.'

It took some months of negotiations to bring Mr. Struve to America. He proved himself to be an able student and an indefatigable worker in the field of stellar spectroscopy to which I assigned him, and he received the degree of Doctor of Philosophy from the University of Chicago for his graduate work done at the observatory. I am justly proud of him whom I now consider the most able spectroscopist of his age in the country.

Mr. Struve's mother, widow of a Russian astronomer, came to America about three years later than her son and also after long negotiations to secure her visa. When I realized that her steamer would be crossing the line of totality of the eclipse of January 24, 1925, I prepared quite an elaborate document appointing her commissioner on the high seas of the Yerkes Observatory of the University of Chicago. I forwarded this to the chief officials of the steamship company in Hamburg and received from the commodore of the fleet the assurance that Madame Struve would have every opportunity to observe the eclipse. At the critical moment, with due ceremony, the captain escorted her to the bridge in spite of the fact that there was a snowstorm at the time.

In May, 1932, I was asked to attend a meeting with some of the officials of the 1933 Century of Progress in Chicago to discuss a suggestion of mine which had come to their attention and which seemed to appeal to them. I had sometimes explained to my guests at the observatory the use of our photo-electric photometer attached to the forty-inch telescope and called their attention to the fact that when the light of a star like Arcturus fell upon the sensitive surface of this instrument, it would generate a current of electricity which could be 'stepped-up' by radio amplification so that it could deliver any desired signal — to the Century of Progress Fair, for instance — and could then be used as a trigger to start any desired action by a powerful electric machine. When this suggestion of mine reached some of the officers of the Fair, I was asked to confirm its accuracy. I later received a letter from Mr. Rufus Dawes expressing the wish that this scheme should be carried into effect and that the Fair should be officially opened in this way. It evidently seemed to these men, as it had to me, that there was real romance in the thought that this apparently feeble starlight which had been forty years in reaching us could be used to actuate powerful modern engines of industry or call into play illuminations millions of times more powerful than the light of the star as it appears from its great distance. And so the Exposition was opened with the luminous impulse of the distant but familiar star Arcturus, Alpha of the Constellation Boötes, shining with the yellow light of the first magnitude as a favorite luminary of the spring and summer sky.

This ceremony, on the evening of May 27, 1933, was an impressive one, occurring in the open air Court of the Hall of Science before an assembled audience of more than thirty thousand, while loud-speakers carried the words to two or three times that number who were within the grounds of the Exposition. Splendid music was furnished by the Chicago Symphony Orchestra and by a great chorus with Lawrence Tibbetts as soloist. President Rufus C. Dawes was the first speaker, introducing me for my short address. Dr. Philip Fox followed, concluding his remarks with the technical ceremony, calling in succession upon the participating observatories. The increasing hum of the motors set in action successively from these centers could be plainly heard, culminating when the Yerkes Observatory closed its switch and sent the final impulse from Arcturus. These complete exercises were broadcast over the principal American radio networks, and many letters have told me how well and how universally they were heard. The occasion seemed to be regarded as a thrilling event.

The following is the text of my address:

'It has seemed appropriate to add a celestrial touch to this ceremony of illuminating the Century of Progress by employing the light of the great star Arcturus in the Constellation Boötes. In so doing, we are literally following the precept of Emerson to "hitch your wagon to a star." Arcturus is one of the brightest stars in our summer sky, and has been known since men first turned their eyes in wonder toward the glories of the heavens. This star is a yellow sun having a diameter about twenty-five times greater than that of our sun and radiating about one hundred times as much light.

'It is highly probable that Arcturus has been sending out its light toward us and in all other directions for thousands of millions of years. It has reached a stage of development not unlike that of our sun, and we know that it contains the same chemical elements that occur in our sun and that are found upon the earth.

'We astronomers call it one of the nearer stars because among the billions of stars forming our galaxy, or the system of the Milky Way, there are hardly more than one hundred known to be nearer to us than Arcturus. However, its distance is enormous, the star being more than two million times as remote as our sun, or about 225 million million miles away.

'The vibrant waves of light surging toward us at the rate of 186,000 miles per second, or eleven million miles a minute, require about forty years to span this bit of the void of space. Therefore the light rays reaching our telescopes tonight and actuating our photo-electric cells, left Arcturus at the time when the eyes of the civilized world were turned toward this central city of our continent at the great Columbian Exposition of 1893.

'One of the striking exhibits at that Exposition was the great forty-inch refracting telescope which had just been presented by Mr. Charles T. Yerkes to the new University of Chicago to serve as the principal research instrument of the Yerkes Observatory, which was soon to be erected at Williams Bay, Wisconsin, on the shore of Lake Geneva. This great refractor still remains the largest of its kind yet constructed.

'As the idea of "borrowing a light" from Arcturus originated with me at this observatory, it has been the plan to use this telescope to catch the light of the star and to focus it upon the photo-electric cell which is to furnish the current needed for our purpose tonight. However, because of the danger of a cloudy sky at any one station, a circuit has been arranged to include the use of the telescopes at Harvard and at the Universities of Pittsburg and of Illinois to insure the success of our experiment.

'The Columbian Exposition did not include the photo-electric cell among its many wonderful exhibits, but scientific men, especially in Germany, were already beginning to study the curious effect of light falling upon surfaces of alkaline metals whereby exceedingly feeble currents of electricity were generated. Impelled by an insatiable curiosity to understand the mysterious workings of nature, scientists have steadily continued this research during the twoscore years that the light now arriving from Arcturus has been coming toward us. And inventors, ever ready to make use of discoveries in pure science, have helped to perfect its technique and have found many practical applications of this photo-electric cell, which in these days is often called "the mechanical eye." It has been of great service to astronomers in enabling them to measure with the highest precision the brightness of the stars without depending upon the capriciousness of the human eye.

'Hence science and invention have prepared the proper apparatus to receive the light from Arcturus and convert it into an electric current which, suitably amplified and transmitted over the tele-graph lines to this Temple of Science, actuates the switch which will in a few moments start the illumination of this Exposition.

'Is not this a fitting illustration of the amazing advances during this wonderful Century of Progress?'

In recent years, my wife and I had sometimes discussed where we should wish to locate after my retirement, but had always come to the conclusion that we preferred to remain among the friends to whom during many years we had become so devotedly attached. Here also the major part of my life-work had been done and we loved this part of the country with its beautiful lakes and hills. No small satisfaction has come to us from keeping friendly contact with the growing families of our friends who have long had country homes on the shores of Lake Geneva. We have in mind at least seven or eight families of which it has been our privilege to know four generations. I am particularly devoted to the youngest group of all, whose regard for me is very touching. We highly prize the friendship of these youngsters, and they are full of splendid promise for the future.

In early spring we decided to build a house on a piece of property adjoining and to the east of the observatory grounds. These twelve to fourteen acres had been turned over to me by the children of my friend Dr. George S. Isham after his death and according to his wishes. We had subdivided the property and had sold a few lots, most of them to friends in the University of Chicago. We called the plat 'University Heights' and had definitely set aside a place for our own use in case we should ever be able to build there.

Our friend Professor Elliot R. Downing built a charming house just south of our lot.

Perhaps one takes a home too much for granted. I might possibly be pardoned for so doing, having lived in only two houses for fifty-two years of my life. Before we found that we could arrange to build a house into which we could put at least some of our choicest belongings, I began to realize how cold the world would seem without a home of my own. I recalled the experience of a neighbor of mine who was offered a substantial sum for his farm. It appeared to be an offer too good to refuse and he accordingly closed the bargain, either party to forfeit three thousand dollars if he failed to keep the contract. Then followed sad days and sleepless nights for both the farmer and his wife. They decided that the loss of the money was nothing as compared with the loss of the home, and cheerfully paid the forfeit.

When it came time for me to retire and hence to leave the director's residence which we had occupied for twenty-seven years, the thought of anything but a small home of my own was very disturbing. *Klein aber mein* was all that I wanted. One of Mrs. Frost's hobbies had been the making of house plans. She had fortunately quite definitely formulated one which seemed best fitted to our needs and one which she thought would be easiest for me, as its plan was not unlike that of the house which we had so long occupied. It gave me a wonderful sense of relief when I found that this simple house, 28 × 38, could not only somehow be financed, but could be erected in seventy days. We were fortunate in many ways, but particularly so in having a friend as our architect and another as our contractor. Mr. Revilo Fuller of Chicago rushed through the plans and specifications, and Mr. Gunard Pihl (one of our village boys who had graduated at the University of Wisconsin) put on a heavy force of fine workmen. Everything was conscientiously done and in record time. We were surprised and delighted to see a red-headed woodpecker on our chimney-top just one week after the first upright was raised.

Being occupied with my duties in the Director's office and endeavoring to clear up my work by July first, I had little time for assisting or even advising in the final plans for occupancy, nor with my lack of vision could I help in the transfer of the garden which

Mrs. Frost had developed for some years. A trailer behind the Ford carried successive loads of plants and bulbs, many of them necessarily being moved at the wrong time of the year. Luckily there was plenty of water to encourage the roots in seeking new quarters and by the time we moved into our home, the garden was a riot of color and much admired.

I had christened the home which we were leaving 'Sternfried' in following Richard Wagner, who named his home in Bayreuth 'Wahnfried,' the place where he had found peace with the personalities whom his imagination had created. We gave to the new home the name 'Brantwood' which had been previously used in Portland, Maine, by my cousin Mary Brant Thompson who only lately passed away.

And so, on June 28, 1932, we moved into our new home on Dartmouth Road with the beautiful observatory woods for a background, a New England stone wall enclosing a considerable portion of our lot, and an unobstructed view of Lake Geneva from our south porch. I have always liked the implication of a sign on a little home in the country not far from us. It reads: 'SUITS US.' We share the families of bluebirds, robins, and other friendly feathered folk with the Downings, and they enjoy our garden visible from their house. We both object to the overabundance of gophers, who, although they are cute little fellows, dig into the garden for their runways. They have apparently found this property, untenanted for many years, a haven for their numerous progeny.

We have a new feeding-table for the birds to encourage more or them to visit us. We do not especially regret the passing of the whip-poor-will whose vociferous unremitting calls disturbed the night hours in the early years of our residence in Williams Bay. He evidently shuns civilization, for we seldom hear him now. Meadowlarks sing near us for a long season. About ten years ago I was surprised to hear the call of the Western meadowlark whose song is much more resonant and melodious than that of the more familiar species. The numbers increased so rapidly that within a short time we had nearly as many of one variety as of the other. Another bird who changed his habitat is the dickcissel. This small member of the finch family, sometimes called the 'little meadowlark,' was common east of the Alleghanies up to forty or fifty years ago. The bird books say that he has entirely disappeared from that region. For over twenty-five years I heard him only occasionally, but about five years ago the bird invaded this section in large numbers and sang his labored ditty from many a fence-post. At the present time they again seem less numerous.

We still have the lazy cowbird, whose nesting habits, by the way, differ from those of other species closely related to him, like the grackles and the red-winged blackbirds. The cowbird's custom of laying eggs solely in the nests of other birds seems to need an explanation. My own hypothesis is that it is a relic of the time when these birds followed the herds of bison in their constant wanderings over the plains. How, forsooth, would it be possible for these birds to build and occupy nests under these conditions?

We once found a summer yellowbird's nest into which a cowbird's egg had been laid. The little warbler cleverly built a new floor over that egg, but the cowbird again invaded the nest. After a second new floor was built, the warblers were undisturbed and succeeded in raising their brood.

One of my greatest difficulties is to get enough exercise. It is not always possible to find someone who is at liberty to walk with me. In order to give me a little independence in this matter, Mrs. Frost had a heavy wire strung from tree to tree at a convenient height for me along a path through the woods to the west of our house. I call this my 'trolley line,' and often take my exercise here. Twice I have continued alone, but not unwatched, about a quarter of a mile, and found my way along an irregular route to the observatory. When I occasionally missed the road, some familiar tree or shrub gave me my location.

The relief from my exacting duties as Director of the observatory was practically a necessity for me as far as my health was concerned, and until we started for the East on August 18 to see the total eclipse of the sun, I took every opportunity to rest. We were loath to leave the new house which we had occupied so short a time, but we were somewhat consoled to know that friends who rented it for a month would enjoy it for us too and would count, as we were doing each morning, the increase in the number of heavenly-blue morning-glories which adorned the porch and which gave us great satisfaction.

BRANTWOOD

The path of the eclipse of August 31, 1932, as charted in Oppolzer's *Canon of Eclipses*, published nearly fifty years ago, passed out to sea from a point in Canada without entering the United States. The scale of his diagram was, however, so small that an error of nearly a hundred miles might be made in reading it. As 1932 approached, rigorous computations were made, from which it was seen that the center of the track of totality would pass from the region of Hudson Bay southeastward across parts of Vermont, New Hampshire, and Maine, finally touching the northeastern portion of Cape Cod. Not only American but some foreign astronomers planned expeditions to observe the eclipse and thousands of citizens flocked into New England for the event.

At this eclipse I had no responsibility in organizing an expedition. Mrs. Frost and I planned to arrive in the eclipse region a few days in advance in order to visit the various stations of our colleagues along the route in New Hampshire and Maine. Weather observations collected for several years past had indicated only fifty per cent probability of clear skies, and many feared to establish stations near the sea on account of the danger of fog. My own choice would have been to locate in Lancaster, New Hampshire, west of Mount Washington. However, a low barometric area, passing down the St. Lawrence, brought clouds which disappointed nearly all the observers along the path. Entirely satisfactory results were obtained at only a few stations, and those chiefly in the southern portion of the track.

As we were visiting our son and his family in Westbrook, a suburb of Portland, it seemed best to me to depend upon the United States Weather Bureau for information and to have the car in readiness to dash toward the point giving the best promise of a clear sky. It so happened that an ocean breeze kept back the clouds obscuring the northern stations and we were fortunate as a family group in having a cloudless sky not far from my son's home.

The corona was a fine one with streamers extending out for two diameters — nearly two million miles. The description given to me during the ninety-two seconds of totality reminded me much of the appearance of the corona as I had seen it in 1900 at Wadesboro, North Carolina. I learned that small grandchildren under seven years of age are not greatly impressed by a phenomenon of such brief duration.

On September 2 we drove to Cambridge, Massachusetts, to attend the meeting of the International Astronomical Union held under the auspices of the Harvard College Observatory. This was the first time that the Union had met in America — four years after the last assembly at Leiden. Sir Frank Dyson, Astronomer Royal, presided as president, and there was an excellent attendance with a good percentage of foreigners. The Union operates almost entirely through the sessions of its committees with an occasional plenary session for the discussion and the ratification of the reports of committees. I was not well enough to attend all of the meetings, but enjoyed the scientific intercourse which such a gathering provides. The program included many visits to points of interest in the vicinity of Boston, and Sir Arthur Eddington gave a public lecture at the Massachusetts Institute of Technology on 'The Expanding Universe.'

From Cambridge we drove back to Hanover, making two short visits *en route* at the homes of friends. Our first stop was at Tewksbury, Massachusetts, at the summer home of our Dartmouth-Wellesley friends, Mr. and Mrs. Henry H. Hilton. I was again reminded, as I am every day of my life, of the unfailing kindness and solicitous concern shown to one handicapped by blindness. So far as I can judge by my own experience, everyone loves a blind man. In this home was a charming little granddaughter who gently but efficiently led me to my place at the luncheon table. Wherever we go we are surprised and impressed by the quick and sympathetic offers of help. I know that blind people often travel alone and I realize why that is possible.

Some miles farther north, we renewed very pleasant associations with a college classmate of Mrs. Frost's. Mr. and Mrs. Heylman live on a beautiful hillside above the lake, known as 'Little Sunapee.' It was a delight to find after a lapse of many years that their interests in life had developed along much the same lines as ours. They also love birds, flowers, and trees, and in their winter home in Porto Rico they have started an arboretum which promises to be a very important one in the testing of trees from various climes.

It is always a satisfaction to me to get back to Hanover which to me is another home. We have not only many friends here, but my brother is still connected with the Medical Faculty. In fact,

in this year of 1933, either my brother or my father or I, separately
or all three of us at the same time, have taught at Dartmouth for
an unbroken period of sixty-five years.

I love the country around Hanover and enjoy the drives — up the
river road to Lyme; down the winding wooded road to West
Lebanon; across the old covered bridge to Norwich, Vermont, and
thence along the Connecticut River to the north to that beautiful
hilltop in Thetford where so many of my forbears had lived and
near which is buried the uncle for whom I was named. I know
every inch of that country and can perfectly act as a guide for my
wife beside whom I sit as she ably drives the car at a pace not too
slow. One might not expect that a blind man would enjoy motoring.
On the contrary, it does interest me very much, and the comfort of
riding in a car is infinitely better than spending the time in a stuffy
train. Mrs. Frost describes everything to me as we speed along — a
familiar mountain in the distance, the winding curves of a rock-
bedded river, the flight of a bird, and always a passing locomotive
whose number we still try to read. On familiar routes, as between
Lake Geneva and Chicago, there is something about the curves
and the occasional grades or even the crossing of a culvert which
makes the route almost as definite in my mind as if I could see its
contours. Thus it happens that I seldom lose my sense either of
distance or time on such a trip.

As we left Hanover for home on Sunday morning, September 11,
I chose the Connecticut River route which would take me to my
birthplace in Vermont. I had stopped in Brattleboro only once
since 1871 and was anxious to see it again. Vermonters are possibly
unduly proud of their State. Although I have not lived in Vermont
since I was five years of age, there has been a strong sense of pride
in being a native of that State which has been the home for at least
four generations of my mother's family.

Upon entering the village at this time, we asked a stranger for
directions to Green Street where we wished to locate the small
brick house in which I was born. We were amused to find, during
our short conversation, that this man's brother had been a student
of mine at Dartmouth. And then he added, to my surprise, 'I have
frequently heard my mother speak of your father, for he was present
when I was born.' Mrs. Frost often says that I couldn't possibly

get lost in Vermont. She was thoroughly convinced of this when we stopped not long ago at a little tea-shop on the road to Burlington to deliver a message to a woman who was a perfect stranger to us. When she heard my name, she asked, 'Are you the Doctor or the Professor?' I replied, 'My brother is the Doctor and lives in Hanover.' 'Oh, yes,' said she, 'I know all about you. I have always lived in Randolph. Your aunt gave me my musical education. When she died, I sang at her funeral service. I sang at your grandmother's too.'

I had been waiting all my life to take the trip from Brattleboro across the lower stretch of the Green Mountains to Bennington and thence into New York State *via* Troy. This was my opportunity. We found the wooded climb very beautiful, and at the highest point there is a wonderful view down through the valley to the south. We saw on the map the name 'Haystack Mountain' and wondered whether we were crossing at that point. We asked the waitress in the restaurant that noon whether that was the case. We got just the answer I expected when she said, 'Oh, that is The Green Mountain.' Vermonters always live on one side or the other of *The* mountain.

If he who reads knows anything about Vermont thrift, he will perhaps recall or freshly enjoy a story which has just occurred to me. A bachelor farmer of these parts had the good fortune to take a little trip out into the world, in fact to Washington, and possibly to be present at the inauguration ceremonies of his fellow citizen, Calvin Coolidge. But his neighbors questioned the man in this wise: 'How can you leave your pig for a whole week?' 'Oh,' replied the farmer, 'I have measured out just the right number of feedings and they will last him *ef he is pru-dent.*'

We have always wanted to try, but have looked askance at the little groups of cottages which one frequently passes now along the highway. On this trip we were definitely committed to make the experiment, and toward the end of the first day we saw the 'Star' cabins advertised. These were for us, of course. What more appropriate! Cabins of this type had been highly recommended to us by many of our friends who had crossed the country on their way to see the eclipse. We did indeed find these small houses not only both clean and comfortable but inexpensive. They have the disadvantage, however, of being located on the main thoroughfares where the noise of the heavy traffic continues throughout the night.

Owing to the difference of time, both daylight-saving and central-standard, and possibly to the persistence of the chauffeuse, we arrived in Chicago at four o'clock on Tuesday afternoon. The thought of the comfort and contentment which would be ours when we reached the home which we had occupied for only seven weeks decided us to push on for the remaining eighty miles, making our drive for the day just four hundred and forty miles.

On Tuesday, October 11, I again entered the hospital, hoping that I might be allowed to part with the troublesome gall-bladder. It was generously arranged that we might have our same connecting rooms and I was fortunate in securing my same excellent nurse, Miss Grace Potts. When it was decided that I was in good enough condition to undergo an operation, I went to the operating-room on my *wagon-lit* perfectly convinced that under my skillful surgeon, Dr. Dallas B. Phemister, I should be given a new lease of life. Blessed be those human benefactors who, both singly and in groups, relieve us of our restricting ailments and make us new again!

I had one or two experiences in the hospital which were very annoying to me, but which were a necessary part of the treatment. Through needles inserted subcutaneously I had to be given the 'Ringer's solution' a process taking some forty-five minutes and which I called 'The Saint Sebastian Act.' For some absurd reason it also seemed difficult for me to take sufficient liquid nourishment. How slow a process it was to drink three quarts a day! I finally decided that if I could combine a bit of sherry with the water, which seemed insipid to me, I should get along better. When one of the doctors saw me with a goblet of water in one hand and a wineglass of sherry in the other, I quoted to him the old German song about Noah which seemed to me appropriate to the occasion.

> Als Noah aus dem Kasten war,
> Da trat zu ihm der Herre dar,
> Der roch des Noah Opfer fein
> Und sprach: 'Ich will dir gnädig sein,
> Und weil du ein so frommes Haus,
> So bitt' dir selbst die Gnaden aus,'

Der Noah sprach: 'Ach lieber Herr!
Das Wasser schmeckt mir gar nicht sehr,
Die weil darin ersäufet sind
All' sündhaft Vieh und Menschenkind:
Drum möcht' ich armer alter Mann
Ein anderweit' Getränke han!'

Da griff der Herr in's Paradies
Und gab ihm einen Weinstock süss,
Und gab ihm guten Rath und Lehr'
Und sprach: 'Den sollt du pflegen sehr!'
Und wies ihm alles so und so:
Der Noah ward ohn' Massen froh.[1]

---

[1] When Noah came out of the Ark, the Lord appeared to him; he smelled the
fine burnt-offering of Noah, and said: 'I will be gracious to you, and since you
and your house are such pious folk, you shall choose for yourself what gift you
would have.' Then spoke Noah: 'Ah, dear Lord, the water does not taste good to
me because in it were drowned all sinful flesh and children of men. So I, poor old
man, would like to have some other form of drink.' The Lord then reached into
Paradise and gave him a sweet vine and gave him good advice and instruction
and said: 'You must take the best care of it,' and explained to him everything
about it,. thus and so, and Noah rejoiced beyond all measure.

CHAPTER XXV

IN RETROSPECT

IN CONSIDERING life from the vantage-point of an experience of two thirds of a century, I am impressed by the fact that it is an experimental science. At every point of our growth and development we are continually trying to do something new, something different, something a little more advanced. We are testing our own powers even in very early youth; sometimes measuring them in terms of those of others; sometimes merely in terms of our own successive experiences; sometimes gauging our physical powers, sometimes our mental capacities, and sometimes our moral forces or wills. The struggle for leadership among his fellows in some cases begins in his earliest school days.

The constant change of motives and desires is always altering the conditions of the experiment and making a new test. Thus, at fifteen, experiences are greatly different from those of ten years of age. New elements of desire and ambition have come to the youth. Of course, in the large and highly organized schools of the cities the boy is swept along in conformity with his fellows and there is far less opportunity for development of individuality or special capacity in unusual lines. This tendency of modern education to turn out students as nearly identical as their individual characters will permit may be for the average benefit of the whole group, but it seems to me that it greatly diminishes the likelihood of developing special genius. The experiment of life is a severe one for many youths as they go to college or enter upon some business employment. Moreover, originality is not greatly desired in either place, and conformity to the usual procedure may often give a serious check to his desire to try new methods instead of following the old ones. Knowing the effect of this repression, I have in my own teaching always tried to encourage the student to proceed with his own line of thought, provided that some basic error is not involved. There are probably few boys who know at sixteen what would be their choice for a life-work. It is ordinarily too early to make a choice.

Later experience or education should show the lines of best capacity. Therefore, it seems to me that, in general, it is better for a youth to defer his choice of occupation until he is twenty, if circumstances permit. Of course many will say that this puts him at a disadvantage as compared with the youth who has gone through the stages from office boy upward and has thoroughly grounded himself in the routine of a certain occupation or business.

For one who expects to enter professional life there may be no little benefit derived from some experience in teaching. As I have said, this was quite a regular practice among the college graduates of a generation or two ago. It doubtless stood them in good stead for the future experiences of life. My father assured me that a few years spent in teaching would never be wasted, whatever might be my final life-work. It is, however, a great pity that so many young men come into their line of occupation rather by chance than by design; some opportunity is offered through a friend of the family and is accepted in the present state of severe competition. I have sometimes asked business friends what proportion of their associates or employees are in their special business by deliberate choice or merely as a result of some more or less accidental circumstance. It appears to be the opinion that a very small percentage of men in the business world are working in just the line they would prefer for their happiness and the full realization of their powers. Those who go into professions have an advantage, because the required training is so long that they are certain to discover whether or not they are likely to be fitted for the field in which they are studying. Of course it would be hard to imagine a state of affairs which would permit everyone to choose his own occupation solely according to his own taste. Perhaps there would be as much confusion and as many misfits as there are under the present system, because a man might have many ideas not suitable to the requirements of the world in which he lived.

It is interesting to find that industry is looking more and more toward the college-bred man of ability to fill positions of responsibility. A degree, after all, begins to mean something practical, and the man is looked upon with less suspicion by the fellow who has spent the same number of years working his way through various departments. Some statistics have been gathered from college presidents to whom leaders of industry have appealed for outstanding men in the graduating classes. These leaders seek intelligence and integrity, and they rightly claim that any successful system of education should train the one and inculcate the other. President E. M. Hopkins voices the general sentiment when he says: 'The man who is most attentive to his college work and secures the best results is altogether likely to be outstandingly successful in the business or profession into which he goes.'

There are still those who scoff at higher education, especially for the man who definitely desires to have a business career. For these skeptics, let me repeat a story applicable to the case and told by Mr. Harold Swift at the annual dinner given by the trustees to the faculty of the University of Chicago. The story is as follows: Father Dorney had an excellent janitor in his church in the stock-yards district, but in the course of time it seemed necessary that in addition to his work as janitor the man must keep the books. Alas, Pat could neither read nor write and was obliged to look for a new job. He had had some experience in cement work, but needed capital in order to accept a contract which was open to him. Fortunately, a banker believed in him, lent him the money, and was promptly repaid. When his friendly creditor remarked: 'Pat, you have done well. I knew you would. What *would* you have been if you had had an education!' Said Pat — 'Janitor of Father Dorney's church!'

There are, of course, many cases of men who are successful both in business and politics — men who have given themselves a liberal education. One such case I should like to cite to illustrate what a man with initiative and brains can do. It is the case of my friend Mr. Charles R. Crane whose father was definitely and openly opposed to college education. His son was not given the opportunity to go to college, but was destined for a business career, although his own inclination was toward study and travel. When his friend Martin Ryerson was being graduated from Harvard Law School, Mr. Crane went East on what was to be a brief visit during Commencement and to see the boat-races at New London. The sea and shipping had always interested him and as usual he walked along the waterfront in New York looking over the ships and their destinations. He found a sailing ship that looked particularly trim and neat and chatted with the captain who was about to sail with a cargo for China. The captain made such a good impression upon him that, on the impulse of the moment, young Charles asked to be taken along as a passenger. After telegraphing his father for permission and for funds, he bought a library of a couple of hundred books, put them on board, and sailed with the ship instead of going to the races. Arriving in China, he spent considerable time in the home of the Anglican Bishop of Canton, returning home by another ship across the Pacific. Thus he started on his career of education and travel which has taken him a score of times to Russia and to many parts of the world. It has brought him many friends among the statesmen and potentates of Central Asia and various countries of Europe. His career in the business world is well known, as is his position as Minister to China under Woodrow Wilson.

It is fortunate for most of us that we must work for our living and must depend upon our own efforts for progress in any field of activity. Favoritism or family connections may have some influence, particularly in business, but for the majority of men and women, they must prove their own value to secure advancement and recognition. The assurance that the necessities and comforts of life will be provided without effort usually removes the incentive for work. There are many who, although financially endowed, are not hampered by it. Money as a means to an end must give one a feeling of comfort and safety, and is absolutely a necessity for the long years of education of one's children. I am thankful that I have children. It has not only been a great joy but an inspiration and has given me a deeper understanding of life. I greatly fear the modern tendencies to avoid the responsibilities of parenthood. I once asked a young woman how many children she had, and met the response, 'We haven't any, Mr. Frost. We have always lived in an apartment and felt that it was no place to bring up children.' My reply was hardly polite, for I promptly answered, 'Then I would buy a tent.'

What a pleasure it is to see the world through the eyes of our children, renewing the study of Nature, of personality, and of human relations. Their questions keep us alert, but we often take for granted too much knowledge and reasoning power on their part. When I once asked my four-year-old son a question on a matter which I supposed that he understood, he replied in surprise, 'Why, Daddy, I don't know much — just a few things that people tell me.' On the other hand, I thoroughly believe in trying to explain things clearly and correctly to children as early as possible. I remember discussing gravitation with my little daughter when she was only three and a half years old. She was much interested, but argued that, 'Perhaps that road out there might stay on if the earth is round, but I don't think a buggy would.' The next day we heard her crooning to herself, 'And God puts us on the ground where gravitation holds us down.'

Perhaps through their college years we change places with our children and they educate us! I remember some very frank talks during those years regarding actual attitudes and habits of some of the new generation. These were certainly illuminating to me. We are first apt to be shocked and to say, 'In my generation, etc.' But I believe in these young folk and their sincerity. They have shed some of the false modesty of my time and have accepted a healthier attitude toward some of the most serious problems of life.

And so, as I near the completion of the most active years of my life, it is natural to look at the picture critically. Where would I have painted it differently? Do the shadows make the high-lights brighter? Have I learned to keep the balance true? At any rate, it has been a labor of head and heart — hard work with its measure of success, and with the daily tasks exalted by the love of wife and family and the warm-hearted devotion of friends. Therewith I am content. Life to me has been far from prosaic. I have loved the wide world, and I have been engaged in a profession which I chose deliberately, never regretting my choice. With my 'wagon hitched to a star,' I have perhaps been saved from the wear and tear of a noisy distracting city, and have not rubbed elbows with uncongenial strangers. How fortunate, too, to be blessed with three intelligent children, and to be the delighted and irresponsible grandfather of three beautiful grandchildren, one of whom is named for me!

Our home is now empty except for friends and as we are enlivened on week-ends by the coming of our son and daughter, their friends, and ours.

I suppose that my keen interest in affairs should lag a bit, that I should wish to relieve myself somewhat of the pressure of daily duties. On the contrary, if I should tell the truth, I should be bored to death with idle hands and a lazy brain.

What couldn't I do if I could see — if I could see...

CHAPTER XXVI

FRAGMENTS OF COSMIC PHILOSOPHY [1]

THESE years since the turn of the century have been golden years of progress in the physical sciences. The University of Chicago has had an honorable part in this advance both in the laboratories and in the Observatory. The introduction of photography into astronomy has made it possible to find the scale of the universe more accurately, to measure the distances of the stars, to determine their speeds in the line of sight, and across the line of sight among their fellows, and to record and map the immense fields of the stellar universe. We may justly say that the life of the University has been contemporaneous with this great advance in the knowledge of the heavens. In recent years there have been equally important discoveries in the field of the minute in the atomic structure of matter. These researches conducted in the laboratories have been interpreted in some respects in terms of the knowledge gained in celestial places. It is quite impossible to find or to produce in the laboratory those conditions which we know must prevail in the stars, and therefore the stars themselves become great laboratories of research and interpretation. Recently, there have been attempts at the explanation and correlation of these results among writers, particularly in England by Sir Arthur Eddington and Sir James Jeans, as well as by some astronomers, physicists, and chemists there and elsewhere. This approach from various sides is advantageous, because the interpretation of the physical and chemical results is complicated, and the solution of the mathematical problems is very difficult. The interpretations of the observations are of course liable to all the defects of our sense perceptions at the telescope as well as to the insufficiency of any system of mathematics to cope with many of the problems. These brilliant English writers, whose works are coming to us very rapidly, tend to give an impression of finality to their conclusions which is somewhat misleading to the average

[1] William Vaughn Moody Lecture given at Mandel Hall, University of Chicago, December 3, 1930.

reader. These authors may perhaps put in enough qualifying clauses to save them from undue criticism from their colleagues who know the full value of these qualifications, but the general reader may easily be deceived and get the idea that the results reached are matters of certainty and not dependent solely upon the premises upon which the authors have based their reasoning.

My first thesis is that the universe is orderly, that it proceeds along the lines of cause and effect, and that for a given cause, with the conditions absolutely identical, the result will be a definite one and not indefinite. This may be determinism, and if so, let it be. In our astronomical research we find that where there is a departure from previous experience from the effect expected of a given cause, it is usually due to a lack of adequate information of the condition. As the knowledge of all the conditions increases, the more do we find that the same result follows the same cause. Of course it is easy to be trite on this subject of an orderly universe, but in his book entitled *The Mysterious Universe*, published in 1930, Jeans gives to the reader the impression that the earth is merely an accident, and Sir Arthur Eddington at about the same time is quoted as having said the same thing in another lecture in England. This, under certain premises, may be the case, and it is one of these premises which I have to discuss. I may say that the fur is flying in England between these distinguished men of research, although this does not appear so much in the works which the public is reading very widely at present.

The premise upon which is based the conclusion that the earth is an accident is that the earth and planets come into being by reason of the close approach of two suns in their aimless wanderings through space. Because such close approaches would occur at extremely long intervals, these writers conclude that the development of a planet is an exceedingly rare event, occurring, as Sir James Jeans states, only about once in five thousand million years. Such is their premise, and if it is plainly stated and is a fact, then the earth may be regarded as an accident. We may, however, object to this assumption that the stars are wandering purely at random, because the more we study stars the more do we find that their motions can be correlated and co-ordinated. Many groups and streams of stars with members in very different parts of the

Elijah (1771–1860)　　　Benjamin (1802–1872)

Carlton Pennington (1830–1896)　　　Edwin Brant, II (1866–　　)

Frederick Hazard (1902–　　)　　　Edwin Brant, III (1930–　　)

FATHERS AND SONS: SIX GENERATIONS OF FROSTS

sky have been found possessing a common motion toward the same vanishing point. A familiar near-by group is the so-called *Bear Family* which includes five of the stars in the Great Dipper, as well as Sirius and other well-known stars. The group of stars including the Hyades known as the Taurus stream also has a common objective. There are many others of these clusters and groups, definitely showing the result of some yet unknown law and order operative among them. Indeed, the latest result of researches on the motions of the stars is that the whole galaxy is turning about a central axis. This is the result of the most precise possible studies of the motions of the stars in the line of sight with the spectroscope and across the line of sight made on photographic plates. Thus we find that what might have appeared to be random motions are perhaps just the motions of the stars as they whirl about the common center of rotation of the galaxy.

There may well be other ways in which planets are derived from suns or in which they are picked up by suns and therefore become members of their systems, rather than by the close approach of two stars. In our own system planets are by no means a rarity, as we already know nearly eleven hundred minor planets between the orbits of Mars and Jupiter in addition to the known greater planets. There may be even another group out beyond Neptune. Pluto may be found to be one of these.

I must very briefly refer to a process, other than the method of close approach, which perhaps is equally capable of producing planets in the neighborhood of a star. I refer to the sudden outburst of a star which increases its brightness many thousand fold in the course of a few hours. We now interpret this as the explosion of a great shell of gas from within the star. Such a case occurred on the evening of June 8, 1918. We had been at our station in the Red Desert in Wyoming for the observation of the total solar eclipse occurring on that afternoon. At about midnight the senior member of our staff, the late Professor Barnard, called us to witness a star of the first magnitude which had not been visible on the previous nights, but which now shone brilliantly, not far from Altair. When earlier photographic plates could be examined, it was found that within thirty-six hours that star had increased its brilliance fully thirty thousand times. It was the explosion of a sun — one of the most gigantic affairs in nature, surpassing anything we can imagine of a terrestrial origin. Observations since that time plainly show that an envelope of gas had been expanding around the star with a speed of about one hundred million miles a day. The diameter of this gaseous ring was visibly increasing year by year and could be measured with the micrometer. This ring of gas now has a diameter of about one two-hundredth of a degree. This is a case of observation, not of theory, and while the mathematics have not been worked out, it is probably not very much more difficult to formulate the result for this case than for the development of planets out of gas extracted from the interior of stars that have had a close approach.

Then the question arises — Is the explosion of a star a rare event? The answer is — By no means! In my own experience in astronomy, at least twenty-five such novæ have been observed which have attained such brightness that they could be very carefully studied with the spectroscope. In the Great Nebula of Andromeda, there flashed out a star in 1885 twenty million times brighter than our sun. This figure assumes that the star was actually in the heart of the nebula and not somewhere in line between us and the nebula. There are fifty thousand chances to one that it actually was within the nebula as it appeared to be. At that time the nebula was supposed to be a great mass of gas, and we thought that a star was forming before our eyes in accordance with the nebular hypothesis of Laplace. We now know that this object is a great spiral galaxy of stars, one of which suddenly flared up and became a so-called nova. Since then there have been found nearly one hundred other cases of the outburst of a nova in that galaxy, and Dr. Hubble estimates that probably thirty occur yearly in that spiral cluster of suns. It is easier to keep watch of a system like this which can be photographed on a single plate than to catch such phenomena that occur in our own galaxy, or Milky Way, which can be covered only by a large number of photographs taken over a considerable period of time. It is estimated that at least ten novæ occur annually in our galaxy. By different methods the geologists calculate that the earth took on substantially its frame as we know it from one to ten thousand million years ago — in other words, perhaps two billion years ago. At the rate of ten novæ per year, there would have been twenty billion cases of the occurrence of novæ in our own system during the past existence of our planet. Thus, instead of being a rarity, some critics say that such an event would be too frequent an occurrence. This result, however, is derived from observation, not from theory. And so I say emphatically that this is a fact far different from an hypothesis of the close approach of two stars with the assumed accidental result of the production of our planet. We must therefore face the question of evolution of planets or stars in terms of cataclysm. It is not necessary that an orderly universe should proceed in a gradual way. There are many processes in physics involving a critical state where abrupt changes occur, and so here we must regard such phenomena, as an explosion of stars, to be a regular process of nature and not accidental. Were such a nova to burst out tonight, we could predict rather accurately from the accumulation of information in the last twenty-five years what would be the probable transformations of its light and spectrum in the succeeding days and weeks. Events that can be predicted are of the nature of law and not of accident, even though we may not know what is the internal trigger-action that causes a sudden explosion.

Among the luminous stars of our galaxy, estimated at many billions in number, there are doubtless millions of yellow suns having physical and chemical conditions and temperatures and atmospheres closely similar to those of our sun. Logically, we have no reason whatever to assume that our dwarf yellow sun is more likely to support planets circulating about it than are these other yellow suns. However, our telescopes cannot give us direct observational evidence, for did our nearest stellar neighbor, only twenty-five million million miles away, have a planet as large as Jupiter revolving about it, its detection would be quite beyond our optical powers. Nevertheless, we have learned by observations with our spectrographs that many stars appearing single in the largest telescopes are actually composed of two or more stars revolving very rapidly about each other. In some cases, one of the companions may be relatively dark and eclipse the brighter companion. Among the stars characterized by the abundance of helium in their atmospheres, which we have especially studied, more than two thirds of the stars are found to be provided with companions and to be double or multiple. These companions are commonly far too large to be called planets, but their existence is evidence that nature tends to produce complex systems of several bodies in a group rather than to develop exclusively into single stars. The mathematical formulation of these processes of cosmology is, of course, extremely difficult, and therefore it is not surprising that mathematicians sometimes confuse the difficulty of the mathematical expressions of evolutionary events with the supposed difficulty for nature to carry out its processes.

Let us now pass to the consideration of a very extraordinary thing, the unity of the universe. It is the spectroscope, usually arranged to record its findings photographically, that enables us to analyze chemically all of the celestial objects that shine by their own light regardless of their immense distances, just as we can study the light of our own star, the sun. We nowhere find chemical elements that have not been detected in the earth itself. In 1868, in the atmosphere of the sun, a golden ray was seen which had the characteristics of a new element, and it was named helium. Twenty-seven years later it was found locked up in certain crystals found in the rocks. When released from its long confinement and made to glow in a vacuum tube, it revealed the same golden ray that had been caught in the sun. It was later found abundantly within the earth and has been applied to practical uses. At the same time, it has been found to be one of the most remarkable of all the chemical elements in its atomic behavior, standing next above hydrogen, which is the fundamental element, number one, in the sequence of the elements. It was thought for some years that the gaseous nebulæ emitted radiations which were due to a new and peculiar element of their own to which until recently the name of nebulium was assigned. It has recently been discovered, however, that these radiations are emitted by the familiar oxygen and nitrogen along with hydrogen. We thus find that our earth is a sample of the universe and that our own bodies are representative of the more common elements, because in them we have the hydrogen, oxygen, nitrogen, calcium, carbon and other elements familiar to us, to the number of about a dozen which are the most conspicuous in the stars found out in these distant galaxies. We know, therefore, that there is one kind of matter in the whole universe, and this points not to any random circumstances, but again to law.

When we consider the units of the universe we are indeed in trouble. Many of these problems are beyond present solution, and our limited knowledge can lead only to fragmentary philosophy of the causes that have been operating and the results that have followed from them. We wish to know which form the structure had at the beginning and which at the end, but we again meet that old problem of the sequence of the hen and the egg. Which precedes the other? Shall we say that the beginning product is dust, or is it an end product of celestial evolution? We find great quantities of dust merely reflecting the light of the stars near it; we also see great non-luminous nebulæ which may be in part merely dust and which obscure the light of the stars behind them; and then we have gaseous nebulæ — a most interesting type. Some of them are in geometric shapes as rings and spirals, while others are rather chaotic. Formerly, these were believed to be the primitive units in the universe. I was taught in Sunday School in the somewhat chilly Calvinistic atmosphere of a New England college town the nebular hypothesis. It was a very beautiful conception, and it has had an extraordinary effect on the development of science since it was proposed by Laplace toward the end of the 18th century. It has lately been found, however, that the nebulæ have been filching their light from stars near them, so that they can no longer maintain their high position as original sources. If it requires the light of a star to incite a nebula into luminosity, then we must regard the star's light as the source, so that, in recent years, the hypothesis has been abandoned by many scientists.

We may now ask if the stars themselves may not be the units of the universe. Every star is a sun, a great glowing sphere of gas with surface temperatures corresponding to the perfect radiator of from five to thirty thousand degrees Fahrenheit, but with their interiors vastly hotter, perhaps as high as fifty million degrees or more. Is it not possible that other units are evolved from stars just as we suppose that our planets were formed from the material of our sun? We may even raise the question whether the vast galaxies, great assemblies of stars often in spiral and spheroidal grouping, represent a stage of beginning or one of later development. One of the finest of these galaxies is that in Andromeda which is faintly visible to the naked eye in our northern sky during the autumn and winter. I prefer not to call it a nebula because that generally implies gaseous material which is not in evidence in any appreciable quantity. It is composed of countless stars, perhaps millions, most of which are so faint and numerous that they give the filmy appearance of a nebula, but with the most powerful telescopes, portions have actually been resolved into stars. The spectrograph shows that their combined light is the same as that of a cluster of stars. The spiral is turning around an internal axis at a very high speed of rotation, and the whole spiral is moving through space at a tremendous rate, approaching us nearly two hundred miles every second. The present estimate of its distance is about nine hundred thousand light years. I should remind you that a light year is nearly six million million miles, being the distance that light can travel in one year. In other words, any conflagration occurring suddenly in that spiral must require nearly a million years before its light can reach us. There are probably not less than two million of these wonderful objects within the reach of our present greatest telescopes. Some of these million galaxies are probably at least a thousand times as distant as the Andromeda galaxy, or on the order of a billion light years.

While we are unable to infer which are the primary and which are the ultimate structures of the universe, we can have no doubt that evolution is proceeding among them. We can classify the stars into many definite groups according to their spectral stage of evolution, and this suggests a rising and a descending branch of the curve of their life histories. We see not a few indications that progress is in cycles involving tremendous periods of time. We question whether one branch of the cycle does not proceed from the simple toward the complex and another later, from the complex toward the simple. Each element has one more free electron than that preceding it in the list. It seems obvious that the complex elements must have been built up out of the simple ones, but this has never been observed in the laboratory or in nature. But as a matter of observation, all transformations of matter are at present in the direction from the complex toward the simple. Thus the element uranium changes spontaneously into a lower radio-active element. While these changes are observed in the case of these elements, from numbers eighty-three to ninety-two in the atomic series, it is widely believed that similar changes at a vastly slower rate are occurring for the other elements.

The eminent chemist, Professor Nernst of Berlin, has recently extended his studies to cosmology. He finds an argument against an infinite past for the universe in the fact that there are so many complex elements still existent and that not more helium has been produced. However, if these elements were developed during that branch of a cycle when the progress was from the simple toward the complex, while they are now evidently on the other branch of the cycle and changing from the complex to the simple, there can evidently be practically infinite time in the succession of cycles. We note in the case of these explosions of temporary stars an apparent tendency for the evolution to proceed from the complex to the simple when a planetary nebula of comparatively simple constitution develops as the nucleus from the remains of a star.

We must now consider briefly one of the interesting developments of the application of mathematical theory to the probable conditions in the interior of a star. In 1905 Einstein announced the equation which showed the equivalent of matter and radiation, that matter can be automatically converted into light and has an equivalent in radiation for every gram of matter. This means that under the terrific temperatures prevailing in the interior of the stars, the negative electrons and the positive protons may combine, going out of existence as matter and forming a tremendous gush of radiant energy. Interatomic energies are so enormous that the annihilation of only four pounds of matter in the sun would give out enough energy to supply the entire earth's demands for one second. Forty or fifty years ago, the leading scientists of the time, Von Helmholtz and Lord Kelvin, could predict a future for the sun of only a few million years, on the theory that its heat was maintained by contraction, but the new doctrine of the actual sacrifice of matter to form light and heat extends the expectation of life of our sun to millions of millions of years. However, Professor E. A. Milne of Oxford contends that there are many mathematical solutions for the formula which Professor Eddington has developed, and that the temperatures within the stars, themselves great laboratories, may be ten thousand times higher than the figures we have given.

There is, moreover, a side of this picture that is highly unsatisfactory to the philosophy of many scientists. It would appear that this radiation is being wasted, and this does not correspond to our ideas of the universe as a great going concern. Astronomers realize that this tremendous outpouring of radiation is being emitted from all the stars, and from some at a vastly greater rate than from our sun, and we feel that there must be some reversal of the process. The search has been both theoretically and practically made as to whether there may not be the possibility that somehow and somewhere radiation may turn back into matter and that the cycle may be complete. My colleague Professor W. D. MacMillan has advanced this view, and it has been thought that the cosmic rays which have been investigated by Dr. R. A. Millikan and others give us some evidence that this may and actually does occur. It certainly would better satisfy our philosophy if ultimately it may be demonstrated as a matter of observation.

There is in our picture of the future of the universe a ghost disturbing to our philosophy, offering the dire prediction that the fate of the universe is stagnation. There is the second law of thermodynamics which states that in all the transformations of heat the tendency is downward. It is called the degradation of energy, or *Wärmetodt* by the Germans. There would be no possibility of producing power or getting anything useful from the heat. Nernst, who himself derived what is called the third law of thermodynamics, has felt as keenly as any the philosophical objection to such an outcome for the universe, and his third law would suggest that under certain conditions the reverse phenomenon may take place, namely, when as a result of some cataclysm or explosion, temperatures as high as a thousand million degrees can be produced. The state of stagnation would be cancelled immediately and reversed and the chemical elements would begin to build up from the simple to the complex.

Let us consider again whether from the infinite past this has not already taken place and accounts for the building up of the elements from number one, hydrogen, to number ninety-two, uranium, which we now find to be proceeding in the opposite direction under the radio-active disintegration. And thus we discover evidence of the perpetuity, future and past, of the universe in a way of cycles such as are suggested in other realms of organic nature.

Everything that we learn from the observational point of view in the study of astronomy seems to me to point precisely and always towards a purposeful operation of nature. When you accept this, it seems to me to be inconsistent with physical sciences not to believe in a mind behind the universe. I cannot imagine, nor can you, the planets getting together and deciding under what law they would operate. Nor do we find anywhere in the solar or stellar systems the debris that would necessarily accumulate if the universe had been operating at random. The order that we do see does not appear to have been produced as the chance outcome of random motions coerced into some measure of uniformity. You cannot fail to recognize that law has been long at work when you examine the wonderful structures of the spirals which have been well reproduced in many books and magazines.

Thus, in a purposeful creation, I find it not at all inconsistent to believe that there must be a mind behind it, developing the purpose. I make the premise that this is a spiritual being, and the further premise that spirit is distinct from matter, and that it is not subject to sense perception, that it is without mass (or is not matter), that it is without length or spatial and probably without time dimension. It is frankly an assumption, but I find it justified in my own mind by the effects which this view has had upon inspired men through all the ages. We receive from this spiritual power some gift, and we may develop it dimly and distantly after the model of the creator's thought. If the universe is purposeful, then it is plain to me that man, who is the highest form of development on the earth, must himself be distinctly a result of purpose rather than of accident. His evolution, whether it is by procedures which are clear to us or not, must be consistent with purpose and not with chance. One thing illustrative of this spiritual attitude is that man has his curiosities, his wonder, his awe, and his reverence for the material universe he sees about him, which may indicate to him a divine power behind it. Thus we may arrive at what Einstein has recently described as a 'cosmic spiritual sense.' It does not need to have in it any supernatural elements. Nature is wonderful enough. It seems that the bringing of the universe more fully into our mental conception is of great value because the greater our view of the material universe so much more must we appreciate and reverence the spiritual power which must lie behind it. How this power applies itself we do not know and perhaps we never shall. But it seems plain that we may gain a finer conception of the Creator by the study of His works, and I believe that the more we appreciate these things and look at matters from the cosmic point of view the more will the great things of life become greater and the small things of life will become smaller. Such a cosmic attitude can tend only towards a betterment of our relations with each other on the planet to which we are attached.

THE END

INDEX

INDEX

Abetti, Angelo, 170, 171
Abetti, Giorgio, 168, 169
Abbot, C. G., 127
Abbott, J. S. C., 12
Adams, Walter S., 121, 122, 140, 245
Æsculapius, 214
Aitken, R. G., 235
Albert, Prince Consort, 11, 124
Alcibiades, 43
Allen, Ira, 14
Allenby, General, 86
Allerton, 2
Alpha Delta Phi Fraternity, 52
Alsace, 71
Altdorf, Switzerland, 162
American Association for the Advance-
    ment of Science, 61, 90, 97, 110, 150
American Astronomical Society, 110,
    146
American Chemical Society, 62
American Institute of Sacred Literature,
    218
American Relief Administration, 210
American Telephone and Telegraph, 26
Amherst College, 22, 70, 95
Amsterdam, Holland, 161
Anaxagoras, 43
Ancestors, 1
Anderson, T., 84
Andover Theological Seminary, 91
Andromeda, the Great Nebula of, 45,
    239, 278, 281
Ångström, A. J., 229
Annalen der Physik, 243
Ann Arbor, Mich., 31, 138
Antwerp, Belgium, 89
Arcetri, Italy, 170
Arcturus, 126, 256, 257, 258, 259
Arequipa, Peru, 237
Arnold, Matthew, 18
Asquam House, 101, 103, 104
Asquith, Prime Minister, 155
Asteroid, 'Frostia,' 210
Asteroid, 'Æsculapia,' 214
Astrogon, 223

Astrographic Chart, 84
Astronomical Spectroscopy, 89, 90
Astronomical Union (International),
    224, 264
Astronomische Nachrichten, 71
Astronomy, 228
Astrophysical Journal, 115, 129, 148, 150,
    189, 208
Athens, Greece, 43, 68, 180
Austria, 147
Austria-Hungary, 167
Ayer, E. E., 114

Babelsburg, 174, 175
Bailey, Mrs., 117
Bailey, Liberty H., 195
Bailey, Solon, I., 39
Baker Library, 92
Baker, Newton D., 134
Balch Hill, 48
Balestiers, 3
Balfour, Arthur J., 155
Ball, Sir Robert, 154
Balmer, J. J., 240
Barnard, E. E., 116, 118, 129, 139, 140,
    142, 143, 144, 203, 277
Barnum and Bailey Circus, 29
Barrett, S. B., 140, 150, 203, 248
Barrows, Pres. David P., 224
Bartlett, E. J., 11, 57
Bartlett, S. C., Jr., 33, 57
Bartlett, Pres. S. C., 41, 91, 178
Bartolli, A., 71
Barton, William E., 213, 214
Basle, 67
Bassot, General, 166
Bayreuth, Germany, 72, 74, 261
Becker, Ernst, 66, 69, 71
Beecher, Rev. Edward, 212
Belapolsky, A., 81, 82
Belgium, 142, 175, 182, 183
Bell, Alexander G., 55
Bennington, Vt., 266
Bensen, E. F., 124
Berkeley, Cal., 224

Berlin, Germany, 69, 74, 75, 78, 79, 80, 81, 174, 175, 182, 254
Berlin-Dahlem, 69, 157
Berlitz School, 165
Berne, Switzerland, 44, 67
Berner Oberland, 66, 67
Beta Lyræ, 90
Big Foot, 128
Bird Calendar, 219
Birds, 29, 86, 120, 198, 261, 262
Bischoffsheim, M., 166
von Bismark, 86
Black Forest, 66, 161
Blaine, James G., 132
Blaisdell, Grandmother, 5
Blaserna, P., 169
B. L. T. (Bert Leston Taylor), 190
Blumbach, F., 81, 82
Bobrovnikof, N. T., 180
Bohr, Nils, 241
Bonheur, Rosa, 66
Bonn, Germany, 161
Boston Journal, 132
Boston, Mass., 6, 10, 15, 28, 34, 64, 94, 102, 151
Bournemouth, Eng., 153, 160
Boutwell, Luman, 56
Bowen, C. I., 242
Boxer Rebellion, 183
Braintree, Vt., 5
Brant, Mary Catherine, 4, 7, 36
Brantwood, 261
Brashear, J. A., 115
Brattleboro, Vt., 2, 3, 8, 14, 88, 265, 266
Brazil, 76
Breasted, James H., 76, 77, 79, 114, 254
Brieg, Switzerland, 108
Broglie Platz, 72
Brooklyn Institute, 150
Brooklyn, N.Y., 62, 70, 104
Brooks, Bishop Phillips, 29, 65
Brown, Rev. Francis, 20
Brown, John, 55
Bruce, Catherine W., 112, 115, 116
Bruce Spectrograph, 116, 233
Brumder, William C., 70
Brünig Pass, 66
Bryan, William J., 134, 135
Buffalo, N.Y., 62, 132, 134, 150
Buffalo Bill (Cody), 68

Bulgaria, 167
von Bülow, 80
Bunsen, Robert, 230
Bureau of Standards, U.S., 75
Bureau of Standards, Imperial, Germany, 174
Burke, Dr. John W., 191
Burlington House, 155
Burnham, U.S., 96, 116, 140, 141, 207, 235
Butler, Gen. B. F., 140
Butterfield Hall, 92

Calendar, Reform of, 225–27
California, 64, 218, 223, 224, 225
California Institute of Technology, 229
Calvert, Mary R., 142, 143
Cambridge, Eng., 155, 156, 160, 254
Cambridge, Mass., 97, 146, 264
Campbell, Gabriel, 43
Campbell, W. W., 62, 115, 122, 147
Camp Collie, 114, 117
Cannon, Annie J., 232
Canterbury, 160
Canterbury, Archbishop of, 155
Cape Cod, 47, 263
Carnegie, Andrew, 121, 124
Carnegie Institution, 126, 138, 140, 141, 142, 209
Carpenter Art Building, 92
Cassini, Family of, 165
Cassini, Place, 165
Catalina Island, 224
C. Cardinalis, 190
Century of Progress, 256, 257, 259
Certosa Monastery, 171
Chalmers, Mr. and Mrs. W. J., 114
Chamberlain, T. C., 220
Chamber of Commerce, U.S., 226
Chandler School of Science, 48, 57, 58, 61, 63, 64, 93
Chaos Club, 220
Chapin, S. B., 128
Chapman, Helen L., 250
Charlottenburg, Germany, 81, 174
Chase, C. P., 50
Chase's Island, 50
Chelsea, Vt., 40
Cherokees, Chief of, 12
Chester, Eng., 152

Chicago and Northwestern R.R., 34
Chicago, Milwaukee, St. Paul and
  Pacific, 34
Chicago *Tribune*, 190, 250
China, 183, 211, 227, 271, 272
Chi Psi Fraternity, 146
Choate, Rufus, 10
Christian Science, 201
Cisco, 204
Claremont, N.H., 8
Clark, Alvan G., 97
Class of '86, Dartmouth, 46
Clemens, Samuel L., 79
Cleveland, Ohio, 150, 243
Cleveland, Pres. Grover, 132, 133
Cluster in Hercules, Great, 84, 206, 239
Cobb, S. W., 10, 12
Colby, Gilbert, 26
Cold Harbor, Va., 8
Collegio Romano, 168
Collie, Joseph, 114
Cologne, Germany, 161, 175
Columbian Exposition, 18, 93, 95, 96, 258
Common, A. A., 84
Comstock, G. C., 110
Concord, N.H., 16, 51, 92
Congregational Church,
  New England of Chicago, 101
  Second of Dorchester, Mass., 101, 103
  First of Williams Bay, Wis., 211
Congress, 133, 136, 185
Connecticut River, 2, 4, 8, 31, 32, 49, 92,
  115, 159, 265
Constantinople, 167, 183
Constellation, Boötes, 257
Constellation, Leo, 7, 168
Contributions of Science to Religion, 218
Cook, C. S., 48, 51, 61
Coolidge, Pres. Calvin, 135, 266
Corniche, Route de la, 167
Cosmos, The structure of the, 281
Coulter, J. M., 218
Crane, C. R., 125, 271, 272
Crawford House, 52
Cricket, Snowy Tree, 199, 200
Crimea, 130
Crookes, Sir William, 154
Crosby, Madame Dixi, 20
Crosby, Mildred, 55, 56
Crump, C. C., 145, 248

Czechoslovakia, 188

Dardanelles, 165
Dartmouth College, 2, 4, 5, 8, 11, 12, 19,
  20, 21, 40, 44, 45, 68, 89, 93, 94, 104,
  110, 112, 121, 146, 151, 264
Dartmouth Halls:
  Conant, 56
  Culver, 48
  Old Dartmouth, 14, 35, 41
  Reed, 35, 44
  Sanborn, 92
  Webster, 92
  Wentworth, 35
  Wilder, 93
Dartmouth Hotel, 20, 33
Dartmouth Medical College, 10, 11, 12,
  15, 25, 35, 91, 98, 99
Dartmouth Medical School Building, 34
Dartmouth Road, 261
Dartmouth Scientific Association, 40
Darwin, Sir George, 156
Davidson, Col. Royal P., 196, 215
Davis, Dr. D. J., 214
Dawes, Rufus C., 256, 257
Delavan, Wis., 114, 127
Denver, Col., 130, 148, 244
Deslandres, M. Henri, 231
Dickens, 12, 123
D. K. E. Fraternity, 52, 114
Dodge, Otis, 119
Domodossola, Italy, 108
Doppler, Christian, 233
Dorchester, Mass., 101, 102, 104, 107
Dotham, Vt., 30
Downing, Elliot R., 260, 261
Downing, Deacon L. B., 12
Drachensfels, Germany, 161
Drake, Tracy C., 114, 125
Dresden, 173
DuBois, Anna Lamson, 6
DuBois, Charles G., 26
DuBois, Earl Cushman, 5
DuBois, Eliza Ann, 5, 99
DuBois, Ellen, 28
DuBois, George, 24
DuBois, Gilman Bradford, 4, 6, 28
DuBois, Joseph, 5
DuBois, Royal T., 27
DuBois, William H., 4, 34, 132

Dudley, Jason, 53
Duncan, W. H., 10, 39
Dyson, Sir Frank, 148, 152, 153, 154

Eastman, Charles, 18
Eastman, George, 226
Eastman Kodak Co., 144
Eaton Hall, 152
Eaton, J. S., 179
Eclipses, 128, 129, 130, 244, 245, 263
Edam, Holland, 161
Eddington, Sir Arthur, 245, 275, 276, 283
Edwards, Jonathan, 36
Egan, W. C., 193
Eighteenth Amendment, 136, 137
Einstein, Albert, 70, 243, 244, 245, 283, 285
Elgar, Sir Edward, 154
Elkhorn, Wis., 118, 256
Ellerman, Ferdinand, 115, 127, 128, 138, 140
Elsass, 73
Elvey, C. T., 238, 247
Emerson, C. F., 44
Emerson, Ralph Waldo, 257
England, 11, 64, 65, 82, 104, 123, 124, 147, 148, 151, 152, 184, 230, 275
Eros, 175
Etna, N.H., 29
Eton, 152, 160
Eugénie, Empress, 124
Europe, 18, 19, 62, 64, 70, 106, 134, 148, 150, 162

Fairbank, Mr. and Mrs. Kellogg, 202
Fairbanks, Arthur, 48, 51
Farrar, 8
Ferdinand, Grand Duke Franz, 174, 183
Fisher, Irving, 136
Fitzgerald, G. F., 243
Flagstaff, Ariz., 146
Fleming, Mrs. M., 232
Fletcher, Robert, 92
Florence, Italy, 107, 169
Florida, 135, 212, 213
Flushing, Holland, 161
Folkstone, Eng., 160
Fontana, Wis., 118, 204
Foote, Henry M., 224
Förster, Wilhelm, 75

Foster, H. D., 101, 102, 104, 105, 110
France, 20, 147, 157, 166, 167, 175, 176, 182, 184
Frankfort, Germany, 69
Frary, Mr. and Mrs. H., 9, 10
Fraunhofer, J., 230
French Academy of Sciences, 166
Frost, Benjamin, 4, 5
Frost, Benjamin D., 4, 145, 151, 176, 196
Frost, Carlton P., 99
Frost, Dr. Carlton P., 2, 7, 34, 36, 91, 98, 99
Frost, Edmund, 1
Frost, Edwin B., I, 7, 8, 124
Frost, Edwin B., II, 27, 47, 58, 79, 83, 93, 103, 157, 213, 251
Frost, Edwin B., III, 273
Frost, Elijah, 4, 5, 7, 8
Frost, Eliza, 5, 99
Frost, Elizabeth, 150, 151
Frost, Frederick H., 131, 146, 176, 217, 218, 250, 273
Frost, Dr. Gilman D., 2, 3, 100
Frost, Grandmother Catherine Brant, 4, 39
Frost, Henry Martin, 8, 47
Frost, Holly, 198
Frost, Jocelyn, 3
Frost, Katharine Brant, 112, 130, 145, 146, 157, 161, 273
Frost, Lydia Heald, 4
Frost, Margaret Thurston, 110
Frost, Mary H. (Mrs. E. B.), 104, 110, 112, 130, 150, 153, 210
Fox, Philip, 180, 207, 221, 257
Friedrich, Dowager Empress, 87
Friedrich, Emperor, 87
Friedrich, Empress, 87
Fuller, Gov., 88
Fuller, Revilo, 260

Gale, H. G., 150
Galesburg, Ill., 212
Galileo, 170
Galileo, The Tribuna di, 170
Galle, Andreas, 178
Garfield, Pres. James A., 132
Garrison Church, Potsdam, Germany, 77
Gay, Willard, 27, 132
Geese, Wild, 203
Geike, Sir Archibald, 154, 155

Gemmi Pass, 67
General Electric Co., 247
Genesis, 17
Geneva, Switzerland, 162, 169
Genoa, 106, 167
Geodetic Institute, Potsdam, Germany, 76, 82, 83
Germany, 43, 46, 74, 79, 82, 86, 147, 148, 161, 167, 168, 170, 176, 182, 230
Gibbs, J. W., 20
Gibraltar, 107
Ginn and Co., 49, 63, 85
Ginori, Count, 170
Goodspeed, Arthur, 100
Goodspeed, E. J., 254
Göttingen, 68, 175
Gounaris, Prime Minister, 68
Grand Canyon, 146
Grant, Pres. U. S., 132
Greece, 43, 68, 180
Greek, 39, 40, 42, 43, 66, 167, 207, 208, 214, 223, 254
Greenwich, Eng., 152, 154
Gregorian Calendar, 227
Grey, Sir Edward, 133
Gwalior, Maharajah of, 154

Haddock, Mrs. C. B., 11
Hagen, Father J. G., 168, 169, 227
Hague, The, 134, 161
Hale, George E., 96, 97, 112, 114, 115, 116, 120, 121, 122, 126, 127, 128, 138, 140, 147, 206, 229, 231, 246
Hale, W. E., 138
Halley's Comet, 217, 225
Hallwachs, W., 69
Halm, J., 71
Hamilton College, 209
Hampton Court, 155
Hancock, N.H., 58
Hanover, N.H., 4, 6, 8, 9, 10, 13, 14, 19, 21, 30, 31, 32, 34, 39, 55, 60, 89, 91, 99, 101, 104, 112, 120, 127, 130, 131, 151, 264
Harding, Pres. Warren G., 135
Hardy, Arthur S., 44
Harper, Pres. William R., 97, 109, 116, 121, 122, 139, 140
Harper's Monthly Magazine, 124
Harper's Weekly, 23

Harriman, H. J., 39
Harris, Dr. T. J., 74
Harrison, Pres. Beniamin, 132
Harrisville, N.H., 58
Hartford, Vt., 30
Harvard College, 2, 15, 94, 232, 237, 256
Havre, France, 176
Hayes, Pres. Rutherford B., 132
Hazard, Carolyn R., 103
Hazard, Edith C., 150
Hazard, Elizabeth Wyman Adams (Mrs. M. C.), 102, 151
Hazard, Marshall C., 102, 114, 151, 212, 213
Hazard, Mary E., 2, 101, 102, 103
Hazen, Allen, 30, 60, 65, 66
Hazen, Charles Downer, 68
Heidelberg, Germany, 96, 108, 161
von Helmholtz, H., 75, 96, 283
Herald, The, N.Y., 11
Herodotus, 254
Herschel, Sir William, 228
Heylman, Mr. and Mrs. Henry, 264
Hill, the Misses, 150
Hills, Col. E. H., 160
Hilton, Mr. and Mrs. H. H., 264
Hirayama, Shin, 81, 162
Hitchcock, Charles Henry, 22
Hitchcock, Pres. Edward, 22
Hitchcock, Mr. and Mrs. Hiram, 14, 15
Hohenzollern Family, 182
Holland, 139, 144, 160, 161
Holmes, Oliver Wendell, 9
Hooker, John D., 229
Hoover, Pres. Herbert C., 135, 136
Hopkins, Pres. E. M., 93, 271
Horticultural Hall, 252
Hospital, Albert Billings Memorial, 253
Hospital, Bobs Roberts Memorial, 255
Hospital, Boston City, 15
Hospital for Crippled Children, 255
Hospital, Mary Maynard Hitchcock, 15, 94
Hospital, Orthopedic, 255
Houston, Texas, 224
Hovey, Richard, 21, 95
Howland, 2
Hubbard, Gardiner G., 55
Hubble, Edwin P., 239, 278
Huggins, Lady, 65, 158

Huggins, Sir William, 65, 157, 158, 229
Huggins, Willetta, 201
Hughes, Sec. of State Charles Evans, 185
Hull, Gordon, 71
Hungary, 188
Hussey, W. J., 138, 235
Hutchins, Pres. Robert M., 254
Hutchinson, C. L., 191, 193, 252
Hyde, Edward, 22

Ide, Hon. Henry C., 107
Illinois Trust & Savings Bank, 216
Imperial Institute, Germany, 75
Indian, American, 12, 18
Isham, Dr. George S., 126, 129, 223, 224, 254, 259
Italian Physical Society, 169
Italy, 157, 166, 168, 176

Janssen, Jules, 229
Japan, 130, 134, 183, 227
Jeans, Sir James, 275, 276
Jena Glass Works, 116
Jenkins, Rev. Paul B., 196
Johnson, Dr. Frank S., 150
Johnson, Samuel, 10
Jupiter, 277

Kaiser Wilhelm II, 75, 86, 87, 88
Kaiserin Augusta Victoria, 77, 86, 87
Kapteyn, J. C., 139, 236
Kayser, Heinrich, 161
Keeler, J. E., 109
Keene, N.H., 58
Kellogg, Sec. of State Frank B., 226
Kelvin, Lord, 283
Kempf, Paul, 237
Kentucky, 4
Kiel, Germany, 71
King Alphonso, 176
King George V, 156, 159
Kinsley, Philip, 250
Kipling, Rudyard, 3
Kirchhoff, G., 230
Kishwauketoc, 128, 211
Kittridge, C. F., 107, 108
Kittridge, Louise, 107, 108
Klumpke, Anna, 66
Klumpke, Dorothea, 66
Knox College, 212

Kobold, H., 71
Kohlrausch, F., 69
Königstuhl, 67
Kundt, A., 75
Küstner, F., 161

Lake Champlain, 6, 7
Lake Chesterfield, 2
Lake Como, Wis., 193
Lake Constance, 172
Lake Delavan, 193
Lake Geneva, Wis., 3, 23, 97, 109, 113, 114, 146, 159, 178, 191, 203
Lake Geneva, Switzerland, 104
Lake Grass, 193
Lake Italian, 107
Lake Lucerne, 162
Lake Michigan, 96
Lake Muskoka, 62
Lake Squam, 101
Lake Sunapee (Little), 264
Lake Wannsee, 80
Lake Geneva Garden Club, 192, 252
Lamson, Anna, 5
Langley, S. P., 81, 230
Laplace, P. S., 45, 278, 281
Larson, J. F., 19
Latin, 39, 40, 42, 43, 66, 157, 223
La Turbie, 167
Laycock, Dean Craven, 21, 110
League of Nations, 134, 163, 185, 186, 226
Leavitt, Henrietta, 239
Lebedew, Peter, 71
Ledyard Bridge, 31, 48
Leeds, Rev. S. P., 54, 55, 56
Leipzig, Germany, 69, 85, 229
Lindsey, Judge Edward, 54
Lindsey, Mildred, 53, 54
Lisbon, Portugal, 11
Liszt, 74
Little, Rev. Arthur, 101, 103
Little, Mary B., 46, 101
Liverpool, 64, 65, 151, 152
Lockyer, Lady, 155
Lockyer, Sir Norman, 40, 46, 229
London, Eng., 40, 65, 66, 82, 108, 148, 151, 152, 153
Lord, John K., 11, 16, 43, 55, 91
Lord, Mrs. John K., 55
Lord, Pres. Nathan, 17

Lotus, 193
Louisville, Ky., 8, 212
Lowater, Frances, 153
Lowell, Percival, 217
Lucerne, Switzerland, 66, 162
Lyman, Theodore, 149
Lyme, N.H., 48
Lyra, Ring Nebula in, 206

Maarken, 161
Macdonald, Dr. W. H., 150, 253
Macedonia, 167
MacMillan, W. D., 253, 284
Madison, Wis., 68
Mahan, Admiral, 86
Maine, 2, 263
Manchuria, 134, 227
Mark Twain, 79
Mars, 217, 277
Marseilles, 167
Marvin, C. F., 227
Mascart, E., 96
Mass. Institute of Technology, 60, 65
Mathews, Shailer, 218
Maury, Miss A. C., 232
Maxwell, J. C., 71
McCarthy, Eddie, 100
McCormick Theological Seminary, 212
McDonald, W. J., 248
McKinley, Pres. William, 7, 83, 133
McLaughlin, A. C., 173
McNally, Dave, 38
Meiringen, Switzerland, 66
Merry del Val, Cardinal, 166
Mexico, 134, 225
Michel, Anthony, 145
Michelson, A. A., 109, 144, 195, 243
Middleburg, Holland, 161
Milan, 107
Milky Way, 45, 116, 142, 144, 228, 239, 240, 258, 278
Millikan, Robert A., 218, 241, 284
Milne, E. A., 283
Milwaukee, Wis., 70
Minerva, 214
Mink Brook, 13, 31
Mitchell, J. J., 216
Mitchell, S. A., 150
von Moltke, Gen., 182

Monaco, 167
Montenegro, 167
Montreal, 150, 151
Moody, Dwight L., 6
Moody, W. V., 275
Moore, Frank G., 68, 101, 102, 103, 105, 110
Moor's Charity School, 12
Morley, E. W., 243
Morril, J. S., 21
Morton, Levi P., 20
Moscow, 187
Mount Ascutney, 5, 43
Mount Chocorua, 52, 101, 102
Mount Gorner Grat, 67
Mount Hamilton, 147
Mount Kearsarge, 52
Mount Matterhorn, 67
Mount Monadnock, 58, 60
Mount Moose, 112
Mount Moosilauke, 5, 51, 99
Mount Sport, 13
Mount Tripyramid, 51
Mount Washington, 51, 52, 263
Mount Wilson, 127, 138, 147, 239
Mountain, Cube, 50
Mountain, Eggishorn, 66
Mountain, Saleve, La Grand, 163
Mountain, Saleve, La Petite, 163
Mountain, Sandwich, 101
Mountain, Stanserhorn, 162
Mountain, Uitliberg, 162
Mountain, Wantastiket, 3
Mountains, Adirondacks, 51
Mountains, Franconias, 5, 50, 51
Mountains, Green, 266
Mountains, Jura, 171
Mountains, Sandwich, 101
Mountains, of Savoy, 167
Mountains, Vosges, 73
Mountains, White, 28
Müller, G., 237
Munich, 83, 172, 173
Museum, British, 157
Museum, Germanic, 73, 173
Museum, Munich, 173
Museum, Rosenwald, 173
Museum, Smithsonian, 172
Museum, South Kensington, 172
Museum, Zwinger, 74, 173

Naples, Italy, 169, 170, 192
Napoleon, 124, 175
Nashua, N.H., 58
Nast, Thomas, 23
National Academy of Sciences, 62, 138, 144, 209
National Astronomical Society, 110
National Physics Laboratory, Teddington, Eng., 155
Nature (weekly Journal), 49, 109, 246
Nebular Hypothesis, 16
Neptune, 277
Nernst, Walter, 284
Newall, H. F., 156
Newcomb, Simon, 61, 110, 243, 244
New England, 2, 5, 6, 7, 26, 29, 36, 54, 104, 105, 114, 125, 152, 263
New Hampshire, 2, 3, 4, 22, 40, 91, 101, 115, 136, 263
New Orleans, 140, 224
Newport, R.I., 57
New Testament, 37
Newton, H. A., 61
New York, 3, 10, 19, 62, 72, 104, 106, 150, 179, 271
New York *Herald*, 11
Nice, France, 106, 164, 165, 166, 167
Nichols, E. F., 71, 126
Nigger Hill, 13, 48
Nigger Island, 50
Night Crawlers, 201
Northampton, Mass., 55
Northumberland, Duke of, 155
Northwestern Military and Naval Academy, 196, 214
Norton Foundation, 212
Norwich, Vt., 265
Nova, 45, 84, 85, 220, 277, 278
Nuremburg, 73, 74, 173

Oak Park, Ill., 112
Observatories:
  Alleghany, 81, 109
  Astrophysical of Meudon, 177
  Astrophysical of Potsdam, 71, 75, 175
  Berlin, 75
  Bonn, 161
  Collegio Romano, 168
  Dearborn, 141, 207
  Dominion, 240
  del Ebro, 225
  Georgetown, 168
  Greenwich (Royal of), 65, 152, 244
  Harvard College, 85, 90, 239, 264
  Harvard College Station at Peru, 237
  Heidelberg, 67, 161
  Imperial Russian, 81
  Lick, 62, 64, 96, 115, 116, 141, 142, 147, 235, 244, 248
  Lowell, 127, 239
  McCormick, 248
  McDonald, 248
  Mount Wilson (Solar Physics), 121, 139, 146, 224, 229, 245
  Naval, 216
  Nice, 166
  Paris, 66, 176
  Pulkova, 81
  Royal of Belgium, 142
  Shattuck (Dartmouth), 71
  Smithsonian, 127
  Solar Physics, Cambridge, Eng., 156
  Strassburg, 66
  Tokyo, 162
  Urania, 174
  Vatican, 168
  Yerkes, 84, 93, 97, 106, 109, 112, 113, 114, 117, 128, 141, 142, 148, 155, 158, 168, 208, 214, 229, 246, 248, 256, 257
  Zurich, 162
Olcott Falls, 50
Olcott Mills, 10
Olympic Games, 151
Oort, J. H., 240
Operas:
  Cavalleria Rusticana, 80
  Flying Dutchman, 173
  Othello, 171
  Parsifal, 72
  Rienzi, 72
von Oppolzer, T., 263
Orford, N.H., 50
Oxford, Eng., 155, 159, 160, 254, 283

Paetsch, Hans, 69
Paraskevopoulos, J., 180
Paris, 66, 68, 97, 108, 110, 115, 165, 175, 176, 182
Park Commission, Walworth Co., 210

Parker, Alice, 16
Parker, Henry E., 16, 18
Parkhurst, J. A., 117, 130, 237
Parkhurst, Lewis, 38, 49, 117
Parras-Mantois, 97, 115
Pasadena, Cal., 138, 224
Pasteur, 98
Paterno di Sessa, Marchese E., 157
Patten, William T., 110
Patten, V. T., 60
Pavlov, I. P., 157, 158
Pease, F. G., 140
Pershing, Gen. John J., 134, 184
Personalia, 209
Petee, C. H., 92
Peters, C. H. F., 209
Phantom Lover, 250, 251
Phelps, Sam, 55, 56
Phemister, Dr. Dallas B., 267
Philippines, 31, 107, 133
Phœnix, Arizona, 224
Piazza Michelangelo, 170
Picard, C. E., 157
Pickering, E. C., 90, 232, 234, 237, 238, 241
Pickering, W. H., 138, 147
Pickwick Papers, 121
Pihl, Gunard, 260
Pilgrim Press, 212
Planck, Max, 149, 241, 246
Planetarium, Adler, 207
Plasket, J. S., 240
Platt, Senator T. C., 133
Plattsburg, N.Y., 6
Pluto, 214, 277
Plymouth, N.H., 57
Pogorelski, A., 180
Poland, 188
Polk, Pres. James, 11
Pompeii, 107
Pope Leo XIII, 168
Pope Pius X, 169
Porter, H. H., 223
Portland, Me., 101, 261
Porto Rico, 264
Potash Hill, 48
Pottawatomies, 211
Potsdam, Germany, 46, 73, 75, 76, 79, 80, 81–89, 108, 115, 162, 174, 175, 182, 234

Potsdam, N.Y., 7
Potts, Grace, 267
Princeton, N.J., 48, 60, 90, 223
Proctor, Senator Redfield, 7, 99

Quadrangle Club, 143
Quebec, 151
Queen of Italy, 168
Queen Mary, 156, 159
Queen Victoria, 11, 123, 159
Quincy, Josiah, 42

Ramsey, Sir William, 154
Randolph, Vt., 4, 5, 6, 27, 28, 33, 34, 40, 64
Rayleigh, Lord, 157
Rechen-Institute, 69
Regiment, Eleventh, Vt., 8
Regiment, Fifteenth, Vt., 7, 99
Regiment, Tenth, Vt., 7
Relativity, Theory of, 243
Renaissance, 73, 173
Repeal of the 18th Amendment, 136, 137
Rhône Glacier, 66
Rice, Edmund, 2
Rice, Tamasine, 2
Richardson, Elder, 17
Richardson, Jane, 17
Riem, J., 69
Ristenpart, F., 69, 73
Ritchey, G. W., 119, 121, 129, 140, 229
Riviera, 166
Rochester, Minn., 215
Rochester, N.Y., 62, 197
Rodés, Father Luis, 225
Rogers, Will, 77
Rollins Chapel, 32
Rome, 168, 169, 170, 224
Röntgen, W. K., 99, 100
Rood House, 55
Roosevelt Dam, 224
Roosevelt, Pres. Franklin D., 136
Roosevelt, Pres. Theodore, 133, 134
Root, Elihu, 185, 209
Rope Ferry Road, 15
Rosenwald Fund, 238, 246
Roses, 193, 195, 197
Ross, F. E., 144
Rowland, H. A., 89, 96, 144, 145, 230

Royal Astronomical Society, 148, 151, 153, 154, 158, 160
Royal Society, 154
Rubens, H., 157
Russell, H. N., 238
Russell, Ex-Governor, William C., 65
Russia, 82, 147, 167, 183, 187, 272
Rutherford, Ernest, 241
Rutland, Vt., 16, 60
Ryerson Laboratory, 70, 109, 150
Ryerson, Martin A., 109, 271

Sachs, Hans, 74
Samoa, 107
Samuels, E. A., 29
Sanborn, Prof. Edwin D., 18, 19
Sanborn, Edwin W., 19
Sanborn Hall, 19
Sanborn, Kate, 19
Sandeys, J. E., 157
San Francisco, 147, 148
Sans Souci, 76, 79
Santa Barbara, Cal., 224
Saturn, 206
Sawyer, Mrs. Z. V., 119
Saybrook, Conn., 50
Scandinavia, 147
Schaffhausen, 66, 162
Scheiner, Julius, 71, 75, 82, 84, 85, 89, 90, 175, 234
Scheveningen, 161
Schiller, 162
Schlesinger, Frank, 121, 228
Schlote, Fräulein, 68
Schumann, Victor, 149
Schuster, Sir Arthur, 152
Schwartzschild, Karl, 70, 175
Science (Weekly Journal), 100, 109
Science and Religion, 212
Scotland, 10
Secchi, Father, 168, 232
Selfridge, Harry G., 159
Serajevo, 174, 183
Serbia, 167
Shakespeare, 9
Shanghai, 134, 227
Shapley, Harlow, 238, 239
Shattuck, Dr. George C., 90
Sherman, Gen. W. T., 188
Siberia, 38

Simplon Pass, 108
Skating, 202
Slipher, V. M., 239
Smith College, 55, 68
Smith, J. M. P., 139
Smith, Dr. William T., 11
Smithsonian Institution, 128
Snow, Benjamin, 68, 74
Snow, Helen M., 126
Socrates, 43
Soissons, 175
Solar Union, International, 144, 146
Sorrento, Italy, 107
Spain, 107
Spalding, C. W., 92
Spear, Polly, 5
Spectroscope, 51
Spörer, G., 81
Spring, Dr. W. A., 174
Springfield Republican, 132, 187
Stars:
    Algol, 234
    Altair, 277
    Arcturus, 126, 256–59
    Beta Aurigæ, 234
    Gamma Ursæ Minoris, 234
    Mizar, 234
    20 Persei, 189
    Pole Star, 237, 238
    Sirius, 234, 236, 245
    Vega, 126
State School for the Blind (Wis.), 201, 218
State School for the Deaf (Wis.), 218
Stebbins, Joel, 173, 238
Stevens, W. Le Conte, 70, 74
Stevens, Roland, 110
Stevenson, Robert Louis, 107
St. John, C. E., 245
St. Johnsbury, Vt., 20, 51, 107
St. Lawrence, the, 151, 263
St. Louis Exposition, 139, 144
St. Peter's, 107
St. Petersburg, Fla., 212, 213
St. Petersburg, Russia, 81, 157
Stockholm, 151
Stockton, Frank, 25
Stoddard, John L., 18
Stokes, G. G., 230
Stone, John Timothy, 212

Strassburg, 66, 68, 70, 71, 72, 73, 84, 108, 161, 182
Stratton, S. W., 75
Struve, Elizabeth, 256
Struve, Hermann, 174, 175
Struve, Otto, 210, 248, 255, 256
Struve, Wilhelm, 234
Stump Lane, 15, 32
Sullivan, N.H., 4
Sumerians, 129
Sunday School, 16
Surrey, Eng., 160
Swift, Harold, 271
Switzerland, 104, 108, 147, 162, 172, 225

Taft, Pres. William Howard, 133, 185
Tarleton Ponds, 50
Teheran, 44
Telescopes:
  Bruce Photographic, 198
  Denver Equatorial, 244
  Snow, 126, 139, 140
  12 in. refractor (Yerkes), 238
  24. in. reflector (Yerkes), 229
  40 in. refractor, 172, 218, 228, 233, 238
  60 in. reflector (Mt. Wilson), 239
  72 in. reflector (Victoria), 240
  100 in. reflector (Mt. Wilson), 229, 239
  200 in. reflector, 229
Tennyson, 3, 39, 123
Teutonic, The, 150
Texas, 248, 249
Thames, the, 159
Thayer School of Engineering, 92
'The Heavens are Telling,' 218
Thetford Academy, 4, 5, 140
Thetford Hill, 4, 30, 140
Thetford, Vermont, 4, 8
Thompson, Mary B., 261
Thompson, Dr. John F., 101
Thompson, Joseph, 70, 95
Thompson, Silvanus, 63
Thrace, 167
Thurston, Margaret, 2, 15
Titanic, the, 151, 152
Todd, Rev. John, 23
Tokyo, 81, 162
Toronto, 61
Tower, G. B. N., 12

Tribune, the Chicago, 190, 250
Treaty of Versailles, 134, 185, 188
Trees, 30, 32, 194, 195
Tucker, Pres. William J., 91, 92, 93, 99
Turkey, 162, 167
Turner, H. H., 66, 139, 159, 160

Union Theological Seminary, 68
University
  of Berlin, 246
  of California, 62, 70
  of Cambridge, Eng., 155
  of Chicago, 70, 96, 97, 109, 138, 146, 148, 164, 213, 221, 248, 259, 275
  Columbia, 150
  Georgetown, 168
  of Illinois, 173, 214, 258
  of Michigan, 62
  of Minnesota, 89
  Northwestern, 61, 226
  of Pittsburg, 258
  Princeton, 128
  of Southern California, 97
  of Texas, 248, 249
  Vanderbilt, 142
  of Wisconsin, 70, 173, 221, 238, 260
  Yale, 61
University Club of Chicago, 220
University Heights, 259
Urso, Camilla, 18

Vale of Tempe, 32
Van Biesbroeck, G., 142, 180, 210, 214
Vatican, the, 166, 168, 169, 227
Vatican Gardens, 168
Vega, 126
Venice, 107, 171
Vermont, 2, 3, 5, 6, 22, 66, 91, 115, 132, 136, 263
Versailles, 177
Versailles, Treaty of, 134
Villefranche, 165
Virginia, 7
Visp, 67
Vogel, H. C., 73, 81, 85, 87, 175, 234
Vollendam, 161

Wadesboro, N.C., 128, 263
Wadsworth, F. L. O., 109

Wagner, Richard, 72, 74, 261
Wales, Elizabeth, 103
War, Balkan, 162,175, 183
War, Civil, 7, 20, 56, 72, 140
War, Franco-Prussian, 71
War of 1812, 6
War, Punic, 12
War, Spanish, 7, 133
War, World, 70, 130, 135, 168, 174
Ward, Artemus, 8
Warming, E., 157
Warner and Swasey, 97, 116, 172
Warren, N.H., 50
Warren, Pa., 54
Washington, D.C., 21, 62, 98, 132, 134, 150, 266
Watson, J. C., 69
Weather Bureau, U.S., 227, 263
Webster, Daniel, 12, 19, 20, 63, 94, 130, 143
Webster Hall, 55, 92
Webster Vale, 14
Wellesley College, 68, 103, 107, 110, 146, 159, 264
Wells, D. Collin, 101, 102
Wentworth, N.H., 50
West, Andrew, 223
Westbrook, Me., 263
Western Electric Co., 26
West Lebanon, N.H., 14, 31, 48, 265
Westminster Abbey, 154
Westminster, Duke of, 152
Wheelock, Eleazer, 36
White, Anna, 68, 102, 103
White, Gaylord, 68
White, Mrs. Gaylord, 68
White Church, The, 92
Whitefield, George, 36
White River, 5
White River Junction, Vt., 29, 34
Wien, W., 149
Wiener, Otto, 69
Wigmore, Dean J. H., 226
Wilde, Oscar, 21
Wilder, C. T., 92
Wilder Hall, 93
Wilder Laboratory, 92, 100
Wilder, Vt., 50
Wilhelm, Crown Prince Friedrich, 87
Wilhelm II, Kaiser, 86

Wilhelm Tell, 162
Willard, Miss Frances, 79
Willard, Joseph M., 50
Willard, Mrs. Mary B., 79, 80
Williams Bay, Wis., 82, 109, 114, 118, 119, 125, 130, 131, 146, 180, 190, 203
Williams, George, 180, 181
Wilmer, Dr. W. H., 191
Wilsing, J., 85, 175
Wilson, Pres. Woodrow, 134, 184, 185, 272
Winchester, Dean of, 154
Winchester, Eng., 160
Windsor Castle, 156
Windsor, Vt., 7, 20
Wisconsin, 23, 112, 146, 152, 165, 216
Wislicenus, Walter, 71
Wolf, Max, 67, 96, 161
Wolfer, A., 162
Woodstock, Vt., 7, 20, 53
Woodworth, Charles, 51
Woodworth, E. K., 51
Worcester, Dean C., 30, 31
Wordsworth, 3, 123
Worthen, T. W. D., 91
Wren, Sir Christopher, 154
Wright, John Henry, 43
Wrigley, William, Jr., 224
Wychwood, 191
Wylie, H. W., 223
Wyoming, 144, 277
Würtzburg, 99

X-Rays, 100, 149, 241, 253

Yerkes, C. T., 97, 98, 109, 115
Yerkes Observatory, Publications of, 122, 141, 142, 143, 208
Y.M.C.A., 127, 128, 162, 184, 202, 210, 221, 255
Yocie, 181
Young, Charles A., 15, 32, 44, 48, 60, 62, 90, 128, 143
Young, Clara, 15, 48
Young, Fred, 15, 27
Ysaye, 166

Zeiss Co., 115
Zermatt, 167
Zurich, 66